LiveMotion™ 2:
A Beginner's Guide

LiveMotion™ 2:
A Beginner's Guide

Simon Dabkowski

McGraw-Hill/Osborne

New York Chicago San Francisco
Lisbon London Madrid Mexico City Milan
New Delhi San Juan Seoul Singapore Sydney Toronto

McGraw-Hill/Osborne
2600 Tenth Street
Berkeley, California 94710
U.S.A.

To arrange bulk purchase discounts for sales promotions, premiums, or fund-raisers, please contact **McGraw-Hill**/Osborne at the above address. For information on translations or book distributors outside the U.S.A., please see the International Contact Information page immediately following the index of this book.

LiveMotion™ 2: A Beginner's Guide

1234567890 CUS CUS 0198765432

ISBN 0-07-219520-7

Publisher   Brandon A. Nordin
Vice President & Associate Publisher   Scott Rogers
Acquisitions Editor   Jim Schachterle
Project Editor   Monika Faltiss
Acquisitions Coordinator   Timothy Madrid
Technical Editor   Alex Hallugian
Copy Editor   Marcia Baker & Dennis Weaver
Proofreader   Mike McGee
Indexer   Irv Hershman
Computer Designers   George Toma Charbak, Tara A. Davis, Lauren McCarthy
Illustrator   Lyssa Wald & Beth Young
Series Design   Gary Corrigan
Cover Design   Greg Scott
Cover Illustration   Kevin Curry

This book was composed with Corel VENTURA ™ Publisher.

*I want to dedicate this book to my father
who's been hospitalized in a coma since 1998.*

*To my mom, Irene, and my younger sister, Agata,
thank you for keeping our family together
when we needed each other the most.*

*To Jeanne and Lucille for helping me through
some of the most difficult times in my life.*

*To all of my friends who've helped me grow as a person
and kept my spirits up—you're irreplaceable.*

*To my amazing girlfriend Jessica,
who miraculously managed to put up with me
over the past months, thank you for everything.
I love you. You're the best thing in my life.*

About the Author

Simon Dabkowski has been working with Adobe's Web development suite for more than five years. Currently, he is the lead art director and Web designer for DesignerOutlet.com, where he's responsible for maintaining and designing DesignerOutlet.com, VerticalOutlet.com, and Auction.DesignerOutlet.com. Simon is an expert graphic designer and he currently uses Adobe's full range of tools, including Photoshop, LiveMotion, GoLive, After Effects, and Illustrator. He also has professional experience with Flash, Dreamweaver, and Fireworks. Simon's work is exemplified by his personal web site, LiveMotionStudio.com, which exhibits his wide range of design skills.

Contents at a Glance

Contents

PART 2

Animation

PART 3
Web and Multimedia Design

Acknowledgments

Writing this book has been a wonderful and, at times, hair-ripping experience. It was a first for me, but I'd love to do it all over again knowing what I know about the process.

I would also like to thank Jim, Tim, Monika, and my technical editor, Alex for guiding me through this uncharted territory. Thanks for making the process such a great learning experience. I would also like to thank all of the LM users I've got to know over the past few months on my forum site. You guys are the best!

Finally, I want to thank everyone at Adobe for creating such a great product and a special thanks to all the LiveMotion beta users.

Introduction

Adobe LiveMotion 2 enables you to create both simple and advanced interactive animations for the Web. With the program's intuitive tool, you can add features such as sound and scripts, and export your work to mediums other than the Web, such as DVD and CD presentations.

If you're currently familiar with some of Adobe's other programs, such as Photoshop, you'll find a shocking resemblance in LiveMotion's similar interface. Adobe's use of palettes, which contain preferences that enable you to alter and further develop the objects you're working with and applying them on, are found in every Adobe program. Palettes are extremely easy and convenient to work with because palettes not only let you free up space, but you can also pick and choose any combination of them and group them into separate groups.

What's New in LiveMotion 2?

Adobe released its first version of LiveMotion in 1999. Many faithful Adobe users praised the new program as the Macromedia FlashKiller because of Adobe's approach to making all its software easy to use. To this day, Flash from Macromedia is the most widely used application for creating interactive SWF files for the Web. Flash also has the upper hand over LiveMotion, because of its capability to ActionScript its TimeLine. Therefore, Adobe's approach in popularizing LiveMotion was to make it compatible with some of its other applications, such as Photoshop and Illustrator, in enabling users to import their native files easily. Adobe's approach to scripting with LiveMotion 1 was behaviors. These adjustable preferences enabled a user to create simple custom scripting effects, which controlled the player's timeline. However, they lacked many of the advanced features Flash allowed.

Enter LiveMotion 2. The most praised feature of LiveMotion 2 is its scripting engine, composed of a Script Editor that enables you to create Player, State, and Handler Scripts. The Script Editor provides a way for you either to add JavaScript or ActionScript commands that will control various elements of your projects. In addition, LiveMotion 2 comes along with a debugger that lets you test the integrity of your scripts. You learn more about these and other new features of LiveMotion 2 as you go through the book.

LiveMotion 1 Users

Those of you who've mastered LiveMotion 1, or at least explored it deeply enough to learn about its capability to add behaviors to your projects, will be glad to know that behaviors aren't completely gone in LiveMotion 2. In fact, behaviors are now a part of the Script Editor, which allows further experimentation and custom capability. At first, the Script Editor will seem complex and Flash-like but, by the end of the book, you'll feel right at home.

You'll also be glad to know that Adobe has bundled several other new features that weren't implemented in LiveMotion 1. LiveMotion 2 now offers tighter integration with Adobe's lineup of applications, such as GoLive, After Effects, Photoshop, and Illustrator. GoLive, for example, now has the capability to open LiveMotion native files and LiveMotion can now import After Effects native files.

Book Structure

LiveMotion 2: A Beginner's Guide is composed of 15 modules, or chapters. These modules are grouped into three parts—Draw in LiveMotion, Animation, and Web and Multimedia Design—that take you from understanding how the program works all the way up to designing web sites with smooth transitions.

Part 1, "Draw in LiveMotion," helps you understand LiveMotion's interface, by discussing the toolbar, the composition, and the palettes. In addition, working with the various types of objects LiveMotion enables you to create or import is discussed. Toward the end of Part 1, you learn to create simple interactive animations composed of objects you've learned about and you also learn to export them, so you can view them in a web browser.

Module 1, "LiveMotion 2 Interface," helps you understand the LiveMotion environment. You learn the purpose of the palettes, the creation of a new composition, and the function of the individual tool in the toolbar.

Module 2, "Work with Simple Shapes," discusses using the four types of tools in the toolbar: Rectangle, Rounded Rectangle, Ellipse, and Polygon tool. Using these tools, you learn to create simple shapes.

Module 3, "Work with Custom Shapes," goes over using various commands to alter and manipulate the shapes learned in Module 2. You learn to use commands such as Transform, Combine, and Group to merge and cut out various parts of shapes.

Module 4, "Work with Text," discusses the creation and importance of type in your work. You learn how to use both the Type tool and the Transform palette to create and manipulate text on your composition.

Module 5, "Import Images," takes you through the steps you need to import images. After doing so, you go over the various palettes and commands which enable you to develop them further.

Module 6, "Buttons and Rollovers," teaches you how to create rollovers from the object you learned about in previous modules. You not only learn how to create simple interactive rollover effects, but also how to create remote rollovers, which enable you to trigger other rollovers.

Module 7, "Export Your Work," discusses the steps needed to export and display your work in a web browser. You learn about the various settings with the Export palette, which lets you set the type of file format to which you want to export your projects.

Part 2, "Animation," introduces you to the timeline, which enables you to animate the objects on your composition (the composition is the area on which you create, import, and edit your objects).

Module 8, "Introduction to the Timeline," teaches you the various parts of the timeline. Before you learn how to animate objects, you learn how the timeline is used by LiveMotion to animate its objects.

Module 9, "Create Simple Animations," takes you through several simple animations composed of the objects you learned about in previous modules.

Module 10, "Advanced Animations and Techniques," takes you on a larger leap into animation by discussing some advanced features of animation.

Module 11, "**Introduction to JavaScript**," is a compact introduction to the world of JavaScript. The module briefly discusses how JavaScripts are composed and covers several useful elements and features.

Part 3, "**Web and Multimedia Design**," teaches you more about scripting. It also explains the use of sound and music in LiveMotion, as well as design techniques.

Module 12, "**Scripting in LiveMotion**," teaches you the various features of scripting in LiveMotion. You learn about the Script Editor and the various types of scripts LiveMotion enables you to work with.

Module 13, "**Advanced Features of Scripting**," discusses some advanced features of scripting in LiveMotion. You learn about such features as Automation Scripting used to control other compositions, instead of the current one. You use this type of scripting to create LiveTabs, which function similarly to LiveMotion's palettes.

Module 14, "**Music and Sound**," takes you through the use of sound in LiveMotion. You learn about both the Sound palette, by discussing adding sound to Object States, and the creation of mini jukeboxes.

Module 15, "**Smooth Design**," wraps up the book by covering several techniques to create smooth transitions between pages when you create web sites in LiveMotion and using well-developed menu bars.

Special Elements

There are some special elements in this book. Each element helps you digest the information learned in each module. The modules themselves are grouped together, ideally for individualized learning. Every module opens up with a list of *Goals*. The *Ask the Expert* sections within the modules are in-depth explorations of a related topic that take you beyond the normal text. To help you quiz yourself along the way, *1-Minute Drills* are located throughout the text. At least one *Project* is located in each module. The project steps you through the creation of topic specific designs. A *Mastery Check* is located at the end of every module, for a more in-depth analysis of what you have learned. The answers to all the Mastery Check questions are in the appendix. The modules may also include hints, notes, or tips. These are short asides that relate to the topic on hand.

Part 1

Draw in LiveMotion

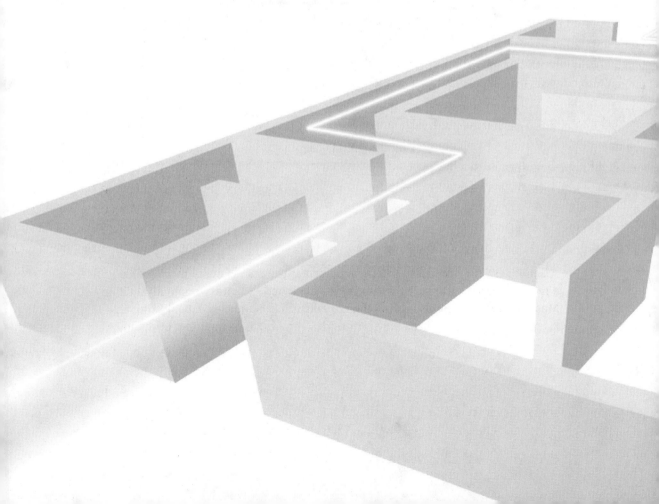

Module 1

LiveMotion 2 Interface

The Goals of this Module

- Understand the purpose of each tool in the toolbar
- Understand the importance of palettes
- Create a new composition
- Learn how to open and save your LiveMotion Projects

This module familiarizes you with the LiveMotion environment, explaining the purpose of each item in the toolbar, the use and importance of palettes, and how palettes relate to each tool. You will also create a new composition, and learn to specify the dimensions and frame rates that will be used within the composition. In conclusion, you'll learn how to open and save your LiveMotion projects, as well as properly exchange files between Macintosh and Windows type computers.

Note

A composition acts as a canvas, on which you'll be creating, editing, drawing, and designing various graphics and animations.

The Toolbar

LiveMotion opens with the toolbar showing on the left side of the screen, as seen in Figure 1-1. When working on a project, the toolbar can be toggled on and off in the Window menu by selecting Tools. Think of the toolbar as an assortment of various brushes you'll be working with on your composition (canvas). Creating and setting the preferences of a composition is explained in the section "Palettes and Ways to Arrange Them."

The toolbar has 22 items. The following describes every one of these items as they appear from top to bottom. In addition, Table 1-1 displays each tool's keystroke, which enables you to switch from tool to tool quickly, without having to select it with your mouse. As you progress through the lessons of this book, the features of each of these items are described in detail.

- **Adobe Online** Adobe has built an Adobe Online feature into all its applications to aid and educate. By clicking the Adobe Online icon, you get access to a huge library of features, such as online help and support, updates, patches, and downloads. You must have Internet Access to use this feature.

- **Arrow Tool** Enables you to select and move all objects on your composition by clicking and dragging them. In addition, the tool enables you to drag the outer points of all your text, graphics, and images to distort them.

- **Sub Group Selection Tool** Can simplify your work by enabling you to select and drag individual objects from within a group, without dragging the entire group itself.

1

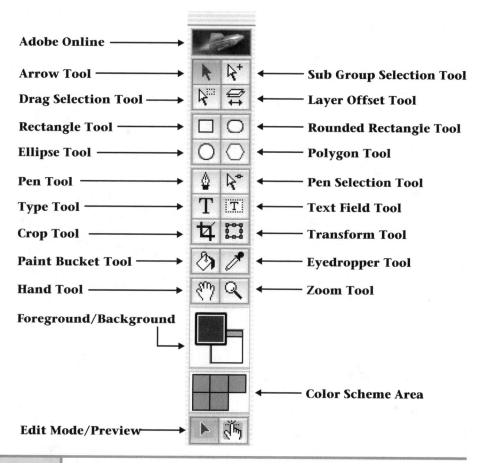

Figure 1-1   The LiveMotion Toolbar

- **Drag Selection Tool**   Enables the selection of objects that might be hidden behind other objects, by clicking and dragging around the hidden object. As you advance within the program, your compositions will often contain many objects, which might overlap each other.

- **Layer Offset Tool**   Enables you to select individual layers of an object, without selecting the entire object itself. This lets you manipulate and make changes to the selected layers, while leaving the unselected layers intact.

- **Rectangle Tool**   Enables you to draw rectangular shapes by clicking and dragging your mouse pointer on your composition. You can also draw perfect

Tool	Keystroke
Adobe Online	n/a
Arrow Tool	V
Sub Group Selection Tool	A
Drag Selection Tool	U
Layer Offset Tool	O
Rectangle Tool	M
Rounded Rectangle Tool	R
Ellipse Tool	L
Polygon Tool	N
Pen Tool	P
Pen Selection Tool	S
Type Tool	T
Text Field Tool	Y
Crop Tool	C
Transform Tool	E
Paint Bucket Tool	K
Eyedropper Tool	I
Hand Tool	H
Zoom Tool	Z
Foreground/Background	n/a
Color Scheme Area	n/a
Edit Mode/Preview Mode	Q

Table 1-1   Toolbar Keystrokes

squares with this tool by holding down the SHIFT key as you click and drag. The preferences for this tool are available in the Transform palette.

● **Rounded Rectangle Tool**   Enables you to draw rectangular and square shapes in the same manner, the edges and corners of which will be rounded. Again, to create squares, hold down the SHIFT key as you click and drag.

● **Ellipse Tool**   Enables you to draw elliptical shapes by clicking and dragging your mouse pointer on your composition. You can also draw perfect circles with this tool by holding down the SHIFT key as you click and drag.

1

- **Polygon Tool** Enables you to create polygons ranging from three to ten sides. Holding down the SHIFT key while dragging keeps all angles equal.

- **Pen Tool** Enables you to create custom shapes by creating points along your composition. As you click your composition to place the second point, the previously placed point connects a segment to the first point. The line that now connects these two points can either be straight or curved. To curve a line between the two points, hold and drag your mouse as you place your next point. Once points are placed, you also have the option to remove them by clicking them. Additionally, by clicking and dragging anywhere along the lines that connect the point together, you have the option of creating new points. The limits of this tool are endless.

- **Pen Selection Tool** An extension of the Pen tool, this tool lets you drag individual line segments between any two points in a shape you've created using the Pen tool. By dragging a line segment with this tool, the object takes on a new shape.

- **Type Tool** Enables you to enter text on your composition. Unlike with the previous version of LiveMotion, LiveMotion 2 lets you enter text with the Type tool on the Composition, instead of into a dialogue box. The tool also lets you create specified boundaries for the text being entered with the tool at a later point by clicking and dragging your mouse with the Type tool. After creating this boundary, all text entered inside it will be kept inside as you type.

- **Text Field Tool** Enables you to enter dynamic text on your composition. Dynamic text is used in scripting and assigned variables that display based on the outcome of a script being run. You learn more about dynamic text and this tool when scripting is discussed in Part 2 of this book.

- **Crop Tool** This tool can be used in two ways. The first way lets you crop unwanted parts of an image or graphic by moving its top, bottom, or sides, and then dragging them. The second way enables you to drag an already cropped object up, down, or sideways by clickingm and dragging its center to crop any unwanted side.

- **Transform Tool** This tool is similar to the Arrow tool with only one difference. By selecting an object with this tool, you can transform its shape. However, unlike the arrow tool, this tool also lets you skew the object.

● **Paint Bucket Tool**   Enables you to set the color and style of any objects. To use this tool, select it and click on an object you want to paint over with a solid color or acquire a specific style. Remember, prior to using this tool, you need to have either a color or style already selected. Styles are introduced in Module 2.

● **Eyedropper Tool**   Enables you to extract a color and style of any object in your composition and save it for later use. This tool works best when used with the Paint Bucket tool.

● **Hand Tool**   Enables you to move the actual composition canvas. If your composition size is larger than your monitor screen, you can use the Hand tool to move to hidden parts of your canvas, instead of having to use the side arrows.

● **Zoom Tool**   Enables you to zoom in and out of your composition. To zoom in, select the tool and click once on your composition. You can zoom in up to 800 percent on your composition. To zoom out, hold down the OPTION key as you click. You can't zoom out further than 50 percent.

● **Foreground/Background**   Below all the tools, notice two squares arranged diagonally on top of each other. The first square displays the current active color, also known as your foreground color. You can change your foreground color in two ways. The first way is by using the Eyedropper tool, which was briefly described earlier, and clicking any object on your composition. You'll notice the foreground box has automatically changed to the color you clicked with the Eyedropper tool. The second way involves using the color palette, which will be explained in the section "The Color Palette." The foreground color box automatically updates with the color chosen from the color palette. The second square is your background color box. By changing the color in that box, you change the background color of your composition. To change your background color, you first need to select the background box, and then proceed with either the Eyedropper tool or the color palette, as you did with the foreground color.

● **Color Scheme Area**   Below the foreground/background boxes is the Color Scheme area. You should see five little squares, each a different color. The Color Scheme area works in conjunction with the Color Scheme palette. The palette and this area are discussed in Module 15.

● **Edit Mode/Preview Mode**   At the bottom of the toolbar, you see two icons. The first icon represents the *Edit* mode, which is the mode you're

1

in currently. The other icon is the Preview mode. When the *Preview* mode is clicked, it shows you a preview of the output for your project. Because animation hasn't yet been covered, you needn't concern yourself with this feature for now. Continue working in the Edit mode by making sure it's selected at all times.

To identify any item in the toolbar, rest the pointer on the icon without clicking the mouse button and its name will appear. You can also move the toolbar to any location on your screen by clicking and dragging the top. To restore its default location, choose Reset to Defaults in the Window menu. Remember, each item will be explained in full detail in upcoming modules of this book.

1-Minute Drill

● What's a quick way to hide the toolbar from your working environment?

● Which four tools in the toolbar enable you to draw shapes?

Ask the Expert

Question: Why don't some of the items in the toolbar have a shortcut key?

Answer: Some of the items in the toolbar aren't tools that you directly work with on your composition. For example, the color scheme item in the toolbar works in conjunction with the Color Scheme palette. By defining colors in this palette, the toolbar displays the colors you chose, so this item doesn't act like a tool.

Question: What are palettes?

Answer: *Palettes* are preferences for the individual tools and items in the toolbar. They're thoroughly explained in the next section of this module.

● Go to the Window menu and uncheck the Tools command.
● The Rectangle tool, the Rounded Rectangle tool, the Ellipse tool, and the Polygon tool.

Palettes and Ways to Arrange Them

In addition to the toolbar, your LiveMotion environment also contains palettes. Palettes are preferences and settings for all the tools in the toolbar. Palettes are the various paints you'll use with your brushes (tools and items in the toolbar) on your composition and they serve the tools in the toolbar the same way paints serve brushes when you're painting. By adjusting these settings as you work with the tools and items in the toolbar, you can create, alter, distort, color, and animate the objects you'll be creating on your composition.

Each palette is embedded in a tabbed window within a larger window containing other palettes within. In LiveMotion 2, there are exactly 18 palettes. As you begin learning each individual tool in upcoming modules, you'll learn which palette to use to alter the state of that specific tool. The tabbed windows each contain a palette that can be moved from one window to another at your discretion. As you familiarize yourself further with LiveMotion 2, you'll begin to adjust the grouping of palettes according to your preference. To move a tabbed window, simply click-and-drag the top of the window, and then move it either in front or in back of another tabbed window. You can also move the tabbed window to another window to group the palettes you think can help you organize your working environment. To set the palettes to their default position, simply go to the Window menu and select Reset to Defaults. The following is a brief explanation of each palette you'll come across while working in LiveMotion 2.

Properties Palette

The *Properties* palette enables you to change font type, size, and style for any text placed on your composition using the Text tool. For shapes created using the Ellipse, Rectangle, Rounded Rectangle, and the Pen tool, the Properties palette lets you change their shape. For imported images, this palette enables you to change the alpha channels, which are explained in Module 5. In addition, the Properties palette also lets you adjust the settings for any of the variables created using the Text Field tool.

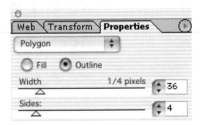

Transform Palette

The *Transform* palette enables you to change the orientation of any object, such as height, width, skew, rotation, and its coordinate position based on the Y- and X-axis. This palette works with all objects, either created or imported into LiveMotion, which include shapes, images, and text objects.

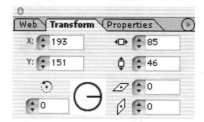

Web Palette

The *Web* palette lets you add a URL (a link) to any object, so when it's exported, it could be used as a link to another page. This palette also provides you with special HTML characteristics for the object it's being used on, such as the object's filename once it's exported as a sliced image and even the targeted frame of the object's link.

Color Palette

The *Color* palette enables you to change the color of shapes and text. In addition, you can also change the color of the background with this palette.

The Color palette lets you display its color wheel in a variety of forms, ranging from Saturation to RGB. You learn more about these forms in Module 2.

Opacity Palette

The *Opacity* palette lets you change the opacity, also known as the transparency of any object, on your composition. As you begin working with layers in upcoming modules, this tool will also enable you to change the opacity of individual layers of an object. In addition, the Opacity palette lets you add a special gradient opacity effect to your objects. These effects range from Linear effects that blend into the background to Radial effects that resemble spirals. You learn more about these and other effects made with the Opacity palette in Module 2.

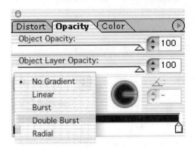

Distort Palette

If you're familiar with Adobe Photoshop, you'll notice the *Distort Palette* tool resembles the Filter menu. In other words, it enables you to apply filters to individual objects by changing their appearance.

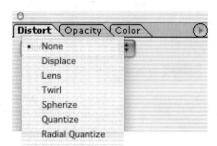

Adjust Palette

The *Adjust* palette lets you adjust settings, such as brightness, contrast, saturation, and tint for any object. In addition, you can posterize objects with this palette.

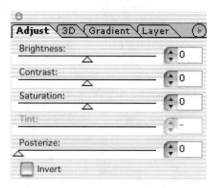

3-D Palette

The *3-D* palette is for giving your object volume. With this palette, you can emboss objects to give them a 3-D-like feeling with a variety of filters, including Cutout, Emboss, Bevel, and Ripple.

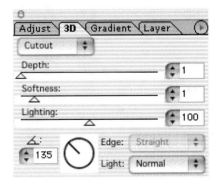

Gradient Palette

The *Gradient* palette enables you to give objects a smooth transition between the type of effect in colors. This effect has several variations, which will be explained in detail in Module 2. The effects of this palette can only be applied to shape and text type objects. Image objects can't be altered.

Layer Palette

As you learn about layers in future modules, you'll learn how to manage the appearance of layers in relation to the objects they're related to with the *Layer* palette. In addition, the Layer Offset tool described previously can be used to perform similar tasks.

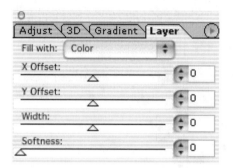

Color Scheme Palette

The *Color Scheme* palette is useful for individuals who want to stay consistent with the use of color on their projects. This palette lets you set colors for your project, and the colors stay saved in the palette and are easily accessible. This palette works in conjunction with the Color Scheme area in your toolbar, which displays the colors set in the Color Scheme palette. You learn more about this palette in Module 15.

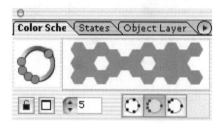

States Palette

The *States* palette enables you to add States to any object on your composition, which results in converting the object into a rollover. *Rollovers* help to add interactivity to your projects. You learn about them in Module 6. This palette lets you create and manage rollovers set for objects.

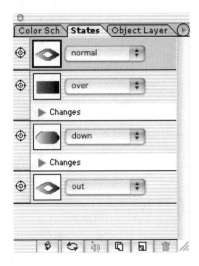

Object Palette

The *Object* palette works in conjunction with the Layer palette. It enables you to create and manage layers for any object on your composition. As you learned earlier, the Layer palette enables us to modify these layers.

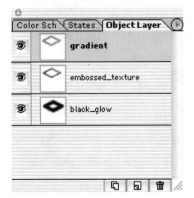

Sounds Palette

The *Sounds* palette holds sound files. In addition, it lets you apply sound files to specific objects and their states. In Module 14, you learn about using sound

1

with your projects by combining a variation of the States and Sounds palette to create interactive rollovers with sound.

Library Palette

The *Library* palette holds various shapes. This palette not only enables you to place shapes, it also lets you save shapes you've created or imported to your composition.

Texture Palette

The *Texture* palette holds textures that could be applied to various shapes. You learn about bringing your own textures into this palette in Module 2.

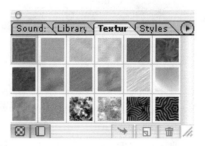

Styles Palette

The *Styles* palette holds styles, which come in various forms. Styles could be saved animation states, rollover effects, layered files, or even files that contain scripts. The Styles palette lets you apply these styles to any object on your composition, as well as create your own custom styles from the object you created on your composition.

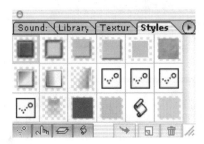

Export Palette

The *Export* palette controls all the settings for exporting your project file. You only need to use this palette when you're finished with your project and want to export your file. You learn more about the settings in the Export palette and the various formats LiveMotion 2 enables you to export your compositions to in Module 7.

Palettes play an important role in the LiveMotion environment. Mastering them enables you to produce compositions with creativity and originality. At times, some palettes might seem more difficult to grasp than others, but they will all be explained fully as the book unfolds.

Ask the Expert

Question: How many individual palettes can I fit in one window?

Answer: If you choose to, you can fit all the palettes in one window, but you should be aware this will take up a great deal of your screen space.

1-Minute Drill

● How would you move one palette on to another window that contains other palettes?

● What's a quick way to restore palettes to their default locations after they've been rearranged by the user?

Create a New Composition

You should now have a basic understanding of the LiveMotion environment. You've learned about the toolbar and its purpose, as well as the palettes and how to use them with the toolbar. Now it's time to learn to create and define the specifications for a composition. For every project you work on, you need to specify various dimensions and frame rates. Typically, you might want to use the same preferences for your composition as with your previous project, so LiveMotion always remembers the composition preferences of your last project.

To start, open your LiveMotion 2 program application and select NEW from the File menu. Notice that a dialogue box displays on your screen asking you for various information. At the top of the window, you're asked to fill in the Width and Height settings which determines the size of your new document. LiveMotion determines and measures these settings in pixels.

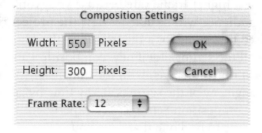

● Drag the top portion of the palette, then drag-and-drop it on to the other window.
● Go in to the Window menu and select Restore to Defaults.

Note

A pixel is a form of measurement. Your computer screen contains thousands of these pixels, each filled with one solid color. Approximately 72 pixels are in one inch.

Determine the Height and Width of Your Composition

In determining the width and height of your composition, consider the resolution of your monitor. Most monitors are set to 1,024 pixels in width and 768 pixels in height. Therefore, creating a composition with the dimensions of 550×500 pixels would take up relatively half the height and width of a monitor set to that resolution. The Internet standard is currently leaning toward this setting. The previous standard was 800×600 pixels.

Determine the Frame Rate for Your Composition

Right below the width and height settings, you'll see the Frame Rate option. A *frame rate* is the amount of frames that will play in a second. The more frames per second, the smoother the animation, although fewer frames rates will considerably reduce your exported file size. Determine your frame rate setting by figuring out on which medium you plan to show your work. If you're designing an animation that will play on your web site, consider using a lesser frame rate, so you keep your file size small. The default amount is set to 12, which most animation designers tend to stick to while creating animations that will play on the Internet. On the other hand, if you plan on designing a CD-ROM presentation, choose a higher frame rate because you won't be limited by file size. Instead, your audience will be able to view the project right from their CD-ROM, as opposed to waiting for a file to load in their browser.

After you fill in all the settings for a new composition and click OK, a blank document will appear on your screen with the dimensions you specified. You can go back and change any of the settings at any time by going into the Edit menu and selecting Composition Settings. Try experimenting with different composition dimensions to find one that suits you.

Save and Open Your Work

LiveMotion native project files are PC and Macintosh backward-compatible. They can be opened with either platform, regardless of where you originally started your project file. There's only one extra step to make sure your LiveMotion project files will open on a PC after they've been created on a Macintosh. The LiveMotion application saves its project files as .liv type files. The *.liv* is a file extension name for all native LiveMotion projects, the same way that a .psd type file is native to Adobe Photoshop. *Native* files can only be opened and edited by the programs that created them. PC applications automatically attach a file extension name to all their documents. On the other hand, Macintosh applications don't, so if you're a Macintosh user, it's important to add a .liv file extension name to all your saved work if you plan to open your documents on a PC. The outcome of trying to open a file that hasn't been tagged with a file extension can sometimes result in the program prompting you that the file is corrupted. Make sure you take the extra precaution if you're planning on sharing your files with others who might use a different type of computer than you, or if you constantly work on different platforms yourself.

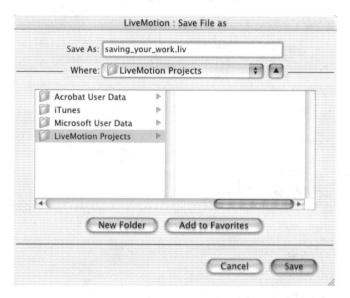

Another important task is always to save your LiveMotion 2 files in the .liv native format. Saving your files in the native format of any program you use enables you to change or add content to your projects in the future. Once a file is exported, that exported file can no longer be opened in LiveMotion. Only the .liv version of that project can be altered in the program. To save a project in LiveMotion to the program's native format, simply use the Save As command from the File menu. Macintosh users, remember the .liv extension if you plan to open your projects on PCs in the future.

Opening files is simple. To open a LiveMotion document, choose Open from the File menu and select the location where your LiveMotion project file is located. The composition of that file's project will open automatically. LiveMotion only enables you to open files with the .liv file extension name. Similarly, you can only save your LiveMotion projects as .liv files. Don't despair if you have graphic or audio files you want LiveMotion to open. There's a different way of bringing these files into LiveMotion (as you learn) in Module 5. If you're planning to export your files to different mediums, you're not limited to only the .liv file type. This feature is also explained in Module 14.

File	
New Composition...	⌘N
New Script	⌥⌘N
Open...	⌘O
Close	⌘W
Save	⌘S
Save As...	⇧⌘S
Revert	F12
Place...	⌘I
Place Sequence...	⌥⇧⌘I
Place as Texture...	
Replace...	⇧⌘I
Export Settings...	⌥⇧⌘E
Export	⌘E
Export As...	⇧⌘E
Export Selection...	
Preview In	▶
File Info...	
Workgroup	▶
Page Setup...	⇧⌘P
Print...	⌘P

LiveMotion is also equipped with a Revert feature. The *Revert* command lets you undo all changes to your project up to your last save. To revert to your last save, choose Revert from the File menu.

1-Minute Drill

● How would you undo all the changes you've made to your project since your last save?

Project 1–1: Create and Save a Simple Composition

In this module, you learned all the basics of LiveMotion. You should now be able to open and save files, and create new documents with various dimensions. In addition, you should have a basic overview of the tools in the toolbar, as well as a brief understanding of all the palettes. You should have a good grasp on arranging your working environment as far as moving the toolbar and arranging all the palettes. The following is a simple project to incorporate everything you learned in this module.

Step-by-Step

1. Begin creating a new composition by choosing New from the File menu.

2. Set the height to 550 and the width to 500.

3. Set the Frame Rate to 12.

4. Even though the composition area is empty, let's end this project in order to have a project file to work with in Module 2. Choose Save As from the File menu and save the file as Project1. (Remember, if you're working on a Macintosh platform, add the .liv file extension name to the end of the filename. If you're working on a PC, ignore it.)

5. Consider creating a new folder where you can easily access all the projects we'll be working on in this book. Create a new folder and save it as LiveMotion Projects. Move the file you just created to that folder.

Project Summary

You should now have a LiveMotion file saved in your LiveMotion Projects folder. As you progress to upcoming modules, you'll have several files in this folder, all of which you'll use as you go through this book.

● Use the Revert command found in the File menu.

Summary

Within this first module, you learned about most of the interface of the LiveMotion environment. You read about all the tools and items in the toolbar, as well as each individual palette and its importance. In addition, you explored creating a new composition and setting its preferences. Finally, you learned about saving and opening your LiveMotion Projects. In Module 2, you'll learn about a variety of tools and palettes to create simple shapes. You'll now use everything you learned about the LiveMotion environment in this module to help you better understand palettes and how they relate to individual tools and items in the toolbar.

Mastery Check

1. What are pixels?

   A. A file extension name

   B. Objects drawn using the tools in the toolbar

   C. A form of measurement

   D. Objects created by the Pen tool

2. If you're planning to design your project for web use, a good idea is to keep your frame rate _____. On the other hand, if you're designing your project for a CD-ROM presentation, you should keep your frame rate _____, for smooth quality.

3. What's a quick way to access the tools in the toolbar?

   A. Clicking them with your mouse pointer

   B. Selecting them from the Windows menu

   C. Using a specified keystroke

   D. Based on user preference

☑ *Mastery Check*

4. How would you move palettes from one window to another?

   A. Using the Pen tool

   B. Clicking and dragging them

   C. Holding down SHIFT as you press a keystroke

   D. Using the Palette tool

5. What's the significance of adding a file extension name during the Save process?

   A. It helps your LiveMotion application on a PC recognize the file.

   B. It helps Macintosh computers better recognize PC files.

   C. It significantly reduces the size of the file.

   D. It makes LM files saved on a Macintosh unable to be open on a PC.

Module 2

Work with Simple Shapes

The Goals of this Module

- Learn how to draw various shapes using specific tools in the toolbar
- Know how to use various palettes to transform your shapes
- Be able to apply and alter various color attributes of shapes
- Know how to add layers and apply 3-D like effects to shapes
- Be able to apply styles and textures to shapes

In the previous module, you got a sense of what the LiveMotion environment consists off and how to set up your working space within it. In this module, everything revolves around the creation of various shapes. This module begins by explaining ways to draw these various shapes using the four basic tools in the toolbar: the Ellipse tool, the Rectangle tool, the Rounded Rectangle tool, and the Polygon tool. In addition, you learn ways of using specific palettes to transform them. In conclusion, how to apply various attributes to these shapes, such as color, gradients, layers, 3-D-like effects, styles, and textures. Many of the palettes you learn about in this module can prepare you for future modules in which you'll also use them. In other words, this module can help you get adjusted to the way you'll use these same palettes, while altering states of other objects, such as images and text.

Draw Various Shapes Using the Toolbar

LiveMotion comes equipped with the four basic tools for creating vector drawings. By understanding how these tools work, you'll find yourself drawing various shapes on your composition. Vectors are objects that stay consistent as you transform their Height and Width attributes. Unlike images, which are referred to as *bitmap objects,* vectors never become pixilated when resized. You learn the differences between these two types of objects in Module 7 when you learn about the export process of your LiveMotion projects.

The previous module ended by creating a simple composition you saved in your LiveMotion Projects folder. You'll remember, at the end of the project, I said you'd use this file in Module 2. Open that file now so you can experiment with the various tools and palettes introduced in this module. Let's begin by individually describing and using the four basic vector tools.

Ellipse Tool

The *Ellipse* tool enables you to create elliptical shapes by clicking and dragging on your composition. Experiment with this tool by first selecting it in the Toolbar, then click and drag on your composition until your ellipse matches the left side shape in Figure 2-1. You've just drawn an elliptical shape but,

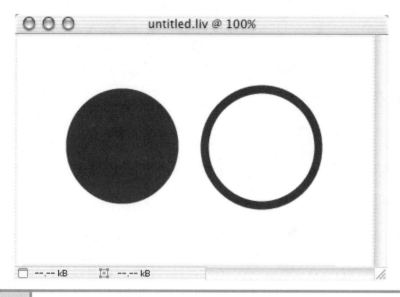

Figure 2-1   Drawing an ellipse

perhaps, you might want this ellipse to be a perfect circle. You can do this in several ways. The first way involves switching back to the Arrow tool and selecting the object if it isn't selected already. Now hold down the SHIFT key and click any of the outer four points located at the corners of the object. Your ellipse should now be a perfect circle. The other way of performing this function is to start from scratch. Select the elliptical object with the Arrow tool and press the DELETE key on your keyboard to remove the object from your composition. Now, switch back to the Ellipse tool and hold down the SHIFT key as you click and drag on your composition. Once again, you should have a perfect circle.

The object you just drew is filled with a solid color. With the Properties palette, you can set the object to reveal only its outline, as seen in the right side object of Figure 1. Look at the Properties palette and notice the Fill and Outline preferences. Make sure your object is selected, and then press the Outline preference on the Properties palette. Your object should now only contain the outline of the shape you created. To control the thickness of the outline, use the Width preference in the palette either to increase or decrease the thickness.

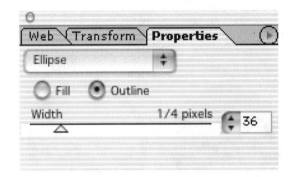

☐ Rectangle Tool

The Rectangle tool lets you create rectangular shapes on your composition. Click and drag on your composition until your shape matches Figure 2-2. Just as the Ellipse tool lets you create a perfect circle, you can create a perfect square by holding down the SHIFT key as you click and drag with the Rectangle tool. You can also convert a rectangle to a square by holding down the SHIFT key as you click the object with the Arrow tool. Remembering to switch tools as you practice creating these various shapes might become a little nerve racking, but

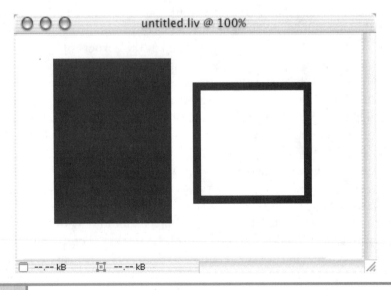

Figure 2-2 Drawing a rectangle

you'll get the feel for it with practice. If you unintentionally create an additional shape when you mean, instead, to select the object, you can always undo your action. To do this, select Undo in the Edit menu. An even easier way to perform this action is to use the keystroke COMMAND-Z.

As with the Ellipse tool, you can change your rectangular object to reveal just its outline using the Properties palette. If you switch back to the Arrow tool, and select your rectangular object, you'll notice that another preference appears at the top of the Properties palette. With this preference, you can turn your object into any of the four vector objects described here: ellipse, rectangle, rounded rectangle, and polygon. In addition, you have an option to turn your shape into a path. Paths are created with the Pen tool and their purpose is described in Module 3. By converting your object into a path object, you allow it to become more editable by the Pen tool.

Rounded Rectangle Tool

As you learned in Module 1, the Rounded Rectangle tool is no different from the Rectangle tool. The only obvious difference between these tools is the Rounded Rectangle tool lets you create rectangles and squares with rounded corners. To control the curvature of corners in your shape, use the Properties palette. Make sure your Rounded Rectangular shape is selected, and then look at the Properties palette. The palette should contain an additional radius preference.

Note

As you work with various tools in the toolbar, notice your palettes sometimes contain different preferences, depending on which tool you're planning to use to create and edit your object.

As you increase the value of the radius, you'll also increase the curvature of the corners of your object and vice versa. Look at Figure 2-3 to see the various shapes you can create with this tool.

Polygon Tool

As you learned in Module 1, the Polygon tool enables you to create various polygons ranging from three to ten sides. Just as with the previous tools, select

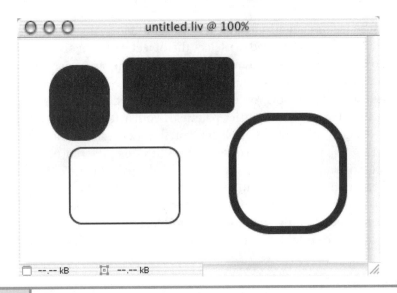

○ ○ ○　　　　　　untitled.liv @ 100%

⬜ --.-- kB　　🔲 --.-- kB

Figure 2-3　Drawing a rounded rectangle

the Polygon tool, and then click and drag to create this shape on your composition. In addition, you can make the angles of your polygons equal by holding down the SHIFT key as you draw the shape with the tool.

To change the amount of sides in your polygon, once again use the Properties palette. In addition to the preferences discussed with the other three tools, notice a Sides preference. Changing the value of this preference increases or decreases the amount of sides in your polygon, respectively. Observe the various polygons you can create with this tool in Figure 2-4.

1-Minute Drill

● Which Palette enables you to control several aspects of shapes drawn with the four vector tools in the toolbar?

● What is the maximum number of sides the Polygon tool lets you create?

● The Properties palette enables you to control several aspects of shapes drawn with the four vector tools in the toolbar.
● The maximum number of sides the Polygon tool lets you create is ten.

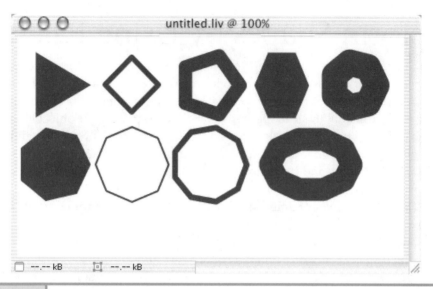

Figure 2-4   Drawing a polygon

Ask the Expert

Question: Am I limited to only these four vector tools in LiveMotion?

Answer: Of course not! In addition to the four shape tools in the toolbar, you also learn how to use the Pen tool in the next module. In addition, ways of adding various shapes from the Library palette are discussed.

Question: Can I import shapes from other applications like Adobe Illustrator?

Answer: Definitely. Not only does LiveMotion enable you to import both native and EPS files created in Adobe Illustrator, it also lets you store them for future use in its Library palette, discussed in the next module.

Question: What's an EPS file?

Answer: An *EPS file* is the format of a file that contains a vector drawing. Adobe Illustrator is one of the programs with the capability to save vector drawings in this format.

Transform Shapes by Using Palettes

Before describing ways of altering your shapes using the Transform palette, let's exercise ways of transforming them right on your composition using the Arrow tool. You've already learned how to drag your objects along your composition using the Arrow tool. Instead, perhaps you'd like to move your object along the X and Y coordinates. To do this, hold down the SHIFT key as you click and drag your object with the Arrow tool. You'll notice your mouse cursor only lets you move up, down, left, and right along your composition, constraining the object to move at 45 degree angles. This is useful when you're trying to move an object vertically on your composition without losing its horizontal position and vice versa.

Notice in Figure 2-5 that when an object is selected with the Arrow tool, seven filled squares and one unfilled square surround the object. By moving your mouse cursor over the unfilled square, your mouse cursor changes into a rotation symbol. If you drag over the unfilled square and hold down the SHIFT key, the rotation is constrained to 15-degree increments. To use one of the other corners to rotate on Windows, use the CTRL key and drag. To use one of the other corners to rotate while constrained to 15-degree increments, hold the CTRL key and the SHIFT key.

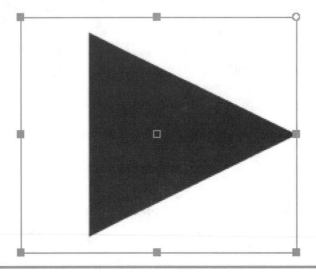

Figure 2-5 | A selected object

The remaining seven filled squares let you transform the width and height of your object. The three filled squares that appear at the corners let you increase and decrease the width and height of your object simultaneously. The remaining four squares enable you to transform the width and height individually. As you might have already noticed, dragging the four corners at the sides of your object increases and decreases them in both directions. To increase or decrease just one side of your object, you'll need to hold down the OPTION key as you click and drag one of the four points. On Windows, use the ALT key and drag to increase or decrease one side.

You can also skew your object directly on your composition without using the Transform palette. To do so, hold down the COMMAND key as you click and drag one of the four filled points located at the sides of your object. On Windows, use the CTRL key to skew.

Now that you've had a hands-on experience using the four basic vector tools in the toolbar and using your composition to transform various attributes of your objects, it's time to introduce two important palettes for transforming your shapes.

1-Minute Drill

● How do you rotate an object without using the Transform palette?

● How would you go about moving your object along the Y-axis?

Properties Palette

You already know about the various preferences you can set as you're working with your four vector shapes, as discussed earlier. Remember, the preferences will change, depending on which tool you're using. In future modules, this palette will also change as you learn about transforming text and images.

Transform Palette

The Transform palette lets you transform various dimensions of your shapes. The first preference lets you change the position of your shape on the

---

● To rotate an object without using the Transform palette, you can use the wheel preference to change the angle of your rotation or you can enter the value of the angle.
● To move your object along the Y-axis, hold down the SHIFT key, and select and drag your object.

composition. The X value field is for your object's X-axis orientation on your composition. By decreasing this value, your shape will move toward the left. By increasing this value, your shape will move to the right. The Y value field changes your object's orientation along the Y-axis. By increasing this field, your object will move further down on your composition. By decreasing this value, your object will move further up. To move your object to the upper-left corner of your composition, you would select the object and fill in 0 for both these fields. If you further decrease these fields, your object will start moving outside your composition, leaving part of it hidden.

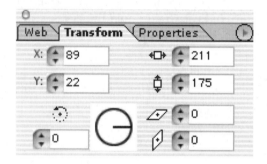

The next preference field in this palette, right below the X and Y fields, is your rotation preference. By default, any shape you create will have an angle value of 0. By increasing the angle, your object will rotate counterclockwise. By decreasing this angle into a negative value, your object will move in the clockwise direction. You can also use the wheel preference to rotate your object. By clicking anywhere in the wheel, you'll notice both the line segment inside the wheel moves toward the location you clicked and the angle value automatically updates to the angle you chose in the wheel. You can also drag this segment around until you choose the appropriate angle for your object.

At the upper-left corner of your Transform palette is the Width and Height setting for your object. By increasing one of these values, you'll stretch either the width or the height of your object. In the same sense, if you decrease one of these values, you'll compress either the width or the height of your object.

The last preference in the Transform palette enables you to skew your objects. The first field lets you skew your object along the X-axis. By increasing this value, your object will begin to skew toward the right. By decreasing this value, your object will skew to the left. The same applies for the Y-axis field. By increasing this value, your object will skew up and, by decreasing, skew down.

2

This completes this part of the tutorial for transforming your objects using the Properties and Transform palettes. It's essential for you to practice using these palettes so you'll develop a better feel for transforming your objects. In the next section, you start using color in your shapes.

Add Color to Shapes

I'm sure you're bored with working in black-and-white by now. So far, all of your shapes have been black and your composition has stayed white. In this section of the module, you not only learn how to add colors to your shapes, you also learn to change values such as opacity, brightness, contrast, gradients, and others.

Color Palette

The Color palette displays colors that you'll use to color your various objects. At the upper-right corner of the palette, there's a small triangle. When you click the triangle, it shows you various displays of colors. You can select any of the colors to help you choose the appropriate color for your object. The RGB (red-green-blue) view shows you the number value for any selected color. All Hypertext Markup Language (HTML) files use these values to display colors correctly for such things as font color, link color, and background. If you know of a specific value and you want to choose its appropriate color in LiveMotion, you can enter that value in the RGB view.

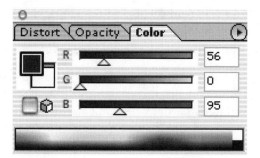

In the upper-left corner of the palette, notice two squares on top of each other resembling those in the toolbar. Just as in the toolbar, these squares represent your foreground and background colors. By selecting the Background square in either the toolbar or the Color palette, and then selecting a color from any one of the color views, you'll notice the background of your composition matches the color you selected. You can change the background to any color you want. The Foreground square changes the color of any object currently selected. Try creating a simple shape. Make sure the shape and the foreground square are selected, and choose a color to apply to the shape.

Right below the Foreground and Background squares in the Color palette, you'll notice a check box next to a small cube. By checking this preference, all the colors in the Color palette will be limited to only the 216 Web Safe colors. This guarantees that all the colors in your project will display correctly to all users.

Two tools work in conjunction with the Color palette. The *Eyedropper* tool lets you extract a color from any object on your composition. When you do this, notice the Foreground box in both the toolbar and the Color palette absorbed that particular color. To apply this color to another object on your composition, you need to use the *Paint Bucket* tool. To do so, select the Paint Bucket tool from the toolbar and click the object you want to apply the color to. Remember, you needn't use the Paint Bucket tool if you want to apply the color to a shape you haven't drawn yet. This is because any shape you draw from now on already contains the color displayed in the Foreground square. The color remains there until you decide to switch it.

Ask the Expert

Question: The background color of my HTML file is 51 153 152. I want to use the same color for the background of my LiveMotion project. How can I exactly match the color in LiveMotion to this value?

Answer: Begin by selecting the RGB view from the drop-down menu in the Color palette. Enter the values in order, starting with 51 in the first field, 153 in the second field, and 152 in the last field.

Question: How do I bring an object in front of another object at will?

Answer: If the object is hidden to begin with, use the Drag selection tool to select it, and then choose Arrange | Bring to Front from the Object menu.

Opacity Palette

The Opacity palette lets you alter the transparency of your objects. By selecting specific preferences in this palette, your objects will become transparent if they either overlap another object or if their color is different from the color of your background. Look at the Opacity palette and notice the various preferences within. The first preference sets the transparency of the object selected. The closer you are to the 0 value, the more transparent your object becomes. In contrast, the closer the value is to 100, the less transparent the object becomes. The next preference sets the transparency of individual layers of your objects. You learned a little about layers in the first module and they'll be further explained in the next section of this module. The Layer Opacity preferences in the palette works the same way as the Object Opacity palette.

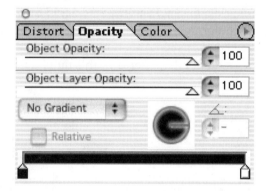

In addition to changing the opacity of objects and layers in the Opacity palette, you have the option to add Transparency Gradient effects to your objects. Don't confuse this effect with the Gradient palette, which is discussed in the next section. You can choose from four effects:

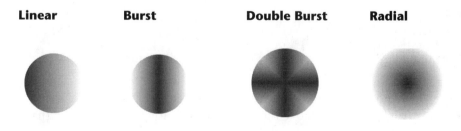

Linear   **Burst**   **Double Burst**   **Radial**

You can also rotate the effect of the transparency by rotating the circle next to the effect preference. As you move about the wheel, the angle field changes with it. Also, notice the two sliders on the bottom of the palette. As you move the left slider toward the right, the transition between the transparent part of your object and the nontransparent part is more sudden. As you move the right slighter toward the left, the transition is more subtle.

Gradient Palette

The Gradient palette is similar to the Opacity palette. A *gradient* is the fading of one color, as it comes in contact with another color. Look at the Gradient palette and notice the similarities to the Opacity palette. You have the same effect options: Linear, Burst, Double Burst, and Radial. Unlike the Opacity palette, you're no longer dealing with transparencies. This time, you're fading one color into another color on your objects. At the bottom of the palette, you have exactly the same sliders, except this time they're in color. Select an object to which you'll add a gradient effect. Perform this quick task:

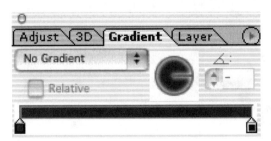

1. Select your shape.

2. In the Gradient palette, select the Radial option from the drop-down menu.

3. Click the left slider and choose a color from the Color palette.

4. Select the right-side slider and select a different color from the Color palette.

Your object now contains a Gradient effect, as seen in Figure 2-6. As with the Opacity palette, you can move the sliders in any direction to increase that specific color amount in your object. In addition, you can use the wheel in the Gradient palette to rotate the effect.

2

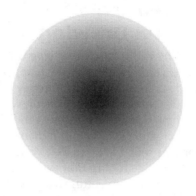

Figure 2-6   A shape with a Gradient effect

Adjust Palette

The Adjust palette will become more useful in Module 5, where you learn about using images in LiveMotion. The palette is useful when you want to increase or decrease values such as Brightness, Contrast, Saturation, and Tint. To change any of these preferences in your object, select the object and move the slider to the right or to the left. Notice the Tint effect is grayed out. You can only change the Tint value in Images. In addition, two Photoshop-like effects exist: Posterize and Invert. *Posterize* is also aimed more toward images and won't be useful to shapes. The Invert effect is a simple check box. By checking this box, the color of your object changes to its opposite color.

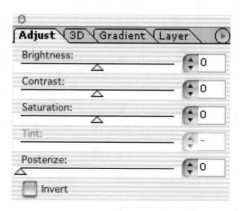

Project 2–1: Create a Two-dimensional Drawing

We've come to a mid point in this module. We've discussed creating and transforming shapes, and you've learned how to apply and adjust colors to your shapes. You also learned about adding transparency to your objects, as well as applying gradients. Practice makes perfect, which is why you should take a break now and practice everything you learned so far in this module by doing a project.

In this project, you'll create a simple two-dimensional drawing. The drawing will be a pair of balloons. as seen in Figure 2-7. You'll use the Ellipse tool, the Polygon tool, and the Rectangle tool to draw your balloons. Then you'll use the Color, Opacity, and the Properties palettes to add some detail. Let's begin.

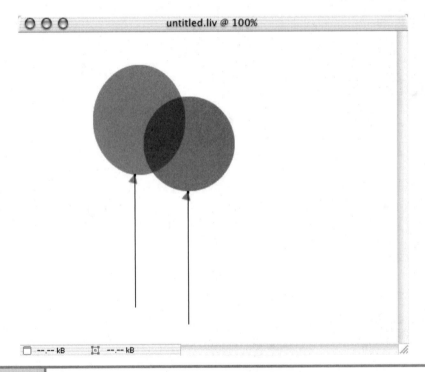

Figure 2-7   2-D balloons

Step-by-Step

1. Choose the Ellipse tool from the toolbar and draw your first balloon. Now, draw your second balloon, except hold down the SHIFT key this time, to make your balloon circular. Position the second balloon slightly over the first one by dragging it with the Arrow tool.

2. Choose the Polygon tool from the toolbar and go over to the Properties palette. Type in **3**, for the Sides preference. Now draw two small triangles on your composition.

3. Notice the triangles aren't positioned properly. Let's fix that by choosing the arrow and selecting both of the triangles. Now rotate the triangles, so their longer edge points up. Next, position them below the two ellipses. To rotate the triangles, you can use the Transform palette or you can drag the unfilled square that's located in the upper-left corner of the two triangles selected.

4. Before adding the small knot and string to your balloons, let's color them. Select the first ellipse and the small triangle below, then choose a color for your first balloon from the Color palette. Do the same for the second balloon, but make sure you choose a different color.

5. Balloons in real life are transparent. You can create this effect by making one of the balloons transparent over the other. To do this, select the second balloon, and lower the Object Opacity in the Opacity palette to about 50.

6. Let's finish this project by creating a knot and a string for each balloon. First, create two small squares with the Rectangle tool. Remember to hold down the SHIFT key as you draw them. Now, position the knots right between the edge of the two triangles and the bottom of the two ellipses.

7. Two strings can be easily made using the Rectangle tool. Select the tool from the toolbar and draw two long rectangles on your composition. To ensure they're as thin as possible, go to the Transform palette and type **1** for their width. Finish by positioning the two strings below the two knots.

Project Summary

You just created your first drawing in LiveMotion. Make sure you save your file and place it in your LiveMotion Projects folder. You'll use this file again at the end of this module to give this drawing an even more 3-D-like feeling.

This project should help you understand how various tools interact with the palettes. If you weren't able to follow some of the instructions, go back in the module and read the part you missed. Building a solid foundation by learning each little concept in the first few modules is important, so you can follow future modules that will rely on your understanding of these concepts. If you've made it this far, take a short break and relax. Make sure you save your file and place it in your LiveMotion Projects folder. You use this file again at the end of this Module to give this drawing an even more 3-D-like feel.

Add Layers and 3-D Effects

Layers and 3-D effects help make your graphics stand out. In this section, you learn about ways to use the Layer palette, the Object palette, and the 3-D palette to spice up your objects.

Object Palette

The Object palette enables you to add, delete, and organize all the layers of an object. A good example of layers is to compare them to the numerous skins of an onion. By adding layers to an object, you're preparing yourself to change individual parts of that object. Each of these parts can be contained within the individual layers of that object. Think back to the last project we completed earlier in this module. We created numerous circles to create a detailed eye. By understanding how layers work and how to create them, you could have sped up the process by creating one object with various layers. Each of those layers would contain one of the circles, which make up the eye.

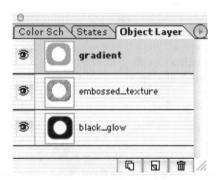

Note

Associating the contents of the Object palette and the Layer palette can get a bit confusing. The Object palette is used for creating and removing layers for an object. On the other hand, the Layer palette is used for editing individual layers.

2

To view the settings in the Object palette, you first need to create an object so the palette will display that object's layer. Create a simple shape and make sure the shape is selected. Now observe the Object palette. Notice the palette displays one layer represented by a small icon of the object that's selected in the composition. Next to the icon is the name of the layer, Layer 1. To the left is a small eye icon. By toggling this icon on and off, the layer to the right of it either shows or hides. On the bottom of the Object palette are three additional small icons. The first icon lets you duplicate the current layer or a layer that's selected. The second icon creates a new layer, while the third icon deletes a layer that's selected. At the moment, the delete icon is grayed out because you can't delete a layer if no other layers exist for that object. To create an additional layer for an object, you can choose to create an exact duplicate from Layer 1 or create a new one. Either way, your new layer will appear directly below Layer 1 in the Object palette. A new layer will always be the color black.

The Object palette lets you create as many layers as the memory on your computer will allow. You can drag and drop layers in front of or behind each other at will. To see them, though, you need to edit them using the Layer palette, which is discussed next, or use the Layer Offset tool.

Layer Palette

The Layer palette enables you to edit layers selected in the Object palette. The X-offset preference lets you move your layers along the X-axis. The Y-offset preference enables you to move your layers along the Y-axis. The Width preference increases or decreases the size of your object in width and height. Finally, the Softness preference lets you blur your layers.

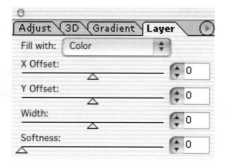

All these preferences are controlled by the small triangular sliders. Each preference has a limit as to how far the slider will let you move in either direction. In addition, at the top of the palette is a drop-down menu, which enables you to select a medium that will fill in your layer. The first option that appears as a default in the palette fills your layer with a solid color. The second option lets you fill the layer with an image. The third option fills your layer with the color of the background, and the fourth, with a texture. Textures and Images will be explained in future modules. For now, let's concern ourselves with the background and the color option. Look at the objects in Figure 2-8. Each of the objects contain various amounts of layers and each is adjusted in the Object palette.

As discussed in Module 1, the Layer Offset tool lets you move layers around on your composition. To use the Layer Offset tool on your selected layer, select it from the toolbar and begin dragging your layers around. There's a boundary as to how far layers can be moved from their associated objects, though. When you reach that boundary, the Layer Offset tool will stop moving the selected layer.

3-D Palette

The 3-D Palette gives you the option of making your objects appear three-dimensional. The drop-down menu at the top-left corner of the palette gives you four effects to choose from: Cutout, Emboss, Bevel, and Ripple. Each effect contains additional adjustments in the palette such as Depth, Softness, and Lighting, which are set using the small triangular sliders. In addition, each effect in the palette also allows you to set the angle of the shadow that the effect creates by using either the wheel at the bottom of the palette or by entering the

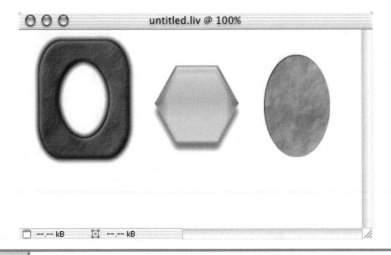

Figure 2-8 Various objects with layers

angle's measurement. Lastly, the two additional preferences located at the bottom right enable you to set the object's Light and Edge.

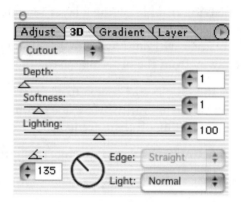

3-D effects could also be applied to individual layers. Simply select the layer you want to apply a 3-D effect to and make the appropriate changes in the Layer palette.

1-Minute Drill

- Which tool enables you to move your individual layers around on the composition?
- Under what circumstances would you be unable to delete a layer in the Object palette?

Apply Styles and Textures

Styles and textures are actual files that are located in your LiveMotion folder on your hard drive. The Styles palette and the Textures palette display these files and allow you to apply them to objects on your composition. Unlike other palettes, which let

---

- The Layer Offset tool.
- You would be unable to delete a layer in the Object palette only if your drawn or imported object contains just one layer.

Ask the Expert

Question: I'm having trouble seeing a layer I created in an object. The layer is hidden behind two additional layers that are on top of it. How can I view my layer without having to go through the trouble of moving one layer away from the other one using the Layer Drag tool?

Answer: Notice the little eye icon next to each layer. By toggling this icon on and off, you can temporarily hide a layer from view. Try hiding the top two layers by toggling off their eye icons.

Question: How many layers does the Object palette let me create?

Answer: As many as your computer's memory will allow.

you set various preferences for your objects and the tools, these two palettes act as resource libraries that you access within the program. LiveMotion comes bundled with quite a few styles and textures available to you. In this section, you learn the process of applying both styles and textures to your objects. In addition, you learn about ways to create and save your own custom textures and styles in their appropriate palette.

Styles Palette

Styles are saved in LiveMotion files containing an object with various adjustments. These adjustments are in the object range anywhere from added custom layers to various animations. Anything you can do with an object in LiveMotion can be saved and imported as a style into the Styles palette. Before you begin learning how to create your own styles, let's look at the functions inside the palette and learn how to apply them to objects.

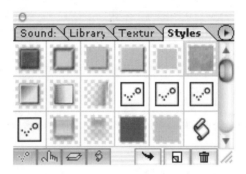

By default, all your styles in the Styles palette will be viewed in a Swatches view. You can change how the palette displays its styles by clicking the small triangle at the top right. You can choose from three different views: Swatches view, Preview view, and Name view. Each view contains a sma-ll icon for the style, which shows the appearance of the style when applied to an object, with the exception that all animation styles are labeled by the same icon. In addition, each style has a name that displays next to its corresponding icon.

Note

The Swatches view is the only view that doesn't display a name for each of its styles. The advantage of selecting this view is you'll get to view more styles in the palette without the need to scroll up and down.

For your convenience, the Styles palette is organized into four categories. These categories are represented by the four small icons at the bottom left corner of the palette. The following are the categories in order, from left to right, as you see them in your Styles palette:

- Styles with Animation
- Styles with Rollovers

- Styles with Layers

- Styles with Scripts

By toggling these icons on and off you can set the palette to display only specific styles. The remaining three icons are the buttons for applying styles, creating a new style, and deleting a style, in that order. Let's go over Applying styles to your objects first:

1. Because you haven't yet covered these features of LiveMotion, toggle off Styles with Animation, Styles with Scripts, and Styles with Rollovers.

2. Create a simple shape on your composition.

3. Finally, select either the icon or the name (depending on which view you're in) of the style you want to apply to the object and click the Apply Style icon in the palette. You should notice the changes to your object instantly.

Now that you know the process of applying styles to your objects, let's go over creating a style of your own:

1. To create your own style, you need to create an object whose appearance you want to save as a style. To begin, create another simple shape.

2. Now, go over to the Layer palette and create an additional layer for that object.

3. Make sure our new layer is selected in the Layer palette, and then go over to the Color palette and select a color for this layer.

4. In the Object palette, increase the width of the layer.

5. The object in your composition should now contain a colored border around it.

6. Now that you've created your own custom style, make sure your object is selected, and then go to the Styles palette and save your style by clicking the New Style icon. A Window screen will appear on your screen.

7. Fill in a new name for your style and notice the remaining preference fields. At the moment, you can fill two preferences. The remaining preferences are grayed out because your object doesn't contain Rollovers, which will be explained in Module 6. The first option asks you if you want to save the layers of the object for the style. Make sure this preference is checked because your object does contain layers. The other preference asks you whether you want to save the color of the first layer for the style. By checking this option on, the objects to which you'll apply this style will be filled with the color of your current object. This option is completely up to you. Remember, the color of your future objects you'll apply this style to will change to the color you chose for Layer 1.

8. Click OK.

9. Now create a new shape and apply your new style to it to see the result.

Deleting is simple. Select the style you no longer want and click the delete icon. Remember, if you accidentally delete a style from your Styles folder, the style will return to the folder once you relaunch LiveMotion. To permanently delete a style, you need to go to the Styles folder in your LiveMotion folder located in your hard drive and drag the style into the Trash Can.

Textures Palette

Textures are similar to styles in the sense that they're applied to objects using the same steps. Unlike styles, though, which are saved LiveMotion Files, textures themselves are image files. These *image* files can be created in nearly any photo editing program and saved to a variety of file formats such as GIF, JPG, and PSD. A good program to use with LiveMotion is Photoshop, which is also made by Adobe.

Note

In Module 5, you learn how to import Photoshop native files containing layers into LiveMotion.

The interface of the Textures palette is similar to that of the Styles palette. The three types of views you learned about in the Styles palette—Swatches view, Preview view, and Name view—also appear in the Textures palette. Applying textures to objects works the same as well:

1. Select an object on your composition.

2. Choose a texture from the Textures palette.

3. Click the Apply icon in the Textures palette.

The New Texture icon next to the Apply icon works a little bit differently. When the New Texture icon is clicked, LiveMotion asks you to find the location of the texture you want to import. Let's go over ways to create your own texture files:

1. Locate an image file on your hard drive that contains a texture you want to import into your Textures palette in LiveMotion.

2. Open the image in your favorite photo-editing program and crop out a small area of the texture you want to use as a texture in LiveMotion.

3. You can now save the cropped part of the image in a variety of file formats, including GIF, JPEG, and PSD.

4. Drag the file into the Textures folder located in your LiveMotion folder on your hard drive.

5. Go back to LiveMotion and click the New Texture icon in the Textures palette. Locate the file you just created in the Textures folder and click Open. Name your new texture, and then click OK. You're done!

Notice the Textures palette also contains new icons at the bottom-left corner. With these icons, you can choose to display large textures, small textures, or both of them at the same time. LiveMotion automatically organizes its textures into its appropriate category, depending on the size of the file.

Project 2-2: Creating a Three-dimensional Drawing

Your previous project consisted of using basic shape tools and palettes to draw two-dimensional balloons. In the following project, you use what you've learned following your last project to create three-dimensional images, as shown in the finished art in Figure 2-9. You'll use your previously saved project to build on the objects you already created. Let's begin:

Step-by-Step

1. Open the LiveMotion file you created for your previous project.

2. Select the ellipse of the first balloon, select copy from the Edit menu, and paste it. Notice LiveMotion pasted the file exactly on top of the file you copied.

3. Go to the Styles palette and apply the style named Bubble to the pasted object.

4. Follow Steps 2 and 3 for the ellipse of the second balloon.

5. Notice the ellipses don't overlap correctly. You can fix that by selecting both ellipses of the second balloon and choosing Bring to Front in the Arrange submenu under the Object menu.

6. Select the strings of both balloons, as well as the pointy triangles and knots. Go to the Object palette and create a new layer. Notice all the objects you selected are modified with the additional layer by this process.

7. Change the color of the second layer to medium gray in the Color palette.

8. In the Layer palette, type **5** for the X Offset preference, type **1** for the Width preference, and type **8** for the Softness preference.

9. Your balloons should now resemble Figure 2-9.

10. Save your files as Project 2-2 in your LiveMotion Projects folder because you'll use it again in Module 3.

Project Summary

You can create three-dimensional objects in a variety of ways. You could use the 3-D palette, for example, to give your balloons a sense of depth. Experiment using the tools and palettes you learned in this module to modify your original two-dimensional drawing. After you do this, take a short break and answer the questions in the Mastery Check.

Summary

You've learned about a huge chunk of the features in LiveMotion in this module. In the beginning of the module, you learned how to draw simple shapes using various tools in the toolbar. In addition, you learned ways of using the Transform palette to adjust the dimensions of your shapes. Later on in the module, you learned how to change the appearance of your objects by using the Color palette to change the color of your objects and using the Opacity palette to change their opacity. In addition, you learned how to add some dimension to your objects by learning how to create and use layers, and apply 3-D effects using

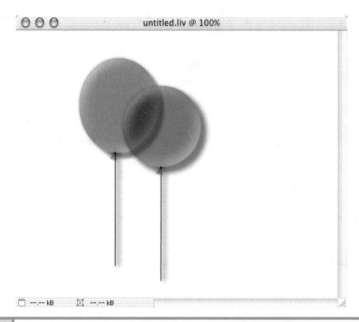

Figure 2-9   3-D Balloons

the 3-D palette. Lastly, you've learned how to add both styles and textures to your objects.

In the next module, you learn how to create more advanced shapes, as well as further convert the shapes you learned about in this module.

☑ *Mastery Check*

1. Which of the following Palettes will allow you to adjust the contrast of your objects?

   A. Gradient palette

   B. 3-D palette

   C. Properties palette

   D. Adjust palette

2. A good example of layers is to compare them to the numerous _____ of an onion.

3. How would you go about creating a new style in the Styles palette?

   A. Create one in an image editing program and save it to your Styles Folder.

   B. Select an altered object and click New Style in the Styles palette

   C. Create one in an image editing program and select it within the Styles palette

   D. Select an altered object and click Apply Style in the Styles palette

4. In order to permanently remove a texture from your Textures palette, you need to:

   A. Drag it out of your Textures folder and move it to the trash.

   B. Select the texture, and click the delete/backspace key

   C. Textures are permanently saved in your LiveMotion program; they can't be removed, only altered.

Module 3

Work with Custom Shapes

The Goals of this Module

- Know how to use the Library palette
- Know how to import shapes
- Learn how to move objects in front of or behind each other
- Learn how to create and edit shapes with the Pen tool and the Pen Selection tool
- Know how to crop shapes with the Crop tool
- Be able to group and combine shapes together

In the previous module, you learned how to draw various shapes with the four basic toolbar tools: the Ellipse tool, the Rectangle tool, the Rounded Rectangle tool, and the Polygon tool. In addition, you learned about several palettes that let you not only adjust the setting for these four Shape tools, but also modify them with features like Opacity, Gradients, 3-D effects, and others. Using these four tools to attempt to draw real-life objects wouldn't be practical, so you'll be glad to know LiveMotion offers plenty of other features that enable you to create, import, and edit shapes that are more complex. In this module, you learn about using features such as the Library Palette, the Pen tool, the Crop tool, and the Object Menu bar to create real-life shapes that resemble real-life objects. You'll use many of the features you learn about in this module again when other types of objects, such as images and text, are discussed.

Use the Library Palette

The Library palette is similar to the Styles and Textures palette, as well as the Sounds palette, which you learn about in Module 14. The Library palette lets you place built-in custom shapes in your composition. The shapes are actual files that reside inside your Library folder, which is located in the LiveMotion folder on your hard drive. In addition to being able to place custom shapes, the palette enables you to replace selected shapes on your composition with the specific shape selected in the palette. In addition, the palette also lets you save shapes inside the palette that you either created or edited. These saved shapes are placed automatically inside your Library folder among the other built-in shape files. At the end of this section, you learn about importing shapes from other vector applications, such as Adobe Illustrator and Macromedia Freehand, into your Library palette.

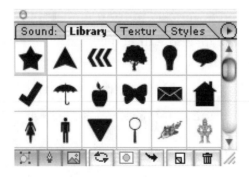

Note

Don't confuse the Library Palette Import feature with the Place Palette Import feature in the File menu. The *Library Palette Import* feature enables you to import shapes directly into your Library palette. *The Place Palette Import* feature, however, imports and places files directly on to your composition.

Let's start by going over the preferences inside the palette. Like the Styles, Textures, and Sounds palettes (the Sounds palette is discussed in Module 14), the Library palette lets you view its contents in three types of views: Swatches, Preview, and Name view. By default, the view is set to the Swatches view. To switch to any of these views, simply select the view from the drop-down menu, which is triggered by the small triangle located at the top right of the palette. In addition, you have three types of category sets for shapes, which are represented by three icon buttons located at the bottom left of the palette. By toggling these sets on and off, the palette displays only the ones selected by their corresponding icon buttons. They are

1. **LiveMotion Objects**   Objects created in LiveMotion.

2. **Vector Objects**   Objects created in other vector applications, such as Adobe Illustrator.

3. **Image Objects**   Objects created in an image-editing application, such as Adobe Photoshop.

The Library palette decides which shapes belong to which one of the three categories by recognizing the file format of the shape. The following are the three categories and the file formats the category accepts:

1. **LiveMotion Objects**   LIV files

2. **Vector Objects**   EPS, PSD, and AI files

3. **Image Objects**   JPEG and GIF files

As with the Styles and Textures palettes, the Library palette enables you to modify objects on your composition. The Replace Object button, located to the right of the three category icon buttons, lets you replace the object selected on your composition with the object in your Library palette. Here's a quick example of how to perform this task:

1. Select or draw an object you want to modify.

2. In the Library palette, select the shape you want to apply to the object.

3. Click the Replace Object button.

4. The shape selected on your composition should now be replaced by the shape from the Library palette.

The *Place Object* button, also located at the bottom of the palette, enables you to place the object selected in the Library palette on your composition. Don't confuse this button with the *Replace Object* button because that button won't let you replace objects.

Note

Notice the Make Active Matte button is grayed out, so you can't perform this action on shapes. This effect is discussed in Module 5, where you learn about working with images.

Now, let's cover importing shapes from both the composition and other vector programs. Here are the steps for importing objects from your composition:

1. Select an object on your composition.

2. Drag the object into the Library palette and let go of your mouse button.

3. Enter a name for your new shape in the pop-up box that appears.

4. The object now appears in the LiveMotion Objects category. In addition, the file for the objects is now saved in your Library folder in the LiveMotion folder located on your hard drive.

The following are the steps for importing shapes from other vector applications:

1. If you created your shape in Adobe Illustrator, save your shape in either the AI or EPS formats. If you're using another vector program, save your file as an EPS file. Finally, if you're using Adobe Photoshop, save your shape as a PSD type file.

2. Drag the file into the Library folder in the LiveMotion folder on your hard drive.

3. In LiveMotion, go to the Library palette, click the New Object button, and then select the file you moved to the Library folder.

4. Open the file and enter the name for your new object.

5. If you saved your shape as an AI, PSD, or EPS type file, the shape will display in the Vector Objects category in your Library palette. If you saved your shape as a JPEG or a GIF type file, your shape will display in the Image Objects category in the palette.

Note

Shapes created and saved in either AI or EPS file formats are the only ones LiveMotion lets you edit. Although LiveMotion has the capability of importing a larger array of file formats, such as JPEG, GIF, PNG, and so forth, shapes saved in these file formats can't be altered.

Finally, you can delete any shape from the Library palette by clicking the DELETE button. Pressing the DELETE button brings up an alert box with the following prompt: "Are you sure you want to delete this object? Doing so will permanently remove it from the Library directory on your disk." Don't proceed until you're certain you want to remove the specific object.

1-Minute Drill

● How is the Library palette different from other palettes, such as the Texture palette and the Styles palette?

● How would you save objects on your composition in the Library palette?

● Unlike the Styles and Textures palette, which alter the appearance of your objects, the Library palette allows you to alter the shape of your object.
● To save objects on your composition in the Library palette, select, drag, and drop the shape on top of the Library palette.

Ask the Expert

Question: I downloaded an image from the Web that contains a shape I want to use in LiveMotion. The file is saved in GIF format. Why does the object become pixilated when I modify its various Transform attributes on the composition?

Answer: Files saved in either AI or EPS format are files LiveMotion recognizes as vector objects. *Vector shapes,* which are located in your Library palette, are considered vector objects. When imported, these objects enable you to edit their width, height, and other characteristics without any pixilation. GIFs and some other file formats are considered raster objects. When stretched, *raster objects* become pixilated. The difference between these two types of objects is covered further in Module 7, where exporting your projects is discussed.

Question: Can you bring this shape into the program in any other way?

Answer: Of course. You can use the Place command located under the File menu. This command enables you to bring a variety of file formats into your composition.

Arrange Menu

The Arrange feature can be accessed from the Object menu. Look at Figure 3-1 and notice the location of the menu in your LiveMotion environment. The Arrange feature lets you bring your selected objects in front of or behind your other objects. Consider your composition as being on Level 0. No object can go below this level. As you begin drawing your various shapes, as well as other objects you'll learn about in Modules 4 and 5, each of them will reside on its own level. So, if your composition consists of five objects, the topmost object, which would be the object you most recently created, will reside on the top level: Level 5. If you move this object around on your composition, you'll notice it covers the other four objects when moved over them. The backmost object, which is also the first object you created, currently resides on the bottommost level: Level 1. If you move that object around on your composition, you'll notice every other object covers it. Another way to envision this is to

3

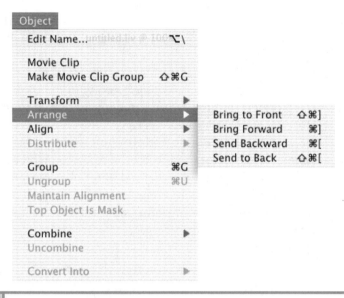

Figure 3-1 The Arrange submenu

think of the composition in terms of containing three dimensions in which all objects are located on the X-, Y-, and Z-axis. Each object on the composition is located at a different level of the Z-axis, so each object either overlaps or is being overlapped by another object. The Arrange menu lets you control on what levels your objects are located, just as the Transform palette enables you to control the X- and Y-axis positions of your individual objects. The following are the Arrange Menu choices and their functions:

1. **Bring to Front**   An object impacted by this function moves to the topmost level on your composition. All the other objects on your composition will reside on levels below this object.

2. **Bring Forward**   This function moves your selected object up one level. If that level is the topmost level on your composition, the selected object is unable to move up any further.

3. **Send Backward**   This function moves your selected object back one level. If the level to which the selected object was moved using this function is Level 1, you won't be able to move the object further back.

4. Send to Back   An object impacted by this function moves to the bottommost level. Every other object on your composition will reside over the selected object.

Important to note is as you create new objects on your composition, they'll always appear on top of one another. Objects previously moved to the topmost level, therefore, now appear behind them.

As you continue to learn LiveMotion and work on new projects, you'll access this feature quite often. Instead of using the Arrange menu each time you want to move an object in front of or behind other objects, you can use keystrokes to access its functions quickly. The keystroke for each function appears next to its name in the Arrange menu under the Objects menu.

1-Minute Drill

● What's the difference between sending your selected shape using the Send Backward command from the Arrange menu and the Send to Back command?

● Newly drawn objects appear on what level in reference to previously drawn objects on your composition?

Use the Pen Tool to Create Custom Shapes

Another way of creating and editing custom shapes is to use a combination of the Pen tool and the Pen Selection tool. These tools were briefly introduced in the first module. In the following section, we'll go over using both of these tools to alter and create new, real-life shapes. Many of the shapes in the Library palette were created using both these tools. Remember, the Pen tool is one of the hardest tools to master in LiveMotion. However, the Pen tool is also one of the most versatile tools in LiveMotion in terms of creating shapes. This is

● The Send Backward command moves your selected object back one level and the Send to Back command moves the object back behind every other object on your composition.

● Newly drawn objects appear on top of the previously drawn objects on your composition.

because the Pen tool enables you to create nearly any type of two-dimensional shape your mind can imagine. The Pen tool works similarly to the Pen tool that appears in other vector programs, such as Adobe Illustrator and Macromedia Freehand. With a sufficient amount of practice, you can learn to control the Pen tool's features.

The Pen Tool

The *Pen* tool works by clicking your composition with the tool. As you click, the points created become joined together with line segments. In other words, the second point will connect to your first point, the third point will connect to your second point, and so on. The area between all your placed points will automatically fill with a solid color that's selected as your Foreground Color.

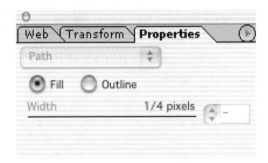

The Pen tool, just as the other four types of drawing tools discussed in Module 2, contains its settings inside the Properties palette. The palette, with the Pen tool selected in the toolbar, enables you to toggle between having the shape drawn either completely filled with a solid color or having its outline appear on the composition. In addition, with the Outline preference toggled on, the palette lets you adjust the width of the outline with the Width preference. Use the sliders either to increase or decrease this preference. Remember, the Properties palette only displays these preferences when the Pen tool is selected in the toolbar. Now, let's practice drawing a simple shape with the Pen tool, as seen in Figure 3-2.

1. Begin by creating a new composition, which you'll work on throughout this module. Set the dimensions to 400×300.

2. Choose a red color from the Color palette. Next, select the Pen tool from the toolbar and place your first point by clicking your composition. Be sure to place the point in the same location as the top-left corner of the drawing in Figure 3-2.

3. Select the location of your second point and click with the tool once more. Try to place the point in the same location as the upper-right corner of the drawing in Figure 3-2. Notice a line segment has been drawn from your first placed point to your second point. This line segment should resemble the top line segment of Figure 3-2.

4. Place your last point at the bottom in the same location, as shown in Figure 3-3. Notice how the area among the three points is automatically filled with a red color. If you placed the points in the same locations as illustrated in Figure 3-3, your shape should resemble the shape of the drawing.

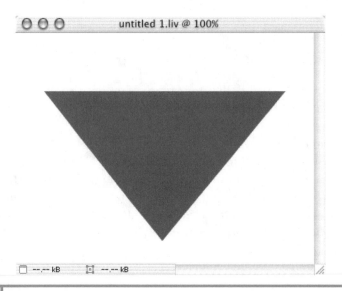

Figure 3-2   A Pen tool drawn shape

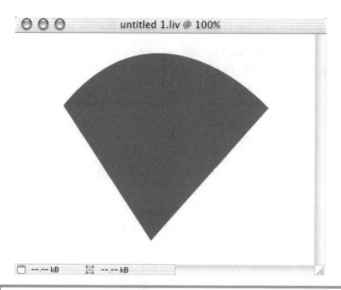

Figure 3-3   Another Pen tool drawn shape

Besides being able to draw straight-lined custom shapes, the Pen tool also lets you draw curved shapes. This process involves dragging with the Pen tool as you place points on your composition. This is where the complexity of the tool comes in. Let's begin by drawing the curved shape in Figure 3-3 on your composition.

1. Begin by placing the bottom point of the shape with the Pen tool.

2. Place your second point in the same location as seen in the right corner of the shape in Figure 3-3.

3. Now place your third point in the same location as the left corner of the shape by clicking and holding down the mouse key. Notice how the line transforms into a controllable curve as you drag your mouse around the composition. In addition, a blue line segment guides you in the direction you move your mouse. To create the curve at the bottom of the shape, you need to drag your mouse toward the bottom-left corner of your composition.

4. Your shape should now resemble the shape drawn in Figure 3-3.

5. Save this file to your LiveMotion Projects folder because you'll use it later in the module. Save the file as Pen Tool Curved Shape.

In addition to drawing shapes with the Pen tool, you can also edit shapes with it that have already been drawn. For example, you can erase any point placed by the Pen tool by going over the point and clicking it with the Pen tool. Notice how a minus (-) sign appears next to the point. You can also add additional points to your shapes. To do so, select the Pen tool and move your mouse pointer along the edges of your shape until a plus (+) sign appears next to it. By adding additional points to your shapes, you can further manipulate them. This is where the old adage, "practice makes perfect" comes in. Creating curved shapes is easy, but trying to draw a shape with a curve in mind is a little more difficult. The more you work with this tool, the easier using it becomes.

Ask the Expert

Question: The shape I drew using the Pen tool contains too many points. I want to delete some of them and place them in other areas. How can I do this?

Answer: Any shape you create with the pen tool can always be further altered in the future, so to erase one of the points of your shape, select the Pen tool and move your cursor over that point. Next to your cursor icon, you'll notice a minus sign appears. Once the minus sign appears, click the point and the point disappears. In addition to creating an additional point, make sure your object is selected. Now move your mouse cursor over any of the segment lines of the object and click to add an additional point.

Question: How can I change the curve of one of the line segments?

Answer: Make sure the Pen tool and the object are selected. Move your mouse cursor over the point closest to that line segment and hold down the OPTION key (if you're using a Mac) or the ALT key (if you're using a PC) as you click and drag the point.

The Pen Selection Tool

The *Pen Selection* tool works ideally alongside the Pen tool and enables you to modify the line segments of shapes as well as their curves. This is an excellent way to touch up the shapes created by the Pen tool. Let's put the Pen Selection tool to work by fixing up the shape you created earlier and modifying it to look like the shape seen in Figure 3-4:

3

1. From your LiveMotion Projects folder, open the file Pen Tool Curved Shape.

2. Begin by selecting the shape with the Arrow tool.

3. Choose the Pen Selection tool from the toolbar and notice how the blue lines surrounding the shape disappear, leaving you with two blue points and one red point. The red point was the first point created.

4. Click the blue point located at the bottom of the blue line segment and drag it up as far as possible. You might need to switch back to the Arrow tool at some point to move your shape down. Continue moving the point up until the shape resembles that in Figure 3-4.

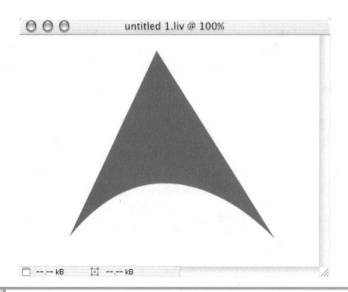

Figure 3-4   A Pen Selection tool edited shape object

You have just transformed the bottom of the curve with the Pen Selection tool. In addition to dragging points, the tool also lets you move line segments of your shapes.

The shape you just created can be further altered with the Pen Selection tool. For example, you could have dragged its line segments to create another shape. The combination of the Pen tool and the Pen Selection tool enables you to create nearly any type of shape you can imagine. As pointed out earlier, if you practice using both these tools, their functions will become more apparent and you'll be able to create even more-advanced shapes.

Remember, you have your Library palette available to you at all times. You might want to save your shape in this palette for future projects. Refer to the section "Use the Library Palette" at the beginning of this module on how to save custom shapes in this palette.

1-Minute Drill

- How does the Pen tool differ from the Pen Selection tool?
- How are curved lines created by the Pen tool?

Crop Shapes

In the first module, the Crop tool was introduced as one of the tools in the toolbar. This tool lets you cut out numerous portions of the shapes you create. The Crop tool is incredibly helpful in hiding certain unwanted portions of shapes. For example, if you want to create a semicircle, you could use the Pen tool to place three points on your composition. When placing your third point, you would continue to hold down your mouse button and drag your mouse to create a curved line. If you're just beginning to master the Pen tool, your semicircle might not look like what you'd expect. A much simpler way of performing this task is to use the combination of the Ellipse tool and the Crop tool. Here are the steps for creating a semicircle, as shown in Figure 3-5:

- The Pen tool enables you to create custom shapes by placing points, which create either straight or curved segments. The Pen Selection tool lets you manipulate shapes created by the Pen tool by letting you drag their points and line segments out of proportion to distort them.
- Using the Pen tool, curved lines are created by simultaneously clicking your composition where you want your point placed, and then dragging your mouse pointer until a curve desired is created.

1. Select the Ellipse tool from the toolbar and create a perfect circle.

2. Select the Crop tool from the toolbar. Click-and-drag any of the sides of the circle until your shape becomes a semicircle.

If you want to create a shape that resembles half a semicircle, click-and-drag any of the shape's corners. Notice both sides of the shape are being cropped simultaneously.

In addition, you can expose any of your cropped shape's sides by clicking the shape and moving your mouse pointer in any direction. Notice how your mouse pointer changes into a hand icon. This is useful if you want to reverse some of the area you cropped out of the shape, or if you want to crop the image further. The best part of this tool is you can always restore all the cropped parts of your shape by clicking and dragging the cropped areas back into their previous location. However, dragging the shape with the Crop tool will convert it to a raster object on export. You learn the difference between raster (bitmap) and vector objects along with exporting procedures in Module 7.

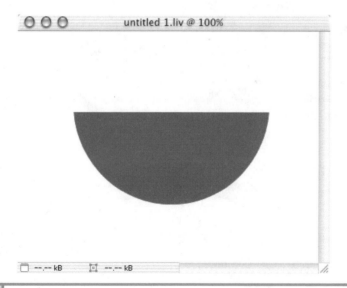

Figure 3-5   A semicircular shape

Group and Combine Shapes

The group and combine functions are useful features in LiveMotion. These are also easily confused, so we discuss them individually here. Let's begin by discussing Group and Ungroup functions.

Group and Ungroup

Look at Figure 3-6 and notice the location of the Group and Ungroup commands (they're located right beneath the Object menu). The *Group* function enables you to group any number of objects on your composition, making them one shape. Unfortunately, many of the palettes you've been introduced to in the last few modules become useless when you work with a grouped object because they won't let you perform any changes on them. The importance of the Group function at this stage is it enables you to move all your grouped objects as a whole, instead of individually. This becomes useful when your composition consists of numerous objects because grouping them helps you organize your

Figure 3-6   The Group and Ungroup commands

projects. Module 8 will discuss the importance of grouping as a way of organizing your objects on the *Timeline,* which lets you animate your objects. The Timeline function is discussed in the second part of this book in Module 8. Let's discuss a quick overview for grouping and ungrouping shapes:

1. Create a variety of shapes on your composition.

2. Select all your shapes using the Arrow tool and choose Group from the Object menu.

All the selected shapes should now be one. If, at any time, you want to ungroup your shapes, you can do so with the *Ungroup* function. To ungroup, choose the Ungroup function from the Object menu. Your shapes will remain in the same location as when you grouped them.

Combine and Uncombine

Like the Group and Ungroup commands, the Combine and Uncombine commands appear beneath the Object menu, as shown in Figure 3-7. Combining your

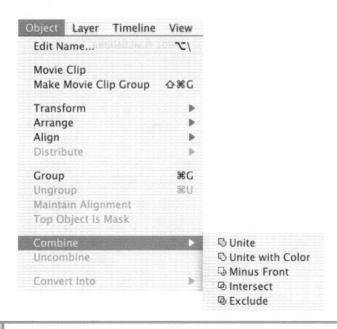

Figure 3-7   The Combine and Uncombine commands

shapes/objects is similar to the grouping function. It's also used to join objects together, though, in a wider variety of ways and, like the Group and Ungroup commands, can be accessed from the Object menu. Combining shapes, however, is much more useful if you intend to continue working with the shapes after they're joined. Unlike grouped objects, when shapes are combined, all the palettes are accessible to the combined shape, so you can perform all the same tasks you would with your original shapes. In addition to joining two or more shapes together, the Combine function also enables you to cut out overlapping areas made by the shapes. The following are modification examples made by some of the other Combine commands under the Combine submenu:

1. **Unite**   This Combine function joins all your selected shapes and converts the colors of the frontmost shapes to the color of the shape that's furthest back on your composition. You can use the Arrange menu to prepare your objects before you perform this function.

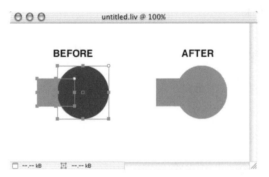

2. **Unite with Color**   Objects combined with this function retain their individual colors. The appearance of your joined objects with their diverse colors remains the same as before you joined them.

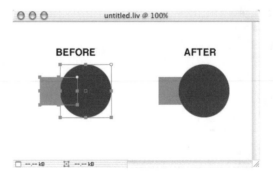

3. is correct.

3. Minus Front   If you combine two objects with this function, the topmost object of the two cuts its overlapping piece into the other object. For example, if your topmost object is a circle and the other object is a square located at the center of the circle, your combined object will result in a square with a hollow circle located at its center. The combined shape will retain the color from the bottommost object.

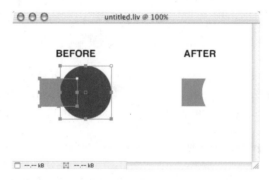

4. Intersect   With this function, the portions of the objects selected that intersect one another will result in the final combined shape. Once again, the color of the final combined shape is the same as the color of the bottommost shape before you combined the shapes using this function.

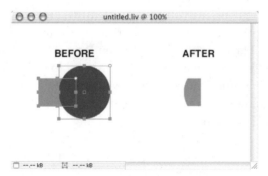

5. Exclude   This function works exactly the opposite of the Intersect function, so your resulting combined shape will consist of all the parts of the objects selected that didn't intersect one another. The color of the combined shape will be the same as the color of the bottommost shape.

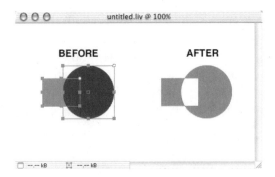

Some palettes won't be accessible to the Unite with Color function. As far as the other functions are concerned, all palettes will be available to them. In fact, the combined shape will behave the same as any other shape.

1-Minute Drill

● What are the differences and advantages of using the Unite Combine function over the Unite with Color Combine function?

Import Shapes

Besides the numerous options you have by creating, cropping, combining, and grouping your shapes in LiveMotion, you're also able to bring in shapes from other applications. Earlier in this module, you learned ways to create shapes in other vector programs and save them in the Library folder on your hard drive to bring them into the Library palette in LiveMotion. You also have the option of bringing your shapes directly into your composition by importing them using the Place command beneath the File menu, as illustrated in Figure 3-8. As previously noted, a wider range of file formats can be brought into LiveMotion by importing them, but LiveMotion won't let you edit shapes saved in any other format than EPS and AI. The steps to import shapes are as follows:

● The differences and advantages of using the Unite Combine function over the Unite with Color Combine function are this: even though the Unite with Color Combine function lets you retain the individual colors of the shape you're combining, the Unite Combine function enables you to use all the palettes available to the individual shapes before they were combined.

1. Create your shape in a program that enables you to save your file as either EPS or AI.

2. Under the File menu in LiveMotion, click Place, and select the file you created in the other program.

3. The object should now reside on your composition.

3

Your imported shape will act exactly as any other shape created or brought in from the Library palette in LiveMotion.

Using Adobe Illustrator in conjunction with LiveMotion lets you use some more advanced features in the program. For example, any shape brought from Adobe Illustrator into Adobe LiveMotion using the Place command acts as a direct link between the two programs. The shape must be saved in the AI format. To clarify, any changes made to the shape in LiveMotion directly impact

Figure 3-8   The Place command

the shape in Adobe Illustrator as long as the file is still opened. In addition, after placing your AI file into LiveMotion, you can use the Edit Original command under the Edit menu to open the file in Adobe Illustrator. Now, any changes made to the shape in Adobe Illustrator will affect the shape in Adobe LiveMotion. Remember, the Edit Original feature of LiveMotion won't work with any other file formats, with the exception of PSD files. This is explored further in Module 5 with an in-depth discussion of images.

Project 3-1: Draw Using Advanced Tools

In the previous module, we concluded with the creation of a drawing that contains three-dimensional balloons. The actual balloons in your drawing look pretty realistic, but the strings you created using the rectangular tool don't look real. In this module, you learned how to use the Pen tool, so now you'll use the pen tool to create a more realistic string for the balloons, as shown in Figure 3-9. In addition, you'll group some of your shapes to maintain some organization in your project files and save your finished file in the LiveMotion Projects folder.

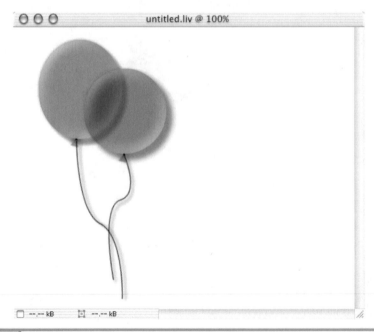

Figure 3-9 An advanced shape

Step-by-Step

1. Open your previous project, called Project 2-2, from the LiveMotion Projects folder.

2. Select and delete the two strings of the balloons.

3. Select the Pen tool from the toolbar and click Outline in the Properties palette. Set the Width preference to 5.

4. Place your first point on your composition and your second point as far away from the first point as the length of the string you want to create.

5. Place your third point between the two and hold down your mouse button. Slowly drag the point either to the top left or to the bottom right. You'll notice the point you're dragging is twisting both the top and the bottom part of the line. Let go of the mouse button when you're satisfied with the curved string.

6. Place the strings right below the knot, then rotate them slightly using the Arrow tool.

7. Your previous strings contained shadows. Instead of going through the process of creating and adjusting new layers for the strings, use the Styles palette to apply a shadow automatically to the two strings. To select both of your strings, choose Drop Shadow 2 from the Styles palette and click Apply.

8. Select all the objects on the composition and choose Group from the Object menu. Finish by saving your project file in your LiveMotion Projects folder on your hard drive.

Project Summary

You used the Pen tool in this project to complete a simple task that involved drawing two strings. As you practice working with the Pen tool independently of this book, you'll soon be drawing other illustrations using only this tool. Notice we ended the project by grouping all the objects on the composition. The purpose of this was to group and organize all the shapes that make up the balloons, so you won't accidentally move or further alter them as you work with this project file in future modules.

3

Summary

This module concludes the section on the creation and manipulation of shapes in this book. Many of the terms and features introduced in this module are used in future modules, so it's important for you to understand every aspect before you proceed to the next module. In Module 4, the shape section is put to rest for a while and you begin using text on your composition. Text and style creates a huge impact on design. In the next module, you learn about the importance of text in design, as well as various ways of creating and manipulating text on your composition.

☑ *Mastery Check*

1. Which one of these four choices displays the correct tools and palettes for creating and importing shapes?

    A. Object palette, 3-D palette, Ellipse tool

    B. Polygon tool, Object palette, Rectangle tool

    C. Pen tool, Library palette, Rectangle tool

    D. Library palette, Pen tool, 3-D palette

2. Which function would you perform if you want your selected object to be brought in front of another object on your composition?

    A. Use the Properties palette to adjust the level the object is on

    B. Use the Arrange menu to bring the object forward

    C. Use the Layer Offset tool

    D. None of the above

3. The _____ tool is used for drawing lines and curves on your composition. The _____ tool is used for editing lines and curves created by the _____.

4. All the Combine functions enable you to combine either all or some parts of the selected objects. Unfortunately, not all of them let you use all the palettes available to you prior to combining your shapes. Which one of these doesn't let you use some palettes?

    A. Unite

    B. Unite with Color

    C. Minus Front

    D. Intersect

☑ Mastery Check

5. Which of the following file formats containing shapes does LiveMotion let you import using the Place command?

A. JPEG and Gif

B. EPS and AIFF

C. GIF and PNG

D. EPS and AI

6. _____ shapes enable you to organize your objects on your composition. You can always _____ them to return them to their previous state.

7. The _____ retains shapes inside until you decide to add them to your composition, while the _____ command automatically places the shapes directly on your composition.

8. What's the quickest and easiest way to create a semicircle?

A. Use the Pen tool and the Ellipse tool

B. Use the Ellipse tool and the Crop tool

C. Use the Pen tool and the Crop tool

D. Use the Crop tool and the Properties palette

9. If you plan to combine two overlapping objects using the Intersect function, which parts of the objects will remain?

A. The overlapping parts of the two objects

B. The unoverlapping parts of the two objects

C. All parts of the objects

D. None of the above

Module 4

Work with Text

The Goals of this Module

- Learn the importance of text in design
- Know how to create and align text
- Be able to transform text using palettes
- Be able to manipulate opacity and color of text
- Learn how to add layers and 3-D effects to text
- Know how to apply styles and textures to text

In this module, you learn about the importance of text in design. In addition, you learn about creating and manipulating text on your composition using various commands and palettes. You've already learned about many of the palettes you use to manipulate, transform, and color your text objects, but the information these palettes display for your text will differ from the information they displayed for shapes. You begin to notice this immediately after selecting the Text tool from the toolbar or after selecting a text object, if one already exists on your composition.

Text, Design, and Style

Text is incredibly important in design. Whether you're creating a logo or a presentation, using text enables you to convey a message to your viewers. Consider the text you see in magazines, on billboards, and even on product labels. Notice how text is used to create a subtle or a strong message about the product the text is selling. Manipulation of text creates a sense of style in your work. The sense of style isn't created only by changing the font of your text and the font's height. LiveMotion enables you to go beyond the manipulation of text that other programs, such as Microsoft Word, do to text. The program lets you apply to text the same effects you applied to your shapes in the past two modules. In that sense, you're able to enrich your text with style and originality—something to catch a viewer's eye. If you ever have a chance to visit New York City, Times Square exhibits the concept this paragraph attempts to convey. No billboard or flashing advertisement is alike. Each one uses a different type of style for its text to stand out from the others.

Style in text is also about consistency and control. After all, you don't want your projects to resemble Times Square. If you did this, your viewer would get lost trying to decipher the message your projects convey. So, stay consistent in the style you choose for your text. Not only does this make your project clean and original, it also helps you to keep the focus of your project's viewers.

Create Text

The Text tool was introduced in the first module. The Text tool enables you to place text on your composition. In the previous version of LiveMotion, creating and typing in text required the user to type it into a fairly large window, which launched upon clicking the Composition with the Type tool. In LiveMotion 2, entering text is much simpler and convenient. The Type tool enables you to type text directly on to the composition with no more dialogue boxes in the way. In addition, the Type tool also lets you create type fields on your composition. By creating one of these fields, users can constrict their text when typing to exist only within the constraints of the field's borders. To create one of these fields, select the Type tool, and then click and drag on your composition until you're satisfied with its proportions. Figure 4-1 shows an example of one of these fields.

Just like shapes, text can be dragged around to any place on your composition with the Arrow tool. You can also transform your text while it's selected with the Arrow tool by dragging any of its outer points. In addition, you can rotate the shape by clicking and dragging the unfilled corner that appears at the top-right corner of your text. You learn about using palettes to transform your text in the upcoming section "Transform Palettes." Until then, you can use the Arrow tool to transform your text exactly as you would with a shape.

LiveMotion also lets you adjust various settings for the text being entered such as Font, Type, Size, Thickness, and many others using palettes. All these features and more can be adjusted in both the Properties and Transform palettes, which are discussed shortly.

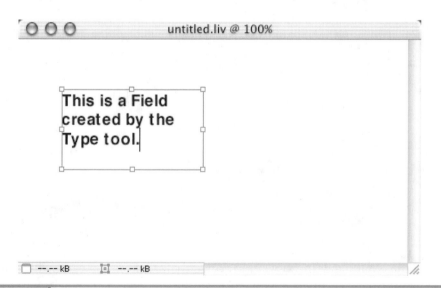

Figure 4-1   A Type tool field

Convert Text Objects

Breaking apart text in LiveMotion is convenient. The Convert Into Submenu, which appears right under the Object menu, enables you to perform just that, as well as convert your text objects into paths, which can be further edited by the Pen tool. For example, if your text contains the word "LiveMotion," selecting the Objects command under the Convert Into Submenu under the Object menu would break apart every letter of the word into nine individual letter objects. Even though you can perform the task without the command by simply typing each letter individually with the Type tool, the command is there to save you time.

The Convert Into/Object process is a useful feature in LiveMotion if you want to transform or manipulate each letter of your text independently from one another. As you learn about animation in the second part of this book, the feature again becomes useful to you by enabling you to animate each letter of your text independently.

On the other hand, if you want to convert your text into a path, which, in turn, would enable it to be editable by both the Pen and the Pen Selection tool, selecting the Path command under the Convert Into Submenu would enable you to do just that. Your text object would now resemble a shape drawn by the Pen tool, as shown in Figure 4-2.

Hi

Figure 4-2 A path-converted object

The remaining command in the Convert Into Submenu—Group of Objects—performs two tasks. First, Group of Objects splits up each letter of your text objects and, second, it groups them together. You briefly learned about the Group command in the previous module, but it will be much more useful to you when you begin animating your various objects, including those that are grouped. You'll also notice several other commands are there. Unfortunately, they're grayed out but for good reason. These commands are specific to image objects that contain numerous layers. You learn about them in the next module.

Align Multiple Text Objects

Aligning text by eye can become extremely tiresome so let LiveMotion do it for you. The Alignment command is available to you under the Object Menu and it enables you to choose among seven different types of alignments:

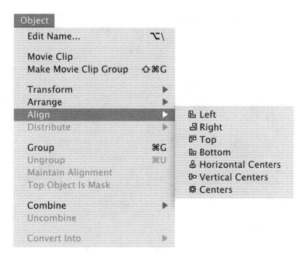

1. **Left:** Aligns all your objects to the left. The objects are aligned relative to the leftmost object.

2. **Right:** Aligns all your objects to the right. The objects are aligned relative to the rightmost object.

3. **Top:** Aligns all your objects to the top. The objects are aligned relative to the topmost object.

4. **Bottom:** Aligns all your objects to the bottom. The objects are aligned relative to the bottommost object.

5. **Horizontal Centers:** Aligns all your objects along the Y-axis of the centermost object.

6. **Vertical Centers:** Aligns all your objects along the X-axis of the centermost object.

7. **Centers:** Aligns all your objects on top of the centermost object.

Distribute Command

The Distribute command is more of a cosmetic feature of LiveMotion. The command takes all your selected objects and spaces them evenly apart among the furthest objects in the selection. As in the Arrange command, Distribute is located under the Object menu.

The Distribute command enables you to choose between two types of distributes: vertical and horizontal. Remember, your selected objects—in this case, text—must already be aligned either vertically or horizontally. To use this command, though, you need to have at least three objects selected.

Transform Text Using Palettes

In Module 2, you used both the Properties palette and the Transform palette to adjust your shapes. Text is no different. In fact, any object you import or create in LiveMotion on your composition is considered an object, which can be further adjusted not only in these two palettes, but in others as well. The only difference is the information displayed in these palettes will vary. In this case, both the Properties palette and the Transform palette will contain different settings and preferences once a text object is selected. Let's review these settings individually.

4

Properties Palette

The Properties palette for text objects contains different preferences than those for shape objects. The preferences inside the palette should look familiar to you if you've used a text editor, such as Microsoft Word, in the past. Starting at the top of the palette, the top two options enable you to set a font and its style. Right below them are other options that enable you to set the point size of your font, leading, and tracking. *Leading* is the distance between the lines of your text. *Tracking* is the distance between each of the individual letters in your text.

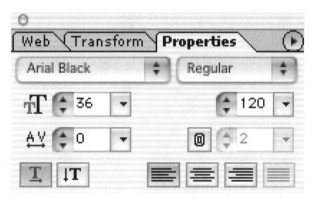

The palette also enables you to toggle between having your text object appear solid or only reveal its outline. When Outline is toggled on, the Width preference enables you to set the outline's thickness. The two buttons at the bottom left of the palette enable you to align your text object to display either horizontally or vertically. By default, the Align Horizontally button is toggled on. Finally, the button at the bottom right of the palette enables you to set the Justification preference for your text.

In the next module, you learn about importing and working with images. Just like text and shape objects, images also contain different settings in not only the Properties palette, but in other palettes as well.

Transform Palette

The Transform palette lets you carefully adjust every transformable aspect of your text. Even though you might use the Arrow tool to transform many of these aspects on your text directly on your composition, the Transform palette enables you to enter specific values for these transformations. You learned about the various properties, options, and preferences inside of the palette in Module 2. To review them, refer to Module 2.

The Transform palette is one of the few palettes that will display the same preferences, no matter what type of object is selected. Notice the preferences are displayed, no matter what object you're working with, so any transformation you've done to shapes, you can also apply to your text. As previously noted, you learn about importing and working with images in the next module. Notice the Transform palette displays the same preferences for images as well.

Ask the Expert

Question: How do I make changes to a specific letter in my text object?

Answer: You need to break apart your text object using the Convert Into/Objects process which you learned about earlier in this module. Doing so enables you to apply a transformation to the individual letters of your text object, independent of one another.

Question: I notice whenever I use the Type tool on my composition, my text appears to the left instead of the proper way, to the right of where I'm clicking. How do I change this?

Answer: To change this while using the Type tool on your composition, set your alignment preference in the Transform palette to the left, so when you type, your text will start at the left and continue to the right of where you clicked with the Type tool.

Question: How can I center my text as I type on the composition using the Type tool?

Answer: Simple. Choose the center alignment the next time you use the Type tool.

4

Add Color to Text

You learned about working with colors and shapes in Module 2. In that module, you learned about all the palettes that let you not only adjust color, but also transparency, brightness, contrast, and even adding gradients to your shapes. Text is no different. In fact, many of the palettes that let you apply these settings display the same preferences they showed when you were working with shapes.

Color Palette

The Color palette is one of the few palettes that always stays the same. Even as you work with other objects in later modules and the Color palette becomes useless for those objects, it still displays the same information. In this module, though, all the features of the Color palette are available. In fact, all the features of the Color palette, which were available to shapes, are available to text objects as well. So, to change the color of your text, select your object, and then choose the color you want to apply to the text from the palette. Remember, if you're planning on designing your projects for the Web, you must check the Web Safe Color preference. As noted in previous modules, this option causes your Color palette to display only Web Safe Colors.

By applying color to your text, all your text becomes colored. If you're tring to apply colors to specific characters in the text, there are two ways of going about it:

1. Instead of typing in a complete word, try creating individual letters of the word instead, and then proceed by coloring them with the Color Palette as desired.

2. Another method involves using the Convert Into | Objects command on your text object, which splits up the entire word into its individual letters. Afterwards, continue by applying various colors from the Color Palette onto the individual broken down letter objects as desired.

If you choose to break up your text in this manner, however, you probably want to use the Group command under the Object menu to group each individual letter of your text. After all, your composition can become quite a mess after breaking up each letter of your text with the Break Apart Text command. You can always choose to ungroup if you plan to continue to work with the individual letters.

1-Minute Drill

- After typing in a word using the Type tool, what is the quickest way to apply a color to every text character except for the first one?

Opacity Palette

The Opacity palette enables you to create transparency in your object. Just as with the shape object, the Opacity palette lets you adjust the opacity in your text objects by adjusting the Object Opacity preference. In addition, the palette also enables you to adjust the opacity of the object's individual layers, that is, if the object contains additional layers to begin with.

- Select your Text object and choose the Convert | Into Objects command found under the Object menu. Then select every text character, except for the first one, and apply a color to them using the Color palette.

Ask the Expert

Question: I created a text object using the Type tool on my composition. How can I make the middle two letters of my text transparent over an object located behind them?

Answer: First, you need to use the Object command in the Convert Into Submenu under the Object menu to alter the letters of your text independently of one another. Then, you need to select the two middle letters and adjust their opacity using the Opacity palette.

Question: How can I revert the Convert Into | Object process?

Answer: Unless you're willing to use the Undo command under the Edit menu to undo every action you performed after breaking apart your text object, there's no other way to put your text back together. Your only option at this point is either to group or combine your text, but you can still add or change the text of your individual text characters.

Transparency is one of the most widely used effects in text when it comes to Flash design. If you've viewed any sites that contain Flash type animations, you might have noticed letters scrolling, appearing, and disappearing. In future modules, you'll learn about animating your text and other objects, as well as exporting them to the Flash format.

Note

Flash animation and design is a SWF type file that's embedded in the HTML you see on sites that use this form of animation. LiveMotion is a powerful Flash-capable animation program. You learn more about animating and exporting to this format in Modules 7 through 15 of this book.

In addition to setting and adjusting opacity in your objects and layers, the palette also enables you to create Gradient effects. In previous modules, you used these effects on your shape objects. The function of these effects works the same for text objects. To apply a gradient effect from the Opacity palette on to a selected object, choose the type of gradient you want to apply and adjust it using the two sliders that appear at the bottom of the palette.

Project 4-1: Create a Logo

The Opacity palette enables you to add some pretty stylish transparency effects to your text. In the following project, you create a logo like the one you see in Figure 4-3.

The text in Figure 4-3 has been individually broken down and modified with the Opacity palette. Here are the steps for creating this effect:

Step-by-Step

1. Create a new composition with the dimensions 400×300.

2. Start by setting the color of your background to black. To do so, select the background square from the toolbar and choose the color black from the Color palette.

3. Click your Foreground box on the toolbar and set its color to white using the Color palette.

4. Select the Text tool from the toolbar and type in the word **LiveMotion**.

Figure 4-3   Logo project

5. Increase the size of your text to 36 and choose Helvetica Bold as your font in the Properties palette

6. Make sure your text is selected on your composition and break apart your object into individual letter objects by performing the Convert Into | Object process under the Object menu.

7. Individually select each letter and begin modifying the letter's transparency, beginning with the letter *L*, by setting the Object Opacity preference in the Opacity palette to 10. Increase the Object Opacity value by ten for every letter following letter *L*. The Object Opacity of the next letter would be 20, the next 30, and so on.

8. Select all the individual letters on your composition. Go back to the Properties palette and increase the font from 36 to 48.

9. Group all your letters using the Group command from the Object menu.

10. Select the Text tool again from the toolbar and type in the Number **2**. Color the text object red, using the Color palette.

11. Using the Properties Palette, type in the following dimensions for the letter: Width: **92** and Height: **243**.

12. Drag the number on top of your previously placed text and choose Send to Back from the Arrange menu under the Object menu.

13. Return to the Transparency palette and choose Radial Gradient for your selected object. Set its angle to 315 degrees.

14. Save and name this project file Project 4-1 in your LiveMotion Projects folder.

Project Summary

You just created a stylish logo for LiveMotion 2. You took the extra step to break apart your text in Step 5, so the word "LiveMotion" would have a less smooth, transparency-like effect. You could have skipped this step and not had to alter each individual letter. Instead, you could have used the Linear effect from the Opacity palette to give the word a smooth transition effect. Try experimenting with this other option and compare it to the current one.

   In the following sections of this module, you continue to access this project file to experiment with the remaining various palettes and their effects on text objects, so keep your project file open as you continue to read.

4

Gradient Palette

The Gradient palette is another helpful palette for giving your text objects a Transparency effect. As discussed in Module 2, the Gradient palette is similar to the Opacity palette except, in addition to fading your text objects, the palette enables you to fade one color into another. To demonstrate the difference better, let's go over the steps for creating this effect by modifying your previously saved file, which you named Project 4-1 Text Effect. Your resulting file should resemble Figure 4-4.

1. Select your LiveMotion grouped object from your composition and ungroup it.

2. Choose Unite from the Combine function under the Object menu.

3. Make sure your combined text object is selected and go over to the Gradient palette. Inside, select the Linear effect.

4. Using the Color palette, set the first slider in the Gradient palette to green. Set the other slider to blue.

5. Select the letter 2 object from your composition and choose the Burst effect from the Gradient palette.

6. The first slider should remain red. Color the second slider a light shade of yellow by selecting it and using the Color palette.

7. Finish by saving your file as Gradient Text Effect in your LiveMotion Projects folder.

Compare the two files to each other by opening both of them in LiveMotion and viewing them side-by-side. This should give you an idea of the similarities and differences the Opacity palette and Gradient palette are capable of performing on your objects. The Gradient palette goes one step beyond the Opacity palette by letting you work with two types of colors. On the other hand, the Opacity palette lets you apply its effect to the object's individual layers by modifying its opacity using the Layer Opacity preference. The Gradient palette isn't capable of performing this task.

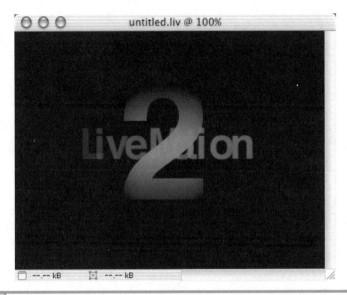

Figure 4-4   Gradient effect on a text object

In addition, objects with gradients take up more space compared to objects modified with the Opacity palette while you're working with animation. This is explained in more detail in Part 2 of this book and needn't concern you for now. File size will play a major role once you begin exporting your work to the SWF format, so minimizing the amount of Gradient effect your project file contains can significantly reduce your file size.

Adjust Palette

The use of the Adjust palette with text objects is similar to its use with shape objects. All the features of the palette are available except for the Tint preference. The palette is directed more toward working with images, rather then shapes and text, which you learn about in the next module. Yet, the palette is still available to your current objects and you can adjust brightness, contrast, and saturation of your text objects at any time. In addition, the palette lets you posterize and invert the color in your text. Remember, though, when you use the Adjust palette with either shape and text objects, the objects themselves will no longer be vector, so using this palette should be kept strictly to image

Figure 4-5 Adjust effect on a text object

(bitmap) objects. The differences between vector and bitmap objects are discussed in Module 6. Let's re-create the image you see in Figure 4-5 by performing the following steps.

1. Open your previously saved file, which you saved as Gradient Text Effect in your LiveMotion Projects folder.

2. Select all your text objects on your composition, and then go to the Adjust palette.

3. Check the Invert box at the bottom of the palette.

4. Select the number 2 text and increase its brightness.

5. Save and name your file Adjust Text Effect in your LiveMotion Projects folder once more.

Notice the color difference of your text. Every color in your text was inverted with this function. To clarify this effect, every color was switched to the opposite color on the Color Wheel. In addition, you brightened your number 2 text object to make it more visible.

1-Minute Drill

● How do the Adjust palette and the Gradient palette differ when working with shape and text objects?

● On what types of objects should the effects in the Adjust palette be used?

Add Layers and 3-D Effects

Layers and 3-D effects are capable of spicing up your text objects the same way they spiced up your shapes in previous modules. On one hand, layers enable you to build on your text by further expanding the details of your text. On the other hand, 3-D effects let you give text objects a sense of volume and depth.

3-D Palette

Being able to control the amount of 3-D effects you use within your project not only significantly decreases the size of your file, it also keeps your overall design in focus. Unless you plan to create three-dimensional designs for your projects throughout your composition, applying 3-D effects at will can distract your audience. This is imperative with text. By the end of this book, you'll feel comfortable enough to design your own web site using LiveMotion, which will be either *static* (nonanimated graphics) or full of animation. Minimizing the amount of 3-D effects on your text can both help your audience view the message you're trying to get across and improve the overall appearance of the site, making it more visually pleasing.

Logos, as in the one you created for LiveMotion 2 previously in this module, should also follow this rule. Applying a 3-D effect to the number 2 text objects would be a much better decision than applying a 3-D effect to the LiveMotion

---

● The Adjust palette and the Gradient palette don't differ when working with shape and text object. Both of these palettes display the same preferences and let you perform the same alterations to your objects.

● The effects in the Adjust palette should be used on image objects.

text object. In some cases, applying 3-D effects to both of the text objects can make them more appealing than applying the effect only to the LiveMotion text object. If you plan to apply a 3-D effect to both the objects, though, it's imperative you use some type of similarities.

The steps you took in applying 3-D effects for your shape objects in previous modules are the same for text objects. Let's use some of the techniques of applying a 3-D effect by applying one to your previously saved file, which you created using the Adjust palette. Your resulting logo should resemble the logo in Figure 4-6.

1. Begin by opening the Adjust Text Effect file from your LiveMotion Projects folder.

2. Select your number 2 text object on the composition and choose Bevel from the 3-D palette.

3. Adjust the following preferences in the 3-D palette: Depth – 40, Softness – 10, and Lighting – 100.

4. Position the LiveMotion text object to the right of the number 2 text object.

5. Save and name your file 3-D Text Effect in your LiveMotion Project folder.

Layer and Object Palettes

The Layer palette and the Object palette need to be discussed together. To use the Layer palette, you need to create layers for objects within the Object palette. On the other hand, to reshape and alter the layers created in the Object palette, you need to adjust them in the Layer palette. One palette needs the other.

As discussed earlier, layers enable you to build on the detail of your objects. In this module, using layers with your text objects is the topic. Sometimes, to have your text appear prominently, you might need a thin outline around it. The combination of the Layer and Object palette is capable of creating such effects, although the same rules apply for keeping some type of control over how many objects in your composition use layers. As with a 3-D effect, a large amount of layers could result in a bloated file size. In addition, creating an outline for nearly every text in your project isn't practical, so you must maintain some type of order over which and how many of your objects use layers that make your individual objects stand out.

Figure 4-6 | 3-D logo

Ask the Expert

Question: I want to add a 3-D effect to my text. Unfortunately, after applying the effect, the letters of the words are too close to each other, making the text impossible to read. Can I do anything about this?

Answer: You should start by using the Properties palette to increase the spacing in your text, and then apply your 3-D effect.

Question: How can I increase the spacing between the first two letters of my word and keep the rest of it as is?

Answer: Begin by typing in your word, using the Text tool on your composition. Inside the text box, highlight the first two letters, and then, in the Properties palette, adjust the tracking preference for these two letters.

Apply Styles and Textures

As discussed in the previous module, styles and textures are actual files that reside in their respective folders in your LiveMotion folder on your hard drive. The palettes that display them differ from other palettes because they don't let you tweak and adjust your objects. Instead, these palettes automatically apply custom-saved settings to your objects.

Styles and Text

As discussed in Module 3, the Styles palette enables you to apply custom styles to your objects. While working with text objects, you have the option of either applying a custom style to the entire selected text or breaking apart your text and individually applying the style to each letter of the text.

Styles come in many forms. They could be saved animation states, layered effects, 3-D effects, filter effects, and others. Any object on your composition can, at any time, inherit any of these forms by being appropriately modified with the Styles palette.

Copy and Paste Styles

LiveMotion lets you copy and paste styles as you please without the use of the Styles palette, so you aren't limited to the styles that appear in that palette. Any time you modify an object on your composition, LiveMotion considers this modification as the object's style. Once you copy that object using the Edit | Copy command, LiveMotion keeps these modifications in the clipboard until you decide to paste them. Pasting a copied style of an object to another isn't performed in the traditional Copy | Paste manner, though. Instead, the Edit menu features a Paste Style command. By using this command, you can apply the style from the clipboard on to your selected object on your composition. Let's practice this feature by performing its function in your last saved file, which you saved in your LiveMotion Projects folder as 3-D Text Effect.

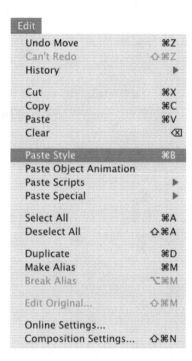

4

1. Select the LiveMotion text object on your composition and choose Copy from the Edit menu.

2. Select your number 2 text object and choose Paste Style from the Edit menu.

   You needn't save this file because it's a quick and simple function. Notice how the number 2 text object inherited all the features from the LiveMotion text object. Remember, you can save any style of an object directly into your Styles palette if you want to use this style in future projects. Also note, just as with the Edit | Copy and Edit | Paste commands function, the Edit | Paste Style command only enables you to paste the style of the most recent copied object. This means any time you copy another object using the Edit | Copy command, the contents of your clipboard will be replaced.

Copy and Paste Parts of Styles

You can copy and paste specific parts of styles back and forth between your objects without the use of the Styles palette. Or, instead, you can use the Paste Special command, which is located in the Edit menu. Whenever you use the Edit | Copy command in LiveMotion, in addition to remembering the style of the object selected, the program also remembers specific elements of that image. The elements the program remembers can be individually re-created in another selected object with the use of the Paste Special command. These elements are:

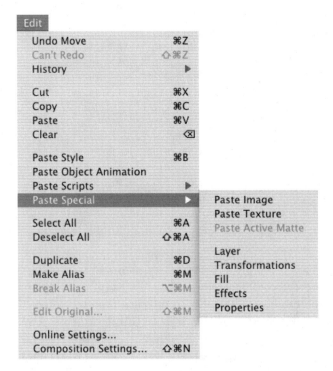

1. **Paste Image:** This command pastes an image on the selected object. If the object from which the Edit | Copy command was used didn't contain an image, this command won't effect your newly selected object.

2. **Paste Texture:** This command pastes the textures object from which the Edit | Copy command was used.

3. Paste Active Matte: If the previous object has an Active Matte, the newly selected object will acquire it as well with this command. Active Matte is introduced in the next module, where working with images is discussed.

4. Layer: All the layers from the object on which you used the Edit | Copy command are pasted on to your newly selected object.

5. Transformation: Any transformations done with the Transform palette or the Arrow tool on the object on which you've used the Edit | Copy command will reflect on your newly selected object.

6. Fill: This command fills your newly selected object with the color of the object on which you used the Edit | Copy command.

7. Effects: Photoshop filters are special effects you work on in the next module. This command will paste filter effects on to your newly selected object.

8. Properties: Any changes done to the object on which you used the Edit | Copy command with the Properties palette will reflect on your newly selected object.

As you can see, LiveMotion allows for many options when it comes to acquiring specific attributes and adding them to other objects. This is a huge time saver. You'll notice this when you work with more advanced projects that contain objects to which you want to apply similar alterations. With the unique Paste command of LiveMotion, you no longer must go through the process of keeping a mental note of all the changes you performed on one object to apply them to another.

Textures Palette

Textures, like styles, can be just as easily applied to your text objects. To apply a texture, select your text object, select the texture you want to apply from the Textures palette, and click the Apply button. You can also apply individual textures to each character of your text. To do so, choose the Convert Into | Objects command found under the Obects menu, individually select each character that was broken down, and apply the texture from the Textures palette. When you finish, you might want to group your characters with the Group command to maintain their alignment and keep them organized.

As you learned in the previous section of this module, you can use the Edit | Copy command with the Paste Special-Paste Texture command to copy a texture from one object and paste it on another. In addition, you can also import custom textures from other applications into the Textures palette in LiveMotion.

Project 4-2: Create a Greeting Card

Logos are one of the most common results of working with text. We previously created a unique text logo for LiveMotion 2. We'll now take a step further and create a simple greeting card utilizing text with various styles and techniques. The overall project should resemble Figure 4-7

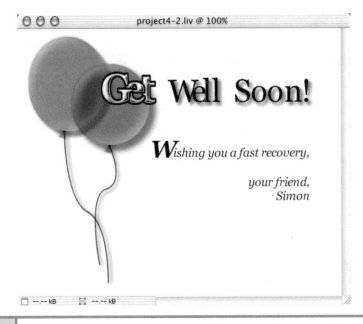

Figure 4-7　Greeting card project

Step-by-Step

1. Open your previously saved project file that you worked on in Module 3. You saved the file as Project 3-1 Balloon.

2. Type the heading of the card, which should read **Get Well Soon**. Use the Type tool to place the text on your composition. In the Properties palette, select the font to Georgia (if you don't have that particular font, use a similar one). Change the font size to 48.

3. To give your heading the unique look you see in Figure 4-7, you must first break apart your text object using the Convert Into | Objects process.

4. Select the first three letters of your heading title—*G, E,* and *T*—and increase their font size to 60 in the Properties palette. In addition, go to the Styles palette and apply the Mercury style to the three selected letters.

5. Move the three letters over the blue balloon. To give these letters the curved appearance you see in Figure 4-7, you must move them behind your Balloons Grouped object. To do this, make sure your three letters are selected, and then choose Send to Back from the Arrange menu under the Object menu.

6. As you might notice, the letters are now hidden by your red balloon. Ideally, you want to move these letters in front of the blue balloon but, at the same time, maintain the letters behind your red balloon. Keeping the letters behind the red balloon will give them the distorted effect you see in Figure 4-7. To perform these functions, you need to ungroup your balloon objects. After doing so, select your three letters once more, and then choose Send to Back from the Arrange menu under the Object menu. Now, continue to repeat choosing Bring Forward from the Arrange menu until the text appears over the red balloon and, at the same time, behind the blue balloon.

7. To keep your composition clean and organized, group all the objects except for the remaining text objects of the words Well Soon! which you work on next.

8. Move your grouped object to the upper-left corner of your composition. After doing so, select the Well Soon! text objects and align them by hand to the Get text object.

9. Next, select the Drop Shadow 2 style and apply it to your selected text objects. Afterwards, group them using the Group command under the Object menu.

10. You're done with the heading, so let's finish by adding a message in your Get Well greeting card. To do so, use the Type tool and type in the following text on your composition, **Wishing you a fast recovery**.

4

11. From the Properties palette, select the font Georgia. Choose Italic, and set the font size to 18.

12. Choose the Break Apart text command from the Object menu. Select the first letter only, and set its size to 48 and its style to Bold from the Properties palette.

13. Finish the greeting message by grouping it using the Group command.

14. Finish by signing the card. To do so, type the following text using the Type tool: **Your Friend,** (Enter your name here).

15. Save your project file as Project 4-2 Balloon in your LiveMotion Projects folder on your hard drive.

Project Summary

You just created a Get Well greeting card. In addition, you finished working with your project file. You won't use your previous project files in future modules to avoid confusion. You can start fresh with a new composition, as you did in Project 4-1 earlier in this module. You'll continue to access the objects created in your previous projects by using the Edit | Copy and Edit | Paste commands to save time, though, so be aware of where these projects are saved.

Summary

You just learned the bulk of working with text in LiveMotion. Most of the terms and ways of altering your text on your composition are similar to the ways you work with shapes. Yet, you also learned that some palettes display and enable you to use different preferences while working with text objects as opposed to shape objects. These palettes will continue to change when you learn about images in the next module. Importing and working with images lets you continue to alter and further advance your LiveMotion projects. All the alteration techniques you learned so far while working with text and shape objects are available to you when you work with images. In addition, you learn about some new techniques that are only specific to images and can't be used with other objects.

☑ *Mastery Check*

1. What's the purpose of adding text in your LiveMotion projects?

    A. To convey a message through your project

    B. To make your project more informative

    C. To be creative

    D. All of the above

2. Unlike Word Processing programs, such as Microsoft Word, LiveMotion lets you add _____ to your text.

    A. Alignment

    B. Size

    C. Color

    D. Style

3. What's the purpose of the Break Apart Text command?

    A. To enable you to work on individual letters of your text

    B. To break apart words from your text

    C. To allow you to use the Pen tool on your text objects

    D. To let you color your text

4. If you want to align all your objects along the Y-axis of the centermost object, which type of alignment would you use?

    A. Horizontal Center

    B. Vertical Centers

    C. Centers

    D. Top

☑ Mastery Check

5. Which of the following palettes remain the same and, in addition, enable you to alter the same preferences, no matter what kind of object you're working on?

A. Properties palette

B. Transform palette

C. Adjust palette

D. Distort palette

6. By applying color to your text object, ＿＿＿ becomes colored.

A. The first letter

B. The last letter

C. All of it

D. None of it

7. While using the Gradient palette, how would you adjust the amount of color used on one side of the object, as well as the other?

A. You can't

B. The darkest of the two colors comes in a greater amount

C. By moving the sliders

D. By first adjusting the object with the Opacity palette

8. Which preference is unusable in the Adjust palette while working on text and shape objects?

A. Contrast

B. Saturation

C. Tint

D. Posterize

☑ *Mastery Check*

9. _____ enable you to build on your text objects, while _____ let you give text objects a sense of depth and volume.

10. The Paste Special command enables you to paste _____ to your objects.

4

Module 5

Import Images

The Goals of this Module

- Learn how to import images into LiveMotion
- Transform images using various palettes
- Distort images
- Add layers to images
- Import Adobe native files into LiveMotion

So far, you've learned a variety of ways to create and manipulate objects by using various palettes, menu commands, and tools in the toolbar. Images are also objects. Unfortunately, unlike text and shape objects, images can't be created within LiveMotion. In addition, LiveMotion won't let you directly open an image on your hard drive using the Open command under the File menu. Like many other photo editing applications, however, LiveMotion does enable you to import images using the Place command, which is described shortly. Once imported, the image becomes an object on your composition, which LiveMotion lets you transform and manipulate.

In the following module, you learn several ways to import and place images using the Place command, as well as how to manipulate these images using the various palettes available in LiveMotion. You also learn new commands that let you import Adobe Native files, which consist of images containing layers.

Import Images

To import an image on to your composition, you need to use the Place command which is available to you under the File menu, as seen in Figure 5-1. Once selected, a window opens, asking you to locate an image from your hard drive. After you select an image, LiveMotion places it directly on your composition.

LiveMotion has limits as to what image file types it lets you import on your composition using the Place command. Some of the most common file formats LiveMotion is capable of importing are GIF, JPEG, and PSD files. GIF and JPEG images are the most widely used file formats. Most of the images you see on web sites are saved in GIF and JPEG file formats, but each has its purpose as to what type of images it displays best. PSD files, on the other hand, are Adobe Photoshop native files, which offer some additional choices in LiveMotion. You learn about the features of PSD files in LiveMotion toward the end of this module in the section, "Work with PSD Files." Of course, other file formats exist, which LiveMotion enables you to import with the Place command, but for now, let's deal with these three.

You can also import an image on to your composition with the use of a scanner. If you currently own a scanner and want to scan an image on to your composition, you can do so with the use of the Import palette. Use the Select Twain option to choose the driver of your scanner so LiveMotion can recognize

File

New Composition...	⌘N
New Script	⌥⌘N
Open...	⌘O
Close	⌘W
Save	⌘S
Save As...	⇧⌘S
Revert	F12
Place...	⌘I
Place Sequence...	⌥⇧⌘I
Place as Texture...	
Replace...	⇧⌘I
Export Settings...	⌥⇧⌘E
Export	⌘E
Export As...	⇧⌘E
Export Selection...	
Preview In	▶
File Info...	
Workgroup	▶
Page Setup...	⇧⌘P
Print...	⌘P

Figure 5-1   The Place command

it. After doing so, use the Import palette, select your scanner, and begin scanning your image directly on to your composition. Even though this is a useful feature in LiveMotion, I advise you to scan the image into an image-editing application prior to bringing the image on to your composition. Despite the fact that LiveMotion offers many different options for color correcting and cropping of the images you import, many other programs specific to editing images offer you more advanced options when it comes to editing. After doing so, you should then use the Place command to import the specific image.

The Import command also lets you copy all the images from your digital camera. Once again, I recommend using an image-editing application to bring in the images from your camera, edit them, and then bring them in to LiveMotion using the Place command.

Graphic Interchange Format

Graphic Interchange Format (GIF) file format is one of the oldest supported file formats for the Web. The advantage of the GIF file format is that it's capable of keeping the file size of your image much lower than any other image file format. Another advantage of GIFs is transparencies because they enable you to save your files with transparent backgrounds. Unfortunately, GIFs aren't the most suitable file formats for saving real-life images, such as people, animals, and landscapes. GIFs are only limited to 256 colors, so if you plan to save your high-quality images in this format, it will reduce their quality significantly. However, GIFs are your best choice when it comes to saving artwork such as images with flat drawings. Cartoons in your local Sunday newspaper are the best example of images that would benefit most from being saved as GIF files. If you currently have any GIF files saved on your computer, they can be easily imported into LiveMotion using the Place command.

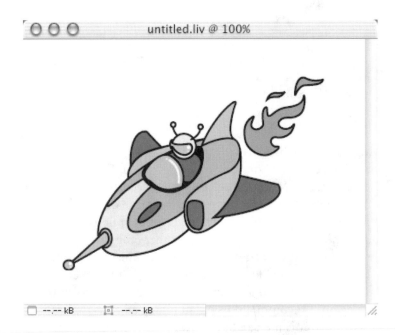

GIF files are also capable of containing animation. Many of the flashing signs and banners you see today while browsing the Internet are actual GIF files. In Part 2 of this book, in addition to creating and exporting your animation to the SWF format, you learn about exporting your work into GIFs.

Joint Experts Photographic Group

Joint Photographic Experts Group (JPEG) files are an ideal choice for images containing real-life objects, such as people, animals, and the environment. Unlike GIFs, JPEGs aren't limited to 256 colors. JPEG compression is 24-bit, meaning it can contain up to 16.7 million colors.

5

JPEG files are one of the most common files you'll find on either your hard drive or the Internet. In addition, most of today's digital cameras import their images into your computer by saving them as JPEG files, so they can just as easily be imported into LiveMotion as GIFs by using the Place command under the File menu.

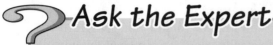

Copy and Transform Images

In addition to using the Place command in LiveMotion to import images, you can also use the Copy and Paste commands in the Edit menu. Look at Figure 5-2 for their exact location. With these commands, you can copy an image from your favorite photo-editing application using the Copy command, followed by the Paste command in LiveMotion. Both ways deliver the same result, so stick with whichever way is most convenient.

Duplicate and Make Alias Commands

As you already learned, LiveMotion is full of helpful features that enable you to be more productive. The Duplicate and the Make Alias commands that follow the Copy and Paste commands are two more commands you'll probably use when you work in LiveMotion.

The Duplicate command, which appears in the Edit menu, illustrated in Figure 5-3, enables you to duplicate any selected object on your composition. The convenience of this command is it performs both the Copy and Paste commands all at once. In addition, the command doesn't replace the contents of your clipboard. The benefit of this feature is you can use the command as you please, without jeopardizing the contents of your clipboard. And, once you use it, the command places your duplicated object exactly on top of its duplicate. You can then use the Arrow tool from the toolbar to move your new object to any part of your composition.

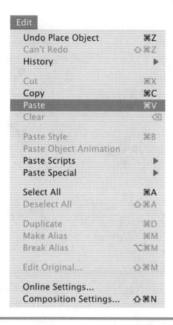

Figure 5-2 The Copy and Paste commands in the Edit menu

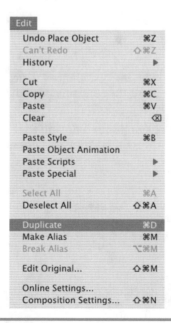

Figure 5-3 The Duplicate and Make Alias commands in the Edit menu

The Make Alias command also appears in the Edit menu, as shown in Figure 5-3, directly following the Duplicate command. The Make Alias command enables you to create an alias object of the selected object on your composition. As with the Duplicate command, the *alias object* is an exact duplicate of the selected object. However, from now on, any changes you make to the original object, automatically impact the changes of the alias object. If, at any time you want to detach the alias from acquiring any further changes, you can do so by selecting the alias object and choosing the Break Alias command in the Edit menu.

Any object created or imported into LiveMotion is capable of taking advantage of these features. Both these features are incredibly useful. In addition, they enable you to save time by being more productive, and spare you the hassle of going back and forth using the Copy and Paste commands.

Crop Images

As discussed in previous modules, the Crop tool lets you remove unwanted parts of the object, in this case, the image. To crop an unwanted part of the image, select the image, choose the Crop tool from the toolbar, and then click-and-drag on any side of the image. You can also crop both sides simultaneously by clicking-and-dragging on one of the corners of the image object.

1-Minute Drill

● Which command would be the best choice for creating an exact duplicate of an object that will mimic all the adjustments and alterations performed on the original?

● In addition to using the Duplicate command to create an exact duplicate of a selected object, what other combination of commands can you use to perform a similar result?

● The Make Alias command.
● You can use a combination of the Copy and Paste commands to perform a similar result. Copying a selected object, followed by using the Paste command to place the object on the composition, creates the same result as the Duplicate command.

Transform Images Using Palettes

As with shape and text objects, images can be modified with palettes. As with shapes, you'll notice some palettes display different preferences that are specific to image objects only.

Note, as with previous objects you've learned about so far, LiveMotion enables you to perform specific transformations on your image objects without the use of palettes. With the help of the Arrow tool in the toolbar, you can transform image objects directly on your composition by clicking-and-dragging any one of the corners or line segments that appear around the object. The Arrow tool also enables you to skew your object by holding down the COMMAND key as you click-and-drag any one of the sides of the object. In addition, the Arrow tool also enables you to rotate objects by clicking-and-dragging on the unfilled corner of the object.

5

Transform Palette

To transform your objects—in this case, images with specific values—you need to use the Transform palette. As with previous objects, the Transform palette lets you adjust all types of dimensional settings for your image objects. If you want to rotate an imported image object to a specific degree, the Transform palette is a much better choice for entering these specific values instead of using the Arrow tool.

The Transform palette also enables you to work with multiple selected objects. To modify the width and height of two objects, and then make them equal in value, you need to enter the Height and Width value into the Transform palette. The values entered appear in both the selected objects.

Properties Palette

Notice how much different the Properties palette appears when an image object is selected as opposed to a text or shape object, shown in Figure 5-4. The Properties palette enables you to modify the Alpha Channel of the selected image object. You can choose from four choices: No Alpha, Use Alpha Channel, Build Alpha from Image, and Active Matte.

Figure 5-4 The Properties palette for images

Alpha Channels are masks of an image. These masks can be created in most image-editing applications such as Adobe Photoshop. Masks let you easily select specific parts of an image. If an imported image contains a mask, LiveMotion enables you to display only the specific part of that image.

To turn on a mask for an object that already has a created mask, you need to select the Use Alpha Channel preference in the Properties palette. On the other hand, if you want to display the same image without using its mask, you would then select the No Alpha preference from the Properties palette.

LiveMotion has the capability to create masks for image objects that previously didn't contain any. Although the quality and precision of the mask won't be as precise as those created in other image-editing applications. LiveMotion creates masks for images automatically. If the composition background is black, LiveMotion will color in all the areas of the selected image that are close to the color of the background, giving the image a chrome-like appearance, as seen in Figure 5-5.

On the other hand, if the composition background is white, the selected image object will appear faded on the composition, as seen in Figure 5-6. To let LiveMotion create an Alpha Channel for a selected image, you need to select the Build Alpha from Image preference from the Properties palette.

The last preference in the Properties palette enables you to use mattes for your selected image objects. *Mattes,* once applied to an image, are shapes the selected image absorbs. By default, the shape in the Properties palette is a circle. By turning on the Active Matte preference in the Properties palette, LiveMotion crops out the selected image object into a circle. To use other shapes, you need to drag a custom shape from the Library palette on to the Properties palette. Look at Figure 5-7. The image object was altered with the Active Matte preference in the Properties palette. The custom shape was dragged from the Library palette and cropped into the image.

Figure 5-5   Alpha Channel on a black background

Figure 5-6   Alpha Channel on a white background

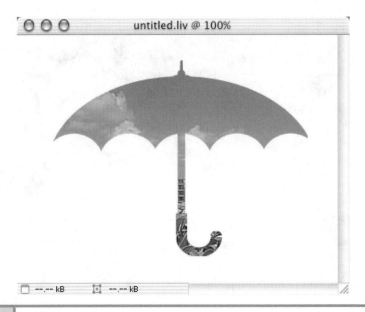

untitled.liv @ 100%

--.-- kB   --.-- kB

Figure 5-7 A matte image

Alpha Channels, masks, and mattes are additional ways to crop out parts of an image without using the Crop tool from the toolbar. By using these features in the Properties palette on your image object, you can modify your images the same way you did with shape objects in previous modules. Unlike shapes, images contain more details, so using the Crop tool to crop out unwanted parts of an image isn't sufficient. Whether you use Alpha Channel, Mask, or Mattes on your image object, the Crop effect will be much more precise.

1-Minute Drill

● What are Alpha Channels?

● By default, the matte in the Properties palette is a circle. How would you change the matte, to use it on a selected image object on your composition?

● Masks of an image.
● By selecting a custom shape from the Library palette, you can drag the shape on to the Properties palette, which automatically updates the selected image on your composition.

Touch Up Images

Regardless of whether you've touched up your images prior to importing them into LiveMotion, the program enables you to make additional corrections using various palettes. As with previous objects, such as text and shapes, these palettes let you adjust the image's brightness, contrast, opacity, saturation, and tint. In addition, they enable you to posterize and apply Gradient effects.

Adjust Palette

In previous modules, you used the Adjust palette to touch up other types of objects. However, you've learned its importance for image objects and know its usefulness is more apparent when you're working with images. If you use your digital camera to take all the images you plan to use in LiveMotion, you'll notice these images need additional touch ups. From my experience, no camera takes a perfect picture, no matter how advanced or costly it is. Therefore, using the Adjust palette can enable you to touch up certain elements of the image, such as brightness, contrast, and saturation.

If you don't currently own or use a digital camera and you plan on using images from other sources, you might also need to adjust certain elements of your image with the Adjust palette. The process of adjusting these preferences within the Adjust palette on your selected images is the same as with shapes and text objects. To adjust the selected image's brightness, you can either brighten or darken it using the slider below it. The same applies for the Contrast and Saturation preference. The Contrast preference enables you either to make the selected image appear sharper or duller on the composition. Finally, the Saturation preference lets you increase the luminosity of color in the image or decrease it.

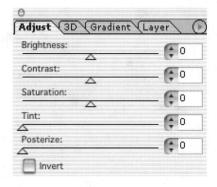

For less realistic and more drastic adjustment of images, the Tint, Posterize, and Invert preferences in the Properties palette can also be used. By default, these three preferences are set to 0. To adjust them and apply them to the selected image, you need to increase their value using their individual sliders located directly below each of the preferences.

Opacity Palette

Using opacity in images enables you to alter their transparency over either the background of the composition or the object(s) located behind it. As with previous objects, the Opacity palette contains Opacity Gradient effects such as Linear, Burst, Double Burst, and Radial. Look at Figure 5-8, which contains four images, individually altered with each effect. Notice the impact of each of these effects on the image.

In addition, the Opacity palette also enables you to alter the transparency of the layers of the selected image using the Object Layer Opacity preference. Layers, which were described in Modules 2 and 3, are explained and associated to image objects in the upcoming sections "Add Layers" and "Layer Palette."

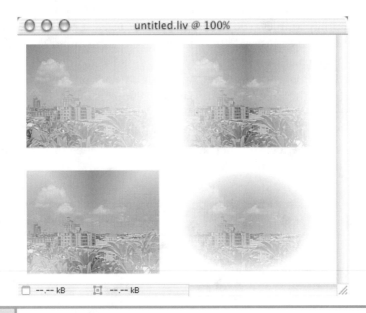

Figure 5-8 Opacity Gradient effects

Gradient Palette

The Gradient palette can't be used with image objects. Because images already contain defined colors, using the Gradient palette to create the fading of one color to another won't alter the selected image. Instead, refer to Modules 2, 3, and 4 to review how the Gradient palette enables you to work with the other two types of objects: shapes and text.

Project 5-1: Transform an Image

Unlike text and shape objects, creating a project using steps of transforming an image is a little tricky. In previous projects, you could draw a shape or type in a specific text by following step-by-step instructions. For you to work on the same image in LiveMotion, as illustrated in Figure 5-9, you need to download and work on exactly the same image. The image you'll use is a view from the top of Hunter Mountain located in Catskills Mountains in New York.

Figure 5-9   Project 5-1

5

Step-by-Step

1. To begin, either find an image you want to use on your hard drive or download one from the Internet.

2. Copy the image to your LiveMotion Projects folder on your hard drive.

3. In LiveMotion, create a new composition with the following dimensions: 400×300.

4. Using the Place command, import the image you previously downloaded to your LiveMotion Projects folder.

5. In the Properties palette, select the Active Matte preference.

6. From the Library palette, select the shape called Apple.

7. Click and drag that shape into the Active Matte box in the Properties palette.

8. Save your finished project as Project 5-1 in your LiveMotion Projects folder on your hard drive.

Project Summary

Your image should resemble the image in Figure 5-9. Notice how the shape selected from the Library palette automatically cropped into the image that you imported from your LiveMotion Projects folder. Using the Properties palette alongside the Library palette enables you to crop your images into some unique shapes. You can experiment cropping your images with some of the other shapes contained in the Library palette. Notice their effect on your image. As described in Module 3, you can also import your own custom shapes into the Library palette by creating them in other vector programs. Refer to Module 3 on how to do this.

3-D Effects, Styles, and Distort Filters

3-D effects and filters enable you to distort the images on your composition. In the following section, you learn about adding 3-D effects to your images, as well as applying filters contained in the Distort palette. In addition, you learn how to import and use filters from Adobe Photoshop in LiveMotion.

3-D Palette

The 3-D palette enables you to apply 3-D-like effects to your objects. In previous modules, you applied these effects to shapes and text. In this module, you apply them to images. In fact, you'll notice how much more detailed these effects appear in images, as opposed to the other two types of objects you worked with. Look at the various effects in the 3-D palette and notice their impact on the images in Figure 5-10.

Each of these effects can be further adjusted inside the 3-D palette, so your effect could vary. These adjustments come in the form of additional preferences, such as depth, lightness, softness, edge, and angle, so each 3-D effect can be adjusted further.

5

Distort Palette

The Distort palette works similarly to the 3-D palette with the exception that the Distort effects within the palette aren't 3-D-like. Look at Figure 5-11, which displays six images containing each of the effects available to you in the Distort palette.

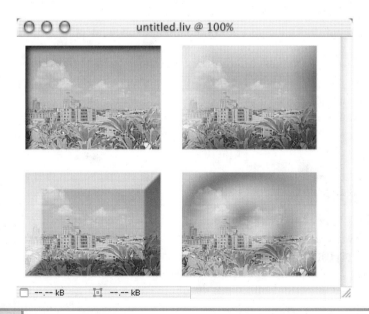

Figure 5-10   3-D effects

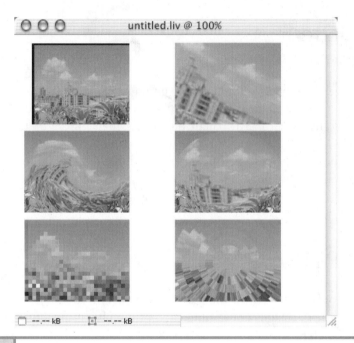

Figure 5-11 Distort effects

Remember, the Distort palette can also be used with other objects, such as text and shapes. However, it's important to apply these effects to objects that contain a lot of color, gradients, texture, and so forth. Doing so makes the appearance of your object that much more distorted. Because images, unlike text and shape objects, already envelop these qualities, working with the Distort palette on images seems more practical.

Styles Palette

Using the Styles palette with your image objects is yet another way of altering your images. As described in previous modules, the Styles palette contains preexisting styles that contain object-altering effects that can be applied to any type of object on your composition. The styles in the Styles palette can contain nearly any type of effect, whether it's a combination of Filter effects, 3-D effects, Distort effects, color, gradient, opacity, and even animation. As previously noted, animation is something that's introduced in Part 2 of this book. Therefore, when using styles on your image objects in this module, we'll steer away from applying those which contain animation styles. In addition, styles can also contain Rollover effects that, when applied, allow the object to perform an interactive effect. Rollover and its effects on objects are explained in the next module.

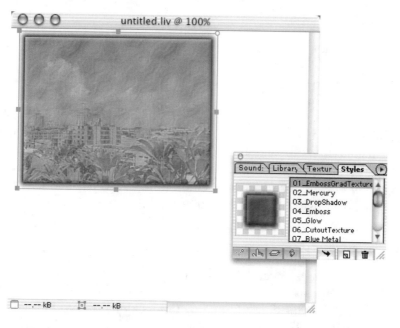

To apply a style to a selected image object, select the image, choose the type of style you want to apply from the Styles palette, and click the Apply button at the bottom of the palette. As noted in earlier chapters, styles can also be saved in the LiveMotion palette (select an object that already contains some type of modifications made by the Filter command or any of the various appearance-altering palettes described in this section of the module). After doing so, click the New Style Palette button at the bottom of the Styles palette and select the modification of the image you want to embed in the style you're saving in the Styles palette. LiveMotion automatically saves the style as a LiveMotion file within the Styles folder in the LiveMotion folder on your hard drive.

To delete a specific style from your Styles folder, select the style you want to delete and click the Delete Style button, which is also located at the bottom of the Style palette. After pressing the Delete Style button, LiveMotion prompts you with the following message: "Do you really want to delete this Style? Doing so permanently deletes the file from the Styles directory on your disk." After clicking OK, the style you chose to delete will be permanently gone from within your Styles palette, as well as the Styles folder within your LiveMotion folder on your hard drive.

Add Layers

Layers enable you to create complex objects. The various parts of those objects are each contained on a separate layer, which is modifiable with the Layer palette. The purpose of doing this enables you to work on different parts of the object, instead of working on the object as a whole. Just like text and shape objects, images can contain multiple numbers of layers.

Plenty of other uses exist for adding layers to an object. Adding a layer to objects and modifying that layer to resemble a shadow is one use. Creating a layer for an object that acts like a border around the object is another use.

Object Palette

The Object palette lets you create and manage the various layers of an object. To create a layer for an object, you first need to make sure the specific object is selected on your composition. After doing this, clicking the New Layer button in the Object palette creates a single layer for that object. The layer created is automatically colored black. To change its color, you first need to select the layer and choose the specific color in the Color palette. In addition, if you want to duplicate the layer from the original image that's selected on your composition, you can do so by clicking the Duplicate Layer button. Layer 2 will now resemble Layer 1.

After you create a layer for an image object, you can now use specific palettes to adjust that layer. In addition to using the Layer palette, discussed in the next section, you're free to use the Style, Texture, Color, Distort, Opacity, and 3-D palette to alter the specific layer. To move the individual layers of an object, you need to use the Layer Offset tool in the toolbar. Using the Arrow tool to move a selected layer around will, instead, move the entire object and its layers as a whole.

Layer Palette

The Layer palette enables you to adjust your layers. These adjustments are similar to those found in the Transform palette. Unfortunately, attempting to adjust the size of a layer in the Transform palette will, instead, alter the entire object and its layers as a whole. A direct approach to modifying only the selected layer of an object in the Layer palette is to use the Layer palette to adjust the specific measurement of a layer.

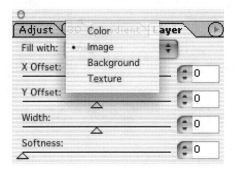

Look closely at the Layer palette while an image object is selected on your composition and compare it to the appearance of the palette when a shape or a text object is selected. You'll notice a slight change in Fill With preference. When you work with shapes and text objects, the Fill With preference is set to Color. On the other hand, when an image object is selected, the preference displays Image instead of Color. Switching this preference to Color when an image is selected will automatically color the entire image object to the color that's set as the Foreground Color at the bottom of the toolbar. If, for any reason, you want to convert an image object to a shape object or vise versa, you can do so by using this preference.

The additional preferences that appear in the Layer palette enable you to offset the X and Y coordinates of your layer, increase its width, and adjust the softness of the layer's width. In addition, you can also use the Opacity palette with your layers to alter their individual transparencies. To do so, you need to select the specific layer and adjust the Layer Opacity preference in the Opacity palette.

Ask the Expert

Question: What happened to filters in LiveMotion 2? LiveMotion 1 used to have a Photoshop palette that let you apply Photoshop-like filters to the objects on the composition.

Answer: Unfortunately, filters are no longer available in LiveMotion 2. If you have access to Adobe Photoshop, you can apply your effects there, and then import your PSD file into LiveMotion. LiveMotion enables you to break down your PSD files into multiple layers, but you can no longer edit the effects on these layers within LiveMotion. Instead, you need to use the Edit Original command to edit the specific layer within your imported PSD back in Photoshop.

Question: Where can I find the Edit Original command and how does it work with Photoshop?

Answer: The Edit Original command appears at the bottom of the Edit menu. LiveMotion enables you to edit any imported PSD file, including AI files back in Photoshop and Illustrator, respectively. After making the necessary changes to the individual layers in the file you applied the edit Original command to, LiveMotion automatically updates these changes on your composition in real time. You learn more about this feature in the next section.

Import Adobe Native Files

One of the most useful features of LiveMotion is its capability to import Adobe Photoshop and Adobe Illustrator native files. These native files are incredibly robust. They can contain layers that are already cropped out. You're currently working with images that appear as rectangles on your composition. In addition, we've introduced ways to crop your images using the Crop tool, the Properties palette, and the Library palette. An Adobe native file, such as one created in Adobe Photoshop, however, is capable of having images cropped out in full detail.

In your previous project, you imported an image of a view from the top of Hunter Mountain in New York. By cropping certain elements, such as individual trees that appear in the image in Photoshop, putting these cropped-out objects on their own layers, and then saving them as a PSD file, LiveMotion enables you to import this file type and break down its individual layers.

Work with PSD Files

To import a PSD-type file into LiveMotion, use the Place command as you would import a JPEG, GIF, or any other type of image. LiveMotion enables you to use the Convert Into command, just as you've done with text objects. Therefore, using this command enables you to break down the individual layers of a PSD file—that is, if the PSD file you're working with contains them. If it does, layers will automatically split apart from the image and become independent objects on your composition. Look at Figure 5-12, which shows you the path to the command. As you might have noticed, the Convert Layers Into command contains other options for converting layers. These options allow the program to organize the individual layers of the PSD file into groups, sequences, and sequences with background. These options are related to animation, which you learn about in Part 2. For now, using the Objects option from the Convert Into command is the best means of breaking down the individual layers of a PSD file.

| **Figure 5-12** | Converting PSDs |

Previously in this module, you learned about using the Properties palette to create Alpha Channels for an image. PSD files are capable of containing Alpha Channels, so once imported with the Place command, any Alpha Channels contained in this file can be turned on with the Use Alpha Channel preference in the Properties palette.

Project 5-2: Create a Picture Frame

In the previous module, you downloaded an image into the LiveMotion Projects folder on your hard drive. You used the tools you've learned up to this point and performed specific alterations on that image. Since then, you've learned about filters, 3-D effects, and Distort effects, which enable you to distort and develop your images further on the composition. In the following project, you use the same image you used in the first project to create a simple picture frame like the one in Figure 5-13.

Figure 5-13 | Project 5-2

Step-by-Step

1. Begin by creating a new composition with the following dimensions: 400×300. Leave the other options as they are.

2. Change the background of the composition to a light orange color from the Color palette.

3. Use the Place command to import the Module5_image.jpg file, which you previously downloaded and saved into the LiveMotion Projects folder.

4. Using the Transform tool, enter the following dimension for the imported image: 329×247.

5. From the Object menu, select the Filter command and choose Water Color Filter under the Artistic category.

6. In the Styles palette, select the Picture Frame style and apply it to the image.

7. Using the Polygon tool from the toolbar, create a triangle with the following dimensions 38×38, then rotate the triangle 90 degrees in the Transform palette.

8. In the Properties palette, choose the outline preference for the triangle object.

9. Using the Crop tool from the toolbar, crop out the bottom piece of the triangle, which leaves you with two remaining sides. Color the object black.

10. Use the Ellipse tool to create a circle with the following dimensions: 8×8, and then drag it at the top edge of the previous triangular object. Color the circle with a dark orange color using the Color palette.

11. Save your file as Project 5-2 in your LiveMotion Projects folder on your hard drive.

Project Summary

Your image object now resembles a watercolor painting hanging from the wall, as seen in Figure 5-13. If you select the image object from your composition and go to the Photoshop palette, you'll notice the watercolor filter appears right inside. You can toggle the effect of this filter on your image by toggling the little eye icon, which appears to the left of the filter in the Photoshop palette. In addition, while keeping your image object selected, look at the Object palette. Notice how the Picture Frame style applied from the Style palette on to the image created additional layers for that image, giving it a picture frame-like appearance. Each of those layers can be further modified if you want to adjust your Picture Frame image object.

Summary

In this module, you learned about every aspect of importing and altering your images in LiveMotion. You learned how to use the Place command to bring in files—such as JPEGs and GIFs—and you learned about importing and breaking down more complex files, such as PSDs. Also, you learned how to crop, distort, and create layers for these images using the various palettes available. This module concludes the introduction of creating and importing objects you'll use to animate in Part 2 of this book. In the next module, you use all the objects you've learned about so far to create some interactivity in your projects by creating rollovers. *Rollovers* are button effects that enable you to trigger numerous actions, such as toggling the visibility of another object on and off, as well as loading web pages. Modules 12 and 13 will describe a way of triggering specified scripts. Scripts in LiveMotion 2 are capable of performing numerous tasks. We'll go over some of these tasks as well as other features of utilizing scripts in your animations in Modules 13 and 14.

Be sure to take the quiz at the end of this module, so you can test your knowledge of all the terms and definitions covered here.

☑ *Mastery Check*

1. _____ type files are more practical to use for saving real-life images, such as those of people, animals, and the environment. On the other hand, _____ file types are more practical to use for images that contain artwork.

2. How would you import an image on to your composition?

   A. Use the Place command

   B. Use the Copy and Paste commands in the Edit menu

   C. Use the Import command

   D. All of the above

3. What is the function of the Make Alias command in the Object menu?

   A. To create an exact duplicate of a selected object

   B. To create an exact alias of a selected object

   C. Both of the above

   D. None of the above

4. Which palette enables you to build Alpha Channels and create mattes for images?

   A. The Properties palette

   B. The Transform palette

   C. The Adjust palette

   D. The Library palette

5. The Adjust palette enables you to _____ your images.

   A. Distort

   B. Reshape

   C. Touch up

   D. Crop out

5

☑ Mastery Check

6. Which of the following palettes will have no effect on an image?

A. The Layer palette

B. The Gradient palette

C. The Object palette

D. The Transform palette

7. To change an image object to a shape object, you need to select Color from the Fill With preference in the _____.

A. Color palette

B. Object palette

C. Properties palette

D. Layer palette

8. Which menu command would you use to import a PSD file type into LiveMotion?

A. The Open command

B. The Import command

C. The Paste command

D. The Place command

9. PSD is the native file format for which Adobe application?

A. Adobe ImageStyler

B. Adobe LiveMotion

C. Adobe Photoshop

Module 6

Buttons and Rollovers

The Goals of this Module

- Learn various ways of creating buttons
- Create rollovers
- Create remote rollovers

The last module was the final one on teaching you how to create various types of objects on your composition. You learned how to draw several different types of shapes, using a large range of shape tools available to you in the toolbar. In addition, you learned how to create and stylize text on your composition. In conclusion, the previous module taught you how to import and manipulate images.

In this module, you use the various objects you learned about to create buttons, rollovers, and remote rollovers. Understanding how Rollover and Remote Rollover buttons work can help you create interactive projects.

Create Buttons

The most basic definition of a *button* in LiveMotion is the part of the area on your composition that, when exported, enables you to trigger its function. So far, you've only learned how to save projects to your hard drive, so you can further apply changes to the project at any time. Your ultimate goal is to export your work to display it, either on the Internet in the form of a web page or as a CD-ROM presentation. In Module 7 of this book, you learn a variety of ways to export your project to several types of file formats, which then enables you to present them on those mediums.

For now, you can view the interactivity of your projects by toggling on the Preview mode at the bottom of the toolbar. Once toggled on, all the palettes, including the toolbar, temporarily disappear from the screen, leaving you with only your composition area. To return to the Edit mode, which enables you to perform further changes to your composition area, toggle on the Edit mode at the bottom of the toolbar. All the palettes and the toolbar will again appear on your screen, enabling you to continue working on your project. A quick way of accessing the Preview mode is by pressing the letter *Q* on your keyboard.

You have an infinite number of ways to create buttons on the composition. Any time you create a shape, text, or image object, and assign that object a function, LiveMotion considers it a button. A simple function you can assign to a button is enabling it to trigger a link, which opens a web site on the Internet. Here are the steps:

1. Create a text object with the Type tool and call it a button.

2. In the Web palette, type in the link to your favorite web site on the Internet.

3. At the bottom of the toolbar, toggle on the Preview mode.

Notice how your mouse cursor changes to a hand cursor when you pass over the button you just created. This signifies the following button is capable of performing some type of function, in the following example, it loads a web page on the Internet. Unfortunately, the Preview mode doesn't let you load web pages. You would first have to export your work and then preview it in a browser. As explained earlier, these steps are explained further in the next module. The Preview mode enables other functions, though, such as rollovers and remote rollovers, to be seen on the screen without going through the export phase.

1-Minute Drill

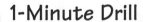

- Which palette would you use to add a link to a button in LiveMotion?
- What's the function of the Preview mode?

6

Advanced Buttons

As explained earlier, you can create buttons in many ways on your composition. In previous modules, you learned how to use the Group and Combine commands from the Object menu to group similarly shaped objects together. The following commands aren't specific only to similar types of objects. For example, you can just as easily group or combine a shape object with a text object or a text object with an image object. Doing so enables you to create more complex buttons. Here are the steps for creating one type of complex button, which consists of different types of combined objects, as shown in Figure 6-1.

1. Choose the Rounded Rectangle tool from the toolbar and draw a shape object with the following dimensions: 107×25.

2. In the Properties palette, toggle on the Fill preference and enter **18** for radius.

3. Choose an orange color for the shape from the Color palette.

4. Using the Type tool, type **BUTTON** on the composition.

- The Web palette.
- It enables you to preview your composition in LiveMotion without the need to export.

BUTTON

Figure 6-1	The Advanced button

5. In the Properties palette, select Arial BoldMT font, enter **16** for size, and enter **5** for Tracking.

6. Place the Text button on top of the orange rounded rectangular shape and choose Minus Front from the Combine command in the Object menu.

7. In the 3-D Palette, choose Bevel for your combined object, and then make the Depth 1, Softness 5, Lighting 108, Edge Straight, and Light Normal.

8. Make sure your finished button is selected and go to the Web palette. In the URL field, type in the full address of your favorite web site, for example, http://www.livemotionstudio.com.

9. Save your project as Button 1 in your LiveMotion Projects folder on your hard drive.

Your finished button should now resemble the button in Figure 6-1. In the next section of this module, you learn how to create rollovers, in which you use the following saved file to create special effects for your button. And in the next module, you learn how to export your project files, which will enable you

Ask the Expert

Question: Can I use an image object as a button in LiveMotion?

Answer: Any object on your composition in LiveMotion can be made into a button, including image objects. Most of the time, image thumbnails are used as Image Object buttons, which load the larger version of an image.

Question: How can I create a rollover effect for an image object in which the object changes once I move my mouse cursor over it?

Answer: In the "Create Rollovers" section, later in this module, you learn how to create these and other types of effects using rollovers. In addition, you learn how to create remote rollovers, which enable you to trigger rollover effects on other buttons.

to preview them in your Internet browsers, such as Netscape Navigator and
Internet Explorer.

Rollovers

Rollovers enable you to add special effects to buttons triggered by the mouse
cursor on your screen. You've probably come across a variety of Rollover buttons
while browsing the Web. Almost every other web page makes use of them.
One of the beneficial reasons for using Rollover buttons on web pages is they
enable the visitor to interact with the web page. By moving your mouse cursor
over a button that contains a rollover, the appearance of the button changes,
letting you know the button is capable of triggering an action. In most cases,
the rollover is accessing another page on that web site.

States Palette

Rollovers are created in the States palette. They rely on *States,* which are different
points of the Rollover stage. By default, all objects on the composition start out
in the Normal State. The *Normal State* stands for the part of the Rollover stage
that stays active when no interaction occurs with the object. The States palette
enables you to create additional States for objects selected on your composition,
so they can perform a rollover on request.

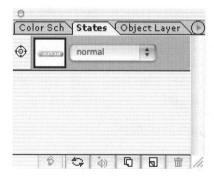

The States palette enables you to create four additional states that, when
activated, enable an object to become a Rollover button. The following
describes each of these States, including the Normal State.

- **Normal State**   The *Normal State* is the part of the Rollover stage that
  stays active when no interaction exists with the button.

- **Over State** The *Over State* is the part of the Rollover stage that happens when the mouse cursor moves over the button.

- **Down State** The *Down State* is the part of the Rollover stage that happens when the mouse button is directly over the button.

- **Out State** The *Out State* is the part of the Rollover stage that happens once the mouse button is released off the button.

- **Custom State** The *Custom State* enables you to trigger other rollovers, which creates an interesting effect. This state is described in later parts of this module when creating remote rollovers is discussed.

The buttons at the bottom of the palette enable you to manage these States. Appearing at the far-bottom left of the palette is the *Add script*, which enables you to add scripted commands to the various States you create for your Rollover buttons. Let's skip this button because its significance is explained in Modules 12 and 13.

The Replace Image button is next to the Add Script button. Once triggered, the *Replace Image* button enables you to replace the image for the currently selected state with an image from your hard drive. You'll probably use this preference when you create rollover objects that were created using image objects. Therefore, if you had an image object selected on your composition and you want to replace the image for that object while in its Down State, you would click the Replace Image button in the States palette to replace the image for specific State. The button right next to it is the *Sound* button, which enables you to select a sound file from your hard drive to apply it to the specific State selected in the States palette. As with the Add Script button, we'll skip this button because using sound in your projects is explained later on in Module 14.

Next to the Sound button are a set of buttons that enable you to create additional States in the States palette. The first button, the *Duplicate State* button, enables you to duplicate any one of the States selected in the States palette. The difference between the Duplicate State button and the Create New State button that appears next to it is this: the Duplicate State button duplicates an exact replica of the State selected. All the alterations done to that specific State are copied to the new duplicate State. The Create New State button, on the other hand, creates an exact replica of the original Normal State.

1-Minute Drill

- How can you change an Over State for an object in the States palette to an Out State?
- What's the difference between the Over and Down State?

Create Rollovers

Several types of buttons can be created from the five various States that the States palette is enabled to create. Note, the Custom State isn't included here because its significance plays a part in the "Create Remote Rollover" section later in this module:

- **Button 1** A button consisting of a Normal State and an Over State changes only when the cursor is moved over the button. After the mouse cursor is moved away from the button, the button returns to its Normal State. This is the most simple and typical type of rollover.

- **Button 2** A button consisting of a Normal State and a Down State changes only when the mouse cursor is positioned directly over the button and the mouse button is pressed down. Because the rollover doesn't contain an Over State, the button won't change when the cursor is passed over the button.

- **Button 3** A button consisting of a Normal State, an Over State, and a Down State changes twice during the rollover process. It changes once the mouse cursor moves directly over the button and again when the mouse button is pressed down.

- **Button 4** A button consisting of a Normal State, an Over State, and an Out State changes twice during the rollover process. It changes once the mouse cursor is moved directly over the button and again when the cursor is moved away from the button.

6

- Click the name of the State you want to change, and then select its replacement from the drop-down menu.
- Over States execute when your mouse cursor passes directly over the corresponding object. Down States, on the other hand, require you to click the object while directly over the corresponding object.

- **Button 5** A button consisting of a Normal State, a Down State, and an Out State changes twice during the rollover process. It changes once the mouse button is clicked while it's over the button and again when the mouse cursor moves away from the button.

- **Button 6** A button consisting of a Normal State, an Over State, a Down State, and an Out State changes three times during the rollover process. It changes once the mouse cursor passes over the object, again when the mouse button is clicked, and again when the mouse cursor leaves the button.

Rollover States enable you to create some type of change to the button for you to be able to view these individual states in action. There would be no point in creating a button containing all four states that doesn't show any appearance changes. While creating a state for an object, therefore, you're enabled to perform some type of appearance change to the object, so you can recognize the state change during the rollover process.

The simplest appearance change you apply to an Object State is a change in color. To do so after having created a State for an object, make sure your new State is selected in the States palette and select a color for that State from the Color palette.

Rollovers with Layers

In addition to using various palettes to alter the appearance of specific States, the combination of the Layer and Object palette enables you to create Rollovers to use layers. If you only make changes to additional layers that you add on to the object, *layers* enable you to maintain the appearance of the initial layer you see once you create an object.

Layers enable you to create two types of rollover effects. The first rollover effect contains layers only on specific States and the second effect contains an equal amount of layers for all its states. The following is an example of the first effect whose Rollover States are illustrated in Figure 6-2.

1. Create a small rectangle on your composition.

2. In the States palette, create an Over and an Out State for that object using the New State button.

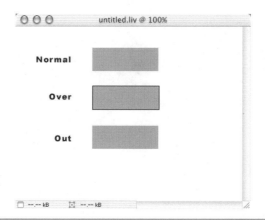

| **Figure 6-2** | Rollover button 1 |

3. Using the Object palette, create an additional layer for the Over State of
your object and choose a unique color from the Color palette.

4. In the Layer palette, increase the width of your second layer by increasing
the Width preference by 2.

5. Use the Preview button at the bottom of your toolbar to view the effect.

Notice how your rollover object changes as you move your mouse cursor
over the shape. The second layer is only visible when your mouse cursor is
directly over the object, as shown in Figure 6-3. The layer disappears once your
mouse cursor leaves the shape. Here's the second effect:

1. Switch back to the Edit mode on your toolbar, and then select your previously
created rollover object and delete it.

2. Use the Ellipse tool and draw a small circular shape on your composition.

3. In the Object palette, create an additional layer for your object. Enter 1 in
the Width preference in your Layer palette.

4. In the States palette, create two additional states using the New State
button: a Down State and an Out State.

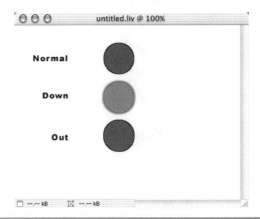

Figure 6-3 Rollover button 2

5. Select your Down State in the States palette. Now select your first layer in the Object palette and pick the color red from the Color palette.

6. Select the second layer in the Object palette, go to the Layer palette, and enter 4 for the Softness preference.

7. Use the Preview button at the bottom of your toolbar to view the effect.

While previewing your Rollover button, move your mouse cursor over the button and click it. Notice how the modified layer for the Down State becomes blurry as you click it. Unlike the previous effect, your object contains the same layer for all of its State. The Down State is the only State that alters its layers further, giving your Rollover button a unique appearance.

Many other rollover effects can be created while using layers. Experiment using them when you create your Rollover button for even more unique effects. In addition, try using some of the other palettes to create unique transitions on the various states of your Rollover buttons.

Rollovers with Images

So far, all your rollovers have been created using shape and text objects, but let's not forget about images. Image objects, just like shape and text objects, can also incorporate all the rollover effects created with these other types of

Ask the Expert

Question: I want to create a rollover effect in which my initial Normal State changes from text to an image. Is this possible?

Answer: That's a unique effect and it's definitely possible in LiveMotion. To create this effect, begin by drawing your text object with the Type tool. In your States palette, create an Over and an Out State. Select your Over State, click the Replace Image button and select an image from your hard drive. Finish by switching to the Preview mode to view the effect.

Question: Why is my image so small?

Answer: Unfortunately, your image will only be as big as your initial Normal State—in this case, your text object—but you can use the Crop tool to align your image properly. In addition, you can also use the Layer palette to move your image along the X- and the Y-axis.

6

objects. In this example, you use the Opacity palette to create a simple Rollover Image button.

1. Import an image into LiveMotion and shrink it down a notch.

2. Create an Over State and an Out State for your image object using the New State button in the States palette.

3. Select the Over State of your Object and, in the Opacity palette, select the Burst effect. Adjust the shading of the opacity in this effect to your preference.

4. Switch to the Preview mode to view your image object's rollover effect.

Project 6-1: Create a Rollover Button

So far, you've learned various ways of creating Rollover buttons on your composition. In fact, you've already created some unique Rollover buttons prior to this project. However, Rollover buttons can get even more advanced by using more layer combinations and combining them with further alterations using other palettes. In the following module, you create a complex Rollover button that uses many different effects applied to it from the various palettes.

The purpose of this project is to make you comfortable using more than one transition effect on the State of your Rollover button. You use the Advanced button you created earlier in this module, which you saved as Button 1 in your LiveMotion Projects folder, and convert it to a Rollover button. Your finished Rollover button should resemble Figure 6-4

Step-by-Step

1. Open the Button 1 project from the LiveMotion Project folder on your hard drive.

2. Select the object and create an additional layer for it using the Object palette.

3. Make sure the new layer is selected in the Object Palette. Increase its Width to 1 and its Softness to 10 in the Layer palette.

4. Select the first layer of your object in the Object palette and go to the Gradient palette.

5. Choose the Burst effect in the Gradient palette, select the rightmost slider at the bottom of the palette, and apply a red color from the Color palette.

6. Go back to the States palette and create an Over, a Down, and an Out State for the object, using the New State button.

7. Select your Over State in the States palette and go to the Gradient palette. Move the leftmost slider closer to the slider on the right about 3/4 of the way down.

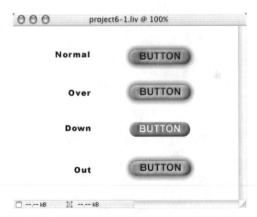

Figure 6-4   Project 6-1

8. Go back to the States palette and select the Down State.

9. In the Gradient palette, choose the Radial effect and move the rightmost slider to the far left.

10. Go back to the Object palette, select your second layer, and decrease the width of the layer to –10 in the Layer palette.

11. Save your project as Project 6-1 in the LiveMotion Projects folder on your hard drive.

12. You can use the Preview mode to view the rollover effect of your new Rollover button.

Project Summary

As you're previewing your new Rollover button, try going over it with your mouse cursor, as well as clicking it. Notice the various characteristics of the button changing as you perform these actions with your mouse. Previous miniprojects in this module in which you created Rollover buttons only changed one characteristic of the button during the rollover process. The following Rollover button in this project, however, uses several different types of alterations at once. This project should give you a better sense of the level of alteration the States palette enables you to create for the various States of the rollover process.

Create Remote Rollovers

Remote Rollovers are buttons that trigger another Rollover button by making use of the Target buttons in the States palette. By using these target buttons, Remote Rollover buttons enable you to change the states of other Rollover buttons. These Trigger buttons appear next to each Rollover State for your selected object in the States palette. These buttons work by clicking-and-dragging them on to the button you want to trigger. Important to note is that the button being triggered should be switched to the state you want to trigger. Here's an example of a Remote Rollover button that triggers another Rollover button, as shown in Figure 6-5.

1. Create your first button with the Type tool in the toolbar and type in the phrase **Click Here**.

2. In the States palette, create an Over and an Out State for your text object, and then drag it to the left side of your composition.

3. Select the Over State of your button and choose a color that's different from the color that appears for the remaining States of that button.

4. Create your second button using the Ellipse tool from the toolbar and choose a color for it from the Color palette.

5. Move the button to the right of your first button.

6. In the States palette, create an Over State for your second Rollover button and apply a color to the shape that's different from the color of the Normal State of that button.

7. Make sure the Over State of your second button is highlighted in the States palette and select your first button on your composition.

8. Click the Target button next to the Over State in the States palette, and then drag-and-drop it over the second button on your composition.

9. Select your second button and highlight the Normal State in the States palette.

10. Go back to the first object once more and select the Out State. Now drag-and-drop the target next to that state on the second button.

11. Click the Preview button in the toolbar to view the effect.

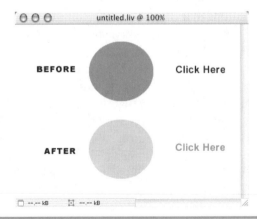

Figure 6-5　Remote Rollover button 1

While previewing your composition, go over your first button and notice how your second button changes. Then move your mouse away from your first button and notice how the second rollover object returns to its normal state. Some of the steps might seem a little tedious since you're going back and forth between the two buttons. Basically, what you're doing in these steps is selecting the States of the second button that you wish to change with the states of the first button. Here's another interesting remote rollover as shown in Figure 6-6, which will trigger another rollover object to appear and disappear.

1. Select the second button that we've previously created and go over to the States palette. Select the Normal State for that button.

2. Go over to the Opacity palette and move the Object Layer Opacity slider to the left so that the object is no longer visible on the composition.

3. Select the Over State for that object in the States palette. Go back to the Opacity palette once more and move the Object Layer Opacity slider all the way to the right.

4. Click the Preview button on your toolbar to view the effect.

5. Save this miniproject as Remote Rollover in your LiveMotion Projects folder.

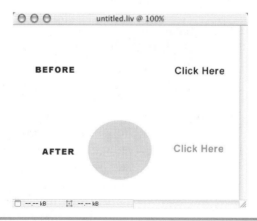

Figure 6-6   Remote Rollover button 2

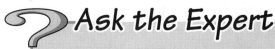

Ask the Expert

Question: How can I make a Remote Rollover effect, which, when triggered, keeps the Triggered rollover in place without returning to its default Normal State.

Answer: Your previous rollover project contained an action on the Out State of the first button that triggered the second button to return to its Normal State. For your second object to remain in its Over State—even after you move your mouse cursor away from your first rollover object—delete the action in the Out State.

Question: I got that to work, but my second Rollover button returns to its Normal State when I move over it. What's wrong here?

Answer: This is because your second rollover object is still active. That button still contains an Over State that enables you to trigger it with or without the first button. In the next section of this module, you learn about using Custom States with objects that are being triggered. The nice thing about using Custom States is they can only be triggered by other rollover objects.

Notice how your second object appears and disappears by going over and away from your first rollover object. The effect was created by making the Normal State of your second object invisible and making the Over State completely visible on the composition. The States of the first button, which trigger the Normal and Over States of the second object, stayed intact.

Remote Rollovers and Custom States

Earlier in this module, you learned that remote rollovers enable you to take advantage of Custom States. The remote rollovers you previously created, you'll notice the second rollover can be triggered without the first Rollover button by moving over it with the mouse cursor. Custom States enable you to create States for objects, which can only be triggered by other rollovers. Therefore, if you previously used a Custom State for the second Rollover button, the button would now change as you move your mouse cursor over it. Only the first button would enable you to trigger the second button's Over State.

1. From your LiveMotion Projects folder, select your previously saved file if it's no longer open on your composition.

2. Select your second Rollover button and choose its Over State in the States palette.

3. From the drop-down menu next to the Over State, select Custom State. Type **hidden** for the state in the dialogue box.

4. You need to edit your first rollover object because it's currently set to trigger the Over State of the second button, which is no longer available. To do this, select the first Rollover button and return to the States palette.

5. In the States palette, select the Over State and notice the particular State displays additional information. Because the current function of the Over State is set to trigger the Over State of the second button, the additional information displayed for that State shows a small icon and the name of the State being triggered. To change this, select Hidden by clicking the Over State name next to the icon. The icon should now display the Over State of the second Rollover button.

6. Do the same for the Out State. Select the Out State for your first object in the States palette and choose the hidden State from the drop-down menu displayed below the Out State.

7. Click the Preview button in the toolbar to view the effect.

8. Save your miniproject as Remote Rollover 2 in the LiveMotion Projects folder.

Notice how you can no longer trigger the rollover of the second object by going over it. The only way to trigger it now is to move over and out of the first Rollover button. You could create this effect by creating and using a Custom State for the second rollover object.

The Remote States palette enables you to create even more unique remote rollover effects, which can trigger more than one Rollover button. In addition, you can also create numerous Rollover buttons, which trigger the same Rollover button. The States palette enables you to create numerous combinations of effects. Be sure to look over the final project of this module, in which you create a small album, displaying various images using remote rollovers.

1-Minute Drill

● How many different Rollover buttons can you trigger with only one Rollover button?

Project 6-2: Create a Remote Rollover Button

As mentioned earlier, remote rollovers enable you to create many unique effects using shape, text, and image objects. In the following project, you create a mini photo album displaying four different images. This photo album consists of one Rollover button, which contains all four images within it and four additional Rollover Text buttons that trigger the appropriate State containing the specific image.

The project calls on four different images from your hard drive. Before moving on with this project, be sure to copy these four images into your LiveMotion Projects folder, so they'll be easily accessible during the project. If you currently don't have any images on your computer, download some from the Internet. Many search engines contain an image search engine, which enables you to search for various images on the Internet. Once you find the four you like, right-click them with your mouse cursor and save them in your LiveMotion Projects folder. You can also refer to the last module for various Internet resource sites that contain images.

Step-by-Step

1. Let's begin by creating a new composition. Enter the following dimensions: **500×300**.

2. Choose a dark red color for the background of your composition.

3. Create the first Rollover button that will contain all the images of the photo album. Use the Rectangle tool and draw a large rectangle on your composition. The shape should take up most of the space. Be sure to leave enough room to the left of the shape, though, so you can fit your Rollover Text buttons that will trigger the images in this Rollover button.

4. Color the shape the exact color of the composition, so the initial Normal State of this Rollover button camouflages to the background.

● The States palette enables you to trigger an unlimited amount of rollovers with only one Rollover button and vice versa.

5. In the States palette, create four additional Custom States for this object by selecting New State at the bottom of the palette and choosing Custom State from the drop-down menu. Name the first **Custom State 1**, the second **2**, the third **3**, and the fourth **4**.

6. Select your first Custom State, called 1, click the Replace Image button at the bottom of the States palette, and select the first image from your LiveMotion Projects folder.

7. Follow Step 6 for each of the remaining Custom States, each time choosing a different image.

8. Use the Crop tool to adjust the appearance of each image on each State until you're satisfied with the way the images display on your composition.

9. You're finished with the first part of this project. Now, you can create the Text Remote Rollover button that will trigger these images.

10. Use the Type tool to create the first text object on your composition. Name the first text object **image 1**.

11. Follow Step 6 to create three additional text objects. Name them **image 2**, **image 3**, and **image 4**, respectively.

12. Use the Align command to align the four text objects properly and move them to the left of your composition. Be sure the images don't overlap the Rollover button, which contains the four images you'll soon trigger.

13. Select all your text objects and create an Over and an Out State in the States palette. By choosing all the text objects, you can create these states for all the objects selected. Once you're going to target specific images in the rollover object that contains them, however, you must work on each of the text objects individually.

14. Select the Over State of these Rollover buttons and apply a color to them that's different from the color of their Normal State in the States palette.

15. Return to the your first Rollover object—the one that contains all your images—and select the Custom State you called 1 in the States palette.

16. Select the first Text button (you named it image 1 in the States palette), select its Over State, and move the Target Circle button over the Rollover button that contains all the images.

17. Go back to the Rollover button that contains the images and select its Normal State in the States palette.

6

18. Once again, select the first Text Rollover button named Image 1. This time, select its Out State and drag the target cursor next to that state over the Rollover button that contains all the images.

19. Perform Steps 15 through 18 for the remaining three text rollover objects. However, be sure to target the appropriate States in the Rollover button that contains all the images. Therefore, the Text Rollover button named image 2 would target the Custom State named 2 in the Rollover button that contains all the images. The Text Rollover button named image 3 would target the Custom State named 3, and the Text Rollover button named image 4 would target the Custom State named 4.

20. Before proceeding to the Preview button, make sure all your targets are intact. All the Text Rollover buttons should target the Custom States 1, 2, 3, and 4, respectively, in the Rollover button that contains the images. Furthermore, make sure the Out States of these Text buttons all target the Normal State of the Image Rollover button.

21. After you make sure everything is intact, proceed by clicking the Preview button.

22. Finish by saving your project as Project 6-2 in your LiveMotion Projects folder.

Project Summary

If you managed to get through the tedious steps of this project, your Preview screen should enable you to move over the four individual Text buttons with your mouse cursor and see their targeted effect on the Image Rollover button, as shown in Figure 6-7. In addition, once your mouse cursor leaves any of the Text Rollover buttons, the Image Rollover button should return to its Normal State and display a camouflaged square.

The following project was an example of a method of creating a mini photo album, using Rollover and Remote Rollover buttons. Before you proceed to the next module, try experimenting with other methods. Make good use of the Library and Properties palette, which enable you to crop various shapes into your image objects. You might even want to use layers instead of colors to signify the rollover effect of your Text Rollover buttons. Numerous possibilities exist and experimenting is the key to achieving an original and unique interface for this photo album.

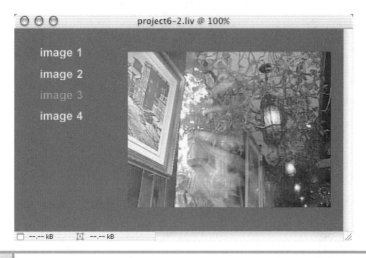

Figure 6-7   Project 6-2

6

Summary

This module introduced you to creating interactive effects using Rollover and Remote Rollover buttons. You learned about creating numerous types of effects with these buttons and discovered the possibility of taking them even further by creating more advanced rollovers that consist of more functions. As mentioned in previous modules, the only way to achieve this goal is to continue practicing. In this case, consider creating your own custom Rollover and Remote Rollover buttons. Before starting the next module, in which you learn various ways to export your work so you can preview it on Internet browsers, be sure to follow along with the previous project, Project 6-2. In addition, be sure to answer the questions in the Mastery Check to test your knowledge of all the terms you've learned in this module.

☑ *Mastery Check*

1. What are buttons in LiveMotion?

    A. Objects that trigger other objects

    B. Objects that act as rollovers

    C. Objects that load links in an Internet browser

    D. All of the above

2. What's the difference between regular buttons and advanced buttons?

    A. Advanced buttons contain more detail

    B. Regular buttons can't trigger a rollover

    C. Advanced buttons can only trigger a remote rollover

    D. Unlike regular buttons, advanced buttons contain Custom States

3. How many different States does the States palette enable you to create for objects?

    A. Three

    B. Four

    C. Five

    D. Six

4. The Normal State is the Default State for an object. On the other hand, the _____ State is the State the rollover object returns to once the mouse cursor leaves the object.

    A. Over

    B. Normal

    C. Out

    D. Over

☑ Mastery Check

5. The Preview mode enables you to view your rollover objects in action, whereas the _____ mode enables you to continue working on your rollover objects.

   A. Work

   B. Alter

   C. Edit

   D. Composition

6. How do you create a State for an object in the States palette?

   A. Create a New State button

   B. Duplicate a State button

   C. Both choice A and B

   D. None of the above

7. What's the main difference between Rollover and Remote Rollover objects in LiveMotion?

   A. Rollover objects, unlike Remote Rollover objects, can change color.

   B. Remote Rollover objects, unlike Rollover objects, can trigger other rollovers.

   C. Rollover objects, unlike Remote Rollover objects, can't contain a Custom State.

   D. No difference exists between Rollover and Remote Rollover objects.

8. What are Custom States?

   A. Custom States are States that can only be triggered by other Rollover buttons.

   B. Custom States are States that can only exist in Remote Rollover objects.

6

☑ *Mastery Check*

    C. Custom States are States that Rollover objects can't contain.

    D. All of the above.

9. Which tool in the toolbar enables you to properly align the various states of either a Rollover or a Remote Rollover button?

    A. Arrow tool

    B. Crop tool

    C. Layer Offset tool

    D. Drag Selection tool

10. The _____ buttons in the States palette enable you to trigger the States of other rollovers.

    A. Link

    B. Replace Image

    C. Target

    D. Arrow

Module 7

Export Your Work

The Goals of this Module

- Learn about HTML
- Learn how to use the Export palette
- Understand the difference between various Export and file format settings
- Learn about compression techniques in various file formats
- Know the difference between vector and bitmap images
- Be able to use several View menu commands to your advantage

In this module, you learn about various techniques that enable you to preview your work in Internet browsers using the Preview In command, as well as export it to HTML files using the Export palette that, ultimately, allows you to upload your work to your web site. In addition, you learn how to use the Export palette to compress and optimize the images on your composition, which will enable you to load them quickly on a web page in your browser. You also learn about the differences between bitmap and vector images, so you can understand how LiveMotion exports these two formats. In conclusion, you use all the export techniques you learn in this module to export the final project of the previous module, in which you created a mini photo album.

What Is Hypertext Markup Language?

Hypertext Markup Language (HTML) is the web standard format for most of the Internet pages you see when you browse the Web. *HTML* is a web browser, capable of reading and displaying its contents. An actual HTML file consists of lines of code an Internet browser uses to load the images and text associated with it. LiveMotion has the capability to compile this code automatically for you during the Export process, which you learn about in the "Export Palette" section later in this module. However, it's important for you to know some of the basics of implementing this code in an HTML editor application to build web sites from the HTML files LiveMotion exports.

All HTML files end in either an HTM or an HTML file extension after the name of the file. The rule of thumb is this: in a web site, the initial page that loads is a file named index.html, index.htm, default.html, or default.htm. The naming process of your HTML files is important, therefore, because it determines which page loads first when the site is accessed from an Internet browser. During the Export process, you're given an option to choose the name of this file, which is also accompanied by either a folder named images, which contains all the images associated with that file, or by a SWF file, depending on which file format you choose to export to in the Export palette. You learn some of the various file formats LiveMotion 2 lets us export to shortly.

As stated earlier, HTML is the web standard for most of the web pages you see when you browse the web, but plenty of other web page file types exist, such as CFM, XML, DHTML, and others. LiveMotion is only capable of exporting your projects into an HTML file format. Nevertheless, all the other web page file types just mentioned include portions of HTML within them. If you plan to use any of these other file formats, simply copy-and-paste the HTML code within the HTML file into the web page file type you want to work with.

1-Minute Drill

- What does HTML stand for?
- Why do you need an HTML file to display your exported projects on the Web?

The Preview In Browser Command

An incredibly helpful and quick way of previewing your projects in LiveMotion is accessible by the Preview In Browser command, which appears under the File menu. Unlike the Preview mode in the toolbar, the *Preview In* command automatically exports your project on the composition and launches an Internet browser, which displays them. The Preview In command does the following: first, it chooses the file type for all your images on your composition, based on the file type selected in the Export palette. By default, the JPEG file format is chosen in the Export palette. Second, the command then exports the HTML file, along with the Images folder, into the Preferences folder for LiveMotion on your hard drive and launches the file in an Internet browser.

- Hypertext Markup Language.
- The HTML file contains lines of code that a web browser reads and can load any images and/or text referenced within it.

LiveMotion automatically locates any Internet web browsers on your hard drive and saves them under the Preview In Browser command. However, if no web browsers appear under this command, you must manually place either shortcuts (Windows) or aliases (Macs) into the Preview In folder located in the helpers folder in your LiveMotion 2 directory on your hard drive. After doing this, the Internet browser appears under the Preview In command in LiveMotion.

After launching this command within the File menu by choosing a browser to preview in, you'll notice an export status bar appear on top of your composition. During this time, you must wait until the process of the status bar is complete if you want to continue working on your project. After the bar finishes exporting, your exported project appears in the browser. This should give you a good idea of how your projects will ultimately come out on the Internet. Therefore, take note of any possible changes you might want to make to your overall projects as a result of its appearance in the browser. For a quick way to access the Preview In command, use the CTRL-ALT-ENTER (Windows) and CTRL-APPLE-ENTER (Mac) keys.

The Export Palette

The Export palette is no different from any other palette you've worked with so far, but the Export palette is of no use to you while working on your projects.

Ask the Expert

Question: My current web site uses CFM files and not HTML files that LiveMotion exports. Can I set LiveMotion to export to CFM instead?

Answer: Unfortunately, LiveMotion can only export to HTML. You can edit the HTML file LiveMotion exports in the program where you create your CFM files, though, and save the file as a CFM file.

Question: Can I replace the HTML file extension to CFM?

Answer: In a way you can, but the file won't properly display in your web site because CFM files require you to adjust some parts of the HTML code for the file to function properly. You can refer to the application you use to create your CFM files and use its help feature to guide you through the process of converting an HTML file to a CFM file.

This palette ultimately becomes useful once you finish with your project, and you want to save it for the Web.

The *Export* palette enables you to save your projects in several different file formats and settings, as seen in Figure 7-1, which is explained further in this section. In addition, each of these file formats has its purpose and benefits, as far as what can be done with the exported file. The other purpose of the Export palette is to compress the overall projects by properly adjusting the individual preferences of the image format you plan on exporting to. A unique feature of the Export palette is it also lets you choose and adjust the file format and compression settings for individually selected objects on the composition.

The Export palette also lets you properly adjust any audio files within your composition. However, because you haven't yet learned about using music, sound, and audio files on your composition, the compression and adjustment preferences of this feature in the Export palette are explained in Module 14.

Remember, the Export palette is only there to adjust the settings before the actual exporting takes place. The process of exporting is explained in the section "Exporting and the Export Commands" in this module. For now, however, you need to learn about the various preferences and options the Export palette lets you adjust for the project being exported.

In addition, the Export palette can be accessed at any time with the Export Settings command, which appears under the File menu, as well as from the Windows menu. Therefore, you can close the Export palette when you work on your composition to get more screen space from your working environment and only launch the command when you need it.

7

Figure 7-1   Export palette Settings

File Formats and Settings

The Export palette enables you to export your work into several different types of file formats. The drop-down menu preference at the top of the palette lets you jump among ten different settings for these file formats and, ultimately, select the appropriate one for your project. Each of these file formats contains its own individual settings. Therefore, if you're exporting your project into the GIF format, the preferences within the Export palette will differ if you were to export your work into the JPEG format. Four preferences stay consistent throughout all the file formats in the palette, though. The first—Export HTML Page—when checked, instructs LiveMotion to create an HTML file that will accompany the file format you chose for your project in the Export palette. The second preference— Export HTML Report—instructs LiveMotion to create a report HTML file, which contains specific details on an exported animated project. This preference is grayed out for all file formats that aren't animated because the report is used only when exporting to the SWF format. You learn about the specific contents of this report when animation is discussed in the next modules. The third preference—Trim Composition on Export—instructs LiveMotion to crop out any unused space on the borders of your composition. For example, if your composition contained only one object at the center, with this preference checked, LiveMotion would export your composition by exporting any and all of the unused empty space around the object. The fourth preference, located at the right side of the Export palette—Preview Export Compression—when checked, displays the actual quality of your project on your composition, based on the quality settings chosen for the file format in the Export palette. This preference can be used as a substitute to preview your work in a browser using the Preview In command because it shows you how your work will display on the Web.

Now, let's discuss each of the file formats the Export palette enables you to export to, as well as their individual preferences and settings, beginning at the top.

Macromedia Flash SWF

The SWF file format is the recommended file format when dealing with animation, but you can also export your current static composition to this format. This format, however, requires web browsers to contain a Flash plug-in. Although most of today's browsers come already equipped with this plug-in, those that don't will display a broken plug-in icon on the page. The plug-in can be downloaded from the Macromedia Shockwave zone site at http://www.shockwave.com.

The SWF format can contain both bitmap and vector objects. However, the main goal when dealing with SWF files is to use more vector than bitmap objects because vector objects significantly reduce the file size of your exported SWF file. These two types of objects are explained in the next section, where you learn which of the objects on your composition belong to which group. The preferences and settings for SWF files in the Export palette enable you to compress and properly adjust your exported composition to this file format. The Export palette enables you to adjust several settings when exporting this way. Starting at the top, just below the five settings that stay consistent throughout all the settings chosen from the drop-down menu at the top, are four tab-like buttons that let you adjust the image compression for this file format, sound, and embed font, and control the flow of animation. Within the image compression tab, the drop- down menu enables you to choose JPEG, Index, or a true-color compression. The quality of these compressions, as well as the quality of opacity effects on your composition, can be adjusted with the following two slider preferences.

In the Sound tab, you're given an option to adjust the MP3 bit rate of any embedded MP3 sound files on your composition. You haven't learned about importing sound into LiveMotion yet, but when you do, you can set the bit rate of your MP3 with this preference. If you're unsure, however, choose Auto Bit Rate and LiveMotion will automatically pick and adjust the best option for you. The tab also enables you to convert your sound files from stereo to mono if you choose, by clicking the Convert To Mono check box.

7

The next tab—the Text tab—enables you to embed fonts used on your composition into the exported SWF file, so they display properly for those users who don't have those specific fonts installed. The first setting simply asks if you want to embed any fonts and, if so, to what extent. The setting enables you to choose None, Full Set (all characters in the various fonts used on your composition), or a partial set that you can further define with the following settings: uppercase letters, lowercase letters, numbers, and punctuation. In addition, the Extra field enables you to add any other types of characters used in your fonts.

The final tab enables you to adjust animation settings for the composition. You haven't learned about animation yet, but this area lets you adjust the frame rate of the composition and enables you to reference specific MovieClips that can be attached using the Script Editor. You learn about this in Modules 8 through 13, when scripting in LiveMotion is discussed.

Auto Layout

The Auto Layout setting in the palette is similar to the GIF, JPEG, and the two PNG settings, which is discussed shortly. The difference is when the Auto Layout setting is used, it exports and slices up your composition into several images. The first preference in the Export palette for this setting enables you to choose a file format for your exported images. Each format displays a different type of image quality slider, which can be adjusted below the slider, as well as additional settings that are specific to that file format. You learn about these individual settings soon.

The setting at the bottom of the palette enables you to choose a name for the folder you'll export to, along with the images inside it. By default, the name of the folder is images.

Live Tabs

Live Tabs are covered in the scripting section of this book and they enable you to control objects on your composition just like palettes do. The difference is you can create objects using various scripting techniques, which are covered in Module 13. With this setting chosen in the Export palette, LiveMotion lets you create these Live Tabs.

Notice the Live Tabs setting doesn't contain any additional settings and preferences. This is because when you create Live Tabs, you use the Save As command, instead of the Export command.

Animated GIF

This setting enables you to export the composition as an animated GIF. The settings are similar to the GIF settings discussed in the following, but two additional settings are specific to the animated GIF setting alone.

The Frame Rate setting enables you to set the frame rate of the animation on the composition. The other setting—Loop—enables you to set how many times the animation will repeat itself. None simply plays the animation once and then stops. Forever loops the animation indefinitely, and the Set option loops the animation by the defined setting chosen to the right.

QuickTime Video

The QuickTime settings enable you to export your composition into the QuickTime MOV format. The Export palette lets you adjust two settings: the quality and compression of the video, and the quality and compression of the sound. These settings are identical to those found in QuickTime Movie Player. If this wasn't previously installed, then it was installed during your LiveMotion 2 installation process.

GIF

The following settings export the entire composition and save it as a single GIF file. This is an excellent choice if the objects on your composition contain solid colors. If the objects contain elements such as linear opacity or gradients, however, selecting the JPEG format in the Export palette would be a much better choice.

The Export palette, with the GIF setting selected, offers several settings and preferences that enable you to adjust the appearance and compression of the object on your composition. Starting with the first preference—the Color setting—lets you adjust the number of colors your exported image will contain. Choosing a higher value for this setting will increase the file size of your exported image and, at the same time, make your GIFs as rich in color as the file format allows; 256 colors is the maximum. On the other hand, choosing a smaller value will reduce the amount of colors in your image, as well as decrease its overall file size. The setting directly below the Preview preference enables you to select the color wheel your exported images will make use of once they're exported. Web Adaptive is the default choice for this setting. This is also the recommended choice if you plan to display your exported project on the Web. You might want to use the other remaining choice, however, if you plan to display your exported projects from within your computer. For example, if you plan to display your work on a Macintosh computer, selecting the Mac OS choice from this preference would ensure the colors of your image would correctly display on this type of computer.

The next settings enable you to toggle Transparency, Dither, and Interlace on and off. By toggling on Transparency, your exported GIF will be transparent over the background. GIFs that are transparent are smaller in file size because the data within them makes use of the background color in the HTML file to display the image correctly. Therefore, by changing the background color of the HTML file, the accompanied transparent GIFS will adjust to display that particular color within them. The remaining settings—Dither and Interlace—affect both the appearance of your files and the way they load in a web browser. Dithered GIFs appear grainy, however, and at the same time their file size will be slightly smaller. Unlike regular GIFs, Interlaced GIFs don't load from top to bottom in a web browser. Instead, these GIFs load as a whole by appearing blurry in a web browser at first and, while loading, they become clear as intended.

JPEG

JPEGs, like GIF files, are capable of displaying in web browsers. In Module 5, you learned the differences between these two types of files and concluded that JPEGs are the better choice when dealing with realistic images, such as photographs and landscapes. Unlike GIFs, however, JPEGs are capable of clearly displaying elements, such as Linear and Gradient effects. So, when dealing with these types of effects, export either your entire composition or the objects in question to this file format.

The main preference for the JPEG setting in the Export palette is the Quality setting, which enables you to set the quality of the image on a percent basis, 100 percent being the best. Remember, though, by raising the quality of your image with this setting, you ultimately increase the overall file size of the image. On the other hand, choosing a lower quality with this setting will decrease the file size but, at the same time, make your file less clear and defined. Three additional settings can be toggled on for JPEGs in the Export palette: Progressive, Reduce Chroma, and Optimized. By toggling on the Progressive setting, the exported image will load blurry at first and become more clear as it loads. The Reduce Chroma setting reduces the amount of glow in your images and, ultimately, slightly reduces their file size. The Optimize setting optimizes your JPEGs for the Web. This box should be checked if you plan to display your work on the Web.

Photoshop

By choosing this file format in the Export palette, your exported composition will be exported into a PSD file. These types of files aren't suitable for the Web. If you try to preview the exported file in a web browser, you'll notice the page contains a broken image icon. This is because web browsers are unable to recognize PSD-type files. Choosing this option is only suitable if you're planning to develop your exported image further in Photoshop.

PNG-Indexed and PNG-Truecolor

The PNG-Indexed and PNG-Truecolor settings are described here as one setting because they're the least-used file formats described in this book. Even though the two most popular web browsers—Internet Explorer and Netscape Navigator— are capable of displaying them, these images are huge in file size because they retain the least amount of compression. On the other hand, compositions exported to these file formats are crisp and clear. Unfortunately, your ultimate goal in using the Export palette is to compress your images to the point where your files are significantly small in size, and remain crisp and clear on the Web, as seen on your composition in LiveMotion.

The settings for the PNG-Indexed file and the PNG-Truecolor format are similar to the GIF settings.

   In addition to adjusting settings for an entire composition, the Export palette also enables you to choose compression and file format settings for the individual objects on your composition. Therefore, you can choose to export an entire composition with one object chosen to export as a GIF file and another as a JPEG file. To create a setting for a specific object, select that object on the composition, and then click the New Object Settings button at the bottom of the palette. With that object still selected, choose a specific setting within the Export palette. To toggle back to the settings chosen for the entire composition (the rest of the objects, in this case), simply unselect the object. If you want to delete the specific settings, select the object once more, and then click the trash can icon at the bottom of the Export palette.

1-Minute Drill

- When should you export your projects to the JPEG format as opposed to the GIF format?
- What is needed for Web browsers to display pages with SWF files embedded within them?

File Size

While explaining the different file format settings within the Export palette in the last section, the importance of compression on these files was stressed.

- When your project contains image objects that contain more than 256 colors, and/or objects with Gradient and Opacity effects.
- The Flash plug-in should be included. Most, if not all, of today's browsers already have the Flash plug-in. You can obtain the plug-in from http://www.shockwave.com.

In addition to using the Export palette to compress these files, you can take steps prior to the export process to ensure the optimal quality and size.

Compress Imported Images

Images, unlike any of the other objects discussed so far, will ultimately increase the file size of your exported images or SWF file. Before rushing to the Export As command, be sure to adjust the export setting properly in the Export palette. Another alternative is to have the corresponding image file already compressed in a photo-editing program. When you work within LiveMotion, however, it's best to import images that are uncompressed and reserve the highest quality. The Export palette is just as capable as the Save for Web command found in Adobe Photoshop.

Vector vs. Bitmap Objects

LiveMotion enables you to work with both vector and bitmap objects. *Vector* objects are objects created with the various Shape tools in the toolbar, as well as the Type tool. Vector objects are also the various shapes in the Library palette, and they're made up of algorithms, which ultimately reduce the file size. In addition, when resized, vector objects don't become pixilated. For example, a rectangle drawn on the composition measuring 5×5 pixels can be stretched infinitely, and still remains as clear and sharp as intended.

Bitmap objects, on the other hand, are made of pixels. Unlike vectors, bitmap images are noticeably larger in file size. When resized and stretched, they appear pixilated. Figure 7-2 shows two identical bitmap objects. Both are taken from the same source file, however the second object has been stretched with the Transform palette. Notice it isn't as clear and sharp as the original.

Most of the bitmap images you worked with so far in LiveMotion are image objects. However, a vector object can become a bitmap object with specific alterations applied from various palettes. Your overall goal while working on your project in LiveMotion is to use more vector objects than bitmap objects. Therefore, it's important to be aware at what point of the process of working on your composition you intentionally convert your vector objects to bitmap objects. In addition, many other ways exist to perform such alterations that won't convert your vector objects.

First, Let's go over some of the ways vector objects become bitmap objects during the editing process. Any time you apply a style from the Styles palette (remember, you aren't including styles that contain only a script and/or animation

untitled.liv @ 100%

--.-- kB   --.-- kB

Figure 7-2   Pixilated bitmap object

7

modification) to a vector object, that object becomes a bitmap image. Effects such as Shading and Gradient effects also convert vector objects. In addition, any time you create an additional layer for a vector object, that object also becomes a bitmap object. If possible, avoid unnecessarily applying such effects to your vectors if you're trying to bring down your file size. Layers can be substituted by stacking several vector objects on top of one another. Styles and Gradient effects, on the other hand, should be used sparingly. Remember, these are only suggestions to bring down the exported file size of your image or SWF file. You're not restricted from using as many effects as you please. In fact, if you're not planning on displaying your exported files on a web site, by all means, have fun and use as many bitmap objects as you please.

Earlier, you learned vector objects can be stretched without being pixilated. Most of the formats the Export palette in LiveMotion enables you to export to are bitmap file formats, so even if your composition contains vector objects, they will ultimately become bitmap images during the export process. However, exporting to the SWF format is different. Unlike the other five file formats, SWF is capable of containing both vector and bitmap objects. When you stretch this file type by hand coding HTML or using it in a web developing application, such as Adobe GoLive, all the vector objects in that file will maintain their clarity and sharpness. Any bitmap objects, however, will become pixilated and blurry.

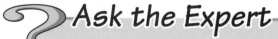

Ask the Expert

Question: All the vector objects on my composition still appear blurry when I zoom in on them in LiveMotion using the Zoom command. Why is this?

Answer: LiveMotion is, unfortunately, unable to display vector objects appropriately on its composition. However, you can test your object by setting it to export to the SWF format—the only file format in LiveMotion capable of displaying vectors—and use the Preview In command to view your vectors in a web browser.

Question: Is there any other way I can assure myself that the object in question is a vector and not a bitmap image without going through the hassle of previewing the composition in a web browser?

Answer: Later in the module, you learn how to use the *Preview Export Compression* command, which is capable of displaying information such as file size and whether the object is a bitmap or a vector.

Exporting and the Export Commands

Now that you know all the compression techniques in the Export palette and on your composition, let's go over the three different types of commands that enable you to export your projects. In addition, you'll learn the breakdown of the files that get exported and the additional information LiveMotion provides us with about the objects on our composition when exporting to the SWF file format.

The Export/Export As Commands

The Export command under the File menu enables you to export your composition. The file becomes automatically named untitled.html and is saved into the default location set by LiveMotion. To set the default location as well as have the option of naming your HTML file, use the Export As command. This command prompts you to choose a name for the file, as well as select the location of where you want to save the file. While exporting, notice a status bar appear on top of your composition. Once the status bar reaches the end, your project has been exported.

During the export process, notice the status bar displaying the various objects that appear on the composition. In Modules 8 and 9, you learn the procedure of naming your projects. This will become useful to you once you introduce the procedure of scripting, which adds another dimension to the interactivity of your projects.

The Export Selection Command

LiveMotion also enables you to export individual objects on your composition. To export a specific object, select it, and then choose the Export Selection command under the File menu. The object is then exported to the file format you choose for that object in the Export palette. Here are the steps for exporting a specific object on your composition with specific preferences chosen for it from the Export palette:

1. Start by either drawing a simple shape with one of the Shape tools in the Toolbar or importing a small image on the composition.

2. Select the specific object and go to the Export palette.

3. At the bottom left of the palette, select Object from the drop-down menu.

4. Click the Create Object Settings button.

5. Choose a file format/setting you want to export your object to and adjust its individual settings and preferences in the palette.

6. Make sure the object is still selected on your composition and choose the Export Selection command under the File menu.

7. Enter a name for your object and choose where you want to save your object on your hard drive.

Your exported object will be accompanied by an HTML file if your composition settings are set to Export HTML. The bounds for the exported selection are determined by the bounding box of the object. Figure 7-3 shows the exported object loaded in a web browser.

If you want to export two objects on your composition into one file, you can do so by using the Group command. Any objects appearing either behind or in front of the selected object won't be included, unless they're grouped along with the object.

The Unable to Export Because of Rollover Overlapping Error

This is one of the most frequent error messages LiveMotion will display if your composition contains several rollovers. Basically, LiveMotion is trying to tell

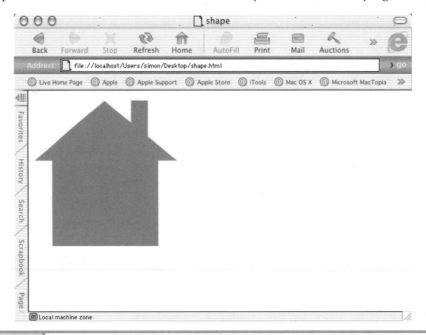

Figure 7-3   Exported object browser preview

you that you have two rollovers overlapping one another. To fix this prior to exporting your composition, try moving one of the rollovers away from the other, and then try exporting again. This error only appears if you're working with JPEG, GIF, PNG, or Photoshop file formats in the Export palette. SWF files are capable of containing rollovers that overlap one another.

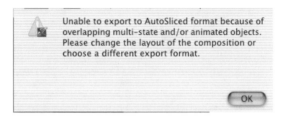

Unable to export to AutoSliced format because of overlapping multi-state and/or animated objects. Please change the layout of the composition or choose a different export format.

OK

1-Minute Drill

● What is the difference between the Export and Export As commands?

● What should you do prior to choosing the Export Selection command?

7

File Breakdown of What Gets Exported

So far, you've learned when a composition gets exported, the exported files consist of the HTML and either an Image folder or a SWF file. When dealing with a SWF file, however, you'll notice LiveMotion exports an additional HTML file along with the initial HTML file that holds the SWF file in it. The file is named exactly the same as the initial HTML file, with the addition of the letter *r* after its name. This file is your export report. Many people decide to throw this file away because it doesn't affect the exported project. However, the information saved in this file can be of much use to you because it tells you about each individual object saved within the SWF file, how much space it takes up, and how long it takes to load from the Internet. In addition, the file tells you at what time interval the specific objects load in the browser, based on its location on the Timeline. You haven't yet learned about animation or the Timeline, which is used to create it. As discussed earlier, you learn about animation in Modules 8 through 13.

● The first time you use the Export command, LiveMotion asks you to name the file and it puts untitled.html by default. You can name it something else if you want to or you can name it under the Export As dialog box. Either way, once you name the file and export it, the Export command uses the same filename you used earlier and overwrites the old one.

● Select the object on the composition you want to export and adjust its setting in the Export palette.

As stated earlier, the report offers valuable information about different aspects of the exported SWF file. By studying this report, you can discover which of the objects exported within the SWF are taking up too much space. This can help you adjust them properly on your composition.

The View Menu

LiveMotion provides you with a few helpful commands that enable you to preview the quality and performance of your projects. LiveMotion is capable of simulating this quality and performance inside LiveMotion, without needing to export to or preview in a browser. These commands are available to you in the View menu.

The Real-Time Preview Command

The *Real-Time Preview* command becomes useful to you when you learn about animating in LiveMotion. With this command on, LiveMotion simulates the animation on your composition in real time. This means LiveMotion is forced to skip any frames during the playback to keep up with the animation. You learn about animation, its properties, and its place in LiveMotion in the next few modules.

The Simulate Slow Download Command

The *Simulate Slow Download* command, when enabled in the View menu, mimics a browser loading your file off the Internet via a slow connection to the Internet. This command becomes useful to you in the next few modules because it enables you to test the length of time users with slow connections to the Internet take to view your projects on the Web.

The Preview Export Compression Command

The *Preview Export Compression* command is the same command found in the Export palette. With this command enabled, LiveMotion allows you to preview the quality of your projects on the composition without needing to export it or preview it in a browser.

The Preview Windows/Mac Gamma Command

The *Preview Windows/Mac Gamma* command varies across systems. For example, on a Macintosh platform, the command is named Preview Windows Gamma and, when activated in the View menu, it enables you to preview your projects in LiveMotion as they would be seen on a PC platform. On the other hand, on a PC machine, the command is named Preview Mac Gamma and it enables you to preview your projects as they would be seen on a Macintosh computer.

7

The Preview Auto Slice Area Command

The *Preview Auto Slice Area* command, also under the View menu, is another helpful feature of LiveMotion. When dealing with all file formats, with the exception of the SWF files, LiveMotion can preview the way it'll slice up the composition into multiple images that were properly selected and adjusted in the Export palette. If your composition area contains rollovers, LiveMotion can preview how they'll be sliced up, along with the objects around them. The areas being sliced will be noted by green lines, as shown in Figure 7-4.

As with the Active Export Preview command, try not to leave this command on all the time. Only turn the Preview Auto Slice Area command on when you need it, so you get the most optimal performance from LiveMotion.

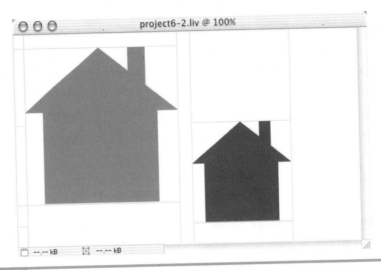

Figure 7-4 Preview Auto Slice composition view

Ask the Expert

Question: What is the purpose of the additional HTML file that gets exported with the SWF format?

Answer: The additional HTML file that gets exported with the SWF format is your export report for the SWF file. It displays information, such as the amount of space each of the individual objects in your SWF file take up in the file. In addition, the report also displays the amount of time each of the objects takes to load on various Internet connections, as well as what time they'll load if your SWF contains animation.

Question: Do I need this report file for my SWF file to function properly?

Answer: You don't. However, keep the file for reference to know which files take up how much space. You can easily point out the objects that take up too much space and appropriately correct them in LiveMotion to shrink the file size of your SWF file.

Project 7-1: Export your Mini Photo Album

In the previous module, you created an interactive mini photo album as your last project. Now that you've learned the various techniques of exporting in this module, let's use them to export your album so you can put it up on the Web. Because you're dealing with images and not graphics, you can export your project to the JPEG format, as well as the SWF format. By doing so, you'll learn how SWF files differ from JPEG files and vice versa. Let's begin.

Step-by-Step

1. Open your previously saved project from the LiveMotion Projects folder, which you saved as Project 7-1. This project contains your mini photo album.

2. Launch the Export palette either by going to the File menu and selecting Export Settings or launching it from the Windows menu.

3. Select the Auto Layout setting inside the Export palette and continue by choosing JPEG as the file format.

4. Choose a value of 60 for the Quality setting.

5. Check On for the Progressive and Optimized settings.

6. At the bottom of the palette, type in **images** if this isn't typed in already. This will be the name of the folder containing your exported sliced images.

7. Choose Export As from the File menu.

8. Create a New Folder in your LiveMotion Projects folder and call it Project7-JPEG, name the file you're exporting as index.html, and finish by saving the file in that folder.

9. Return to your Export palette and select the Export settings command for Macromedia Flash SWF.

10. Select JPEG for image compression, choose 60 for the Quality preference, and choose 6 for Opacity Resolution. Leave the rest of the settings as they are.

11. Choose Export As from the File menu and create a new folder in your LiveMotion Projects folder. Name this new folder Project7-SWF, name the file you're exporting index.html, and save it to that folder.

12. Finish by launching the index.html file from your Project7-JPEG folder and the index.html file from your Project7-SWF folder. Remember, you saved both these folders in your LiveMotion Projects folder, where you've saved all your projects so far.

7

Project Summary

While previewing both of these files in your web browser—whether it be on Internet Explorer or Netscape Navigator—look closely at the index.html file from your Project7-JPEG folder in the web browser. Notice the page displaying this file is composed of several images that individually load on the page. The images are loaded from the Image folder, located in your Project7-JPEG folder. LiveMotion automatically scripted your index.html file to create the rollover effects you created on your composition in LiveMotion for this mini photo album.

Now look closely at the index.html file from your Project7-SWF folder in the web browser. The SWF embedded in that HTML by LiveMotion loads as a whole in the web browser, as opposed to the other index.html file. This is because SWF files are capable of containing all the images, rollovers, and remote rollovers within them. In addition, SWF files can be further controlled with the right mouse button. By right-clicking them, you can choose to zoom in on your SWF files. Notice how your images become pixilated as you zoom in. This signifies they're bitmap objects. The individual Text buttons, however, stay consistently clean and sharp as you zoom in because they're vector objects. You can also control the animation aspect of the SWF file with functions such as Play and Stop. However, because you haven't yet learned about animation and your file doesn't contain any, this feature won't affect the SWF file in question.

Remember, always save your files using the LiveMotion Save As command because the files you export using the Export command won't be allowed to be edited further in LiveMotion. This is true for all the file formats you export with the Export palette, including the SWF file format. You can, however, use a web developing application, such as Adobe GoLive, to work in the HTML code that LiveMotion exported in the index.html file. Remember, the Images folder included with index.html you've exported to the JPEG file format needs to remain in the same location as the index.html file. Therefore, if you plan to upload these files to your web site, remember to keep them together and keep the directory paths intact. This rule is also the same for your exported SWF files. The code in the index.html file exported with it requires the SWF file to remain in the same directory. If you're comfortable editing the script within the HTML file, however, you can do so and set to call the file in its appropriate location.

Summary

Now you've covered all the steps you need to take to export your projects. You've learned ways to use the Export palette to choose both the file type and the level of compression for the objects on your composition. You've also learned the importance of using vector instead of bitmap objects to keep the file size of your projects to a minimum, as well as the difference between the two. Finally, you learned several helpful simulation commands found under the View menu. You learned how they enable you to preview both the quality of your objects and the way LiveMotion plans to export them by simulating their performance.

You have now finished Part 1 of this book. You should now be comfortable working with the three types of objects in LiveMotion and be able to export them. In Part 2, "Animation," you learn the principles of animation, including elements such as the Timeline, and you learn to animate all the objects used so far. In addition, a new feature of LiveMotion 2—Scripting—is introduced for those who've previously used LiveMotion 1. Scripting enables you to create advanced animations.

Be sure you feel comfortable with the Export procedure, as well as working with all the objects discussed so far—creating buttons, rollovers, and remote rollovers—before you proceed to the next part of the book. Also, take the time to answer the Mastery Check at the end of this module.

7

☑ *Mastery Check*

1. Which of the following file formats is LiveMotion capable of exporting to?

    A. DHTML

    B. XML

    C. HTML

    D. CFM

2. What's the function of the Preview In command?

    A. It enables you to preview your projects on the composition

    B. It enables you to preview your projects in a Web browser

    C. It enables you to preview your composition on your hard drive

    D. It enables you to preview your composition in your projects

3. What's the purpose of the HTML file that gets exported with the Export command along with either a SWF file or an image folder?

    A. The HTML file holds all the files together.

    B. The HTML file acts as a page that displays these files.

    C. The HTML file contains scripts that trigger the different files in the Image folder, as well as scripts that trigger the various objects in a SWF file.

    D. All of the above.

4. How many different settings are available to you in the Export palette?

    A. Five

    B. Eight

    C. Nine

    D. Ten

☑ Mastery Check

5. Which of the following statements is true for compression?

I. The exported file size of a compressed image file imported into LiveMotion is significantly lower than the exported file size of an imported image that isn't compressed.

II. Bitmap objects significantly reduce your exported file size in comparison to vector objects.

III. Vector objects can be resized without becoming pixilated.

A. I

B. II and III

C. I and III

D. II

6. _____ objects are made up of complex algorithms, which ultimately reduce the file size. _____ objects, on the other hand, are made of pixels. Unlike _____, _____ images are noticeably larger in file size. When resized and stretched, they appear pixilated.

A. Vector/Bitmap/vector/bitmap

B. Vector/Vector/bitmap/vector

C. Bitmap/Vector/bitmap/vector

D. Bitmap/Bitmap/vector/bitmap

7. What will happen to a shape drawn on the composition once an additional layer has been applied to it from the Object palette?

A. The object becomes a vector object.

B. The object becomes a bitmap object.

C. The object becomes both a vector and a bitmap object.

D. The object remains as is.

7

☑ Mastery Check

8. Which command enables you to export a specific object on your composition?

   A. The Export palette

   B. The Export As command

   C. The Export command

   D. The Export Selection command

9. Which of the following commands lets you preview the file size of both individual objects on your composition, as well as the composition itself?

   A. The Auto Slice Area command

   B. The Export Compression command

   C. The Preview In command

   D. The Real-Time Preview command

10. The Auto Slice Area command enables you to view which of the following?

    A. The way LiveMotion will slice up your composition when exporting

    B. The way LiveMotion will slice up your vector objects when exporting

    C. The slices that enable you to convert vector objects to bitmap objects

    D. The slices that enable you to convert bitmap objects to vector objects

Part 2

Animation

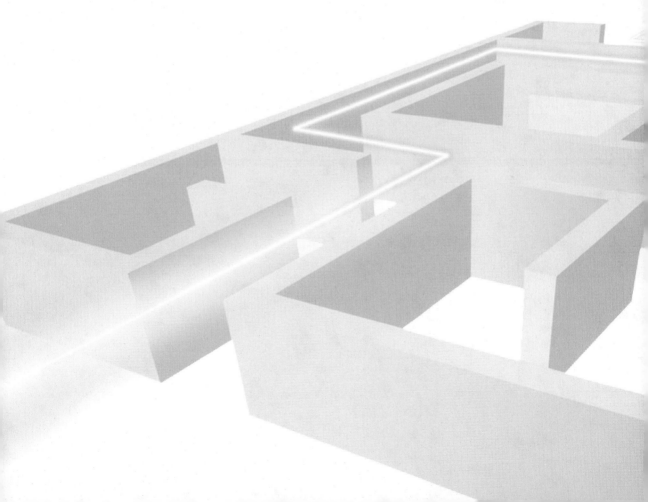

Module 8

Introduction to the Timeline

The Goals of this Module

- Learn the purpose of the timeline
- Know about the different components of the timeline
- Be able to assign names to your objects
- Know how to create keyframes and Motion Paths for your objects
- Be able to create MovieClip and MovieClip Groups
- Learn how to utilize the Timeline menu for additional timeline features

Part 1 of this book paved the way for us in terms of explaining the various ways to create and work with static objects on the composition. In the following part of the book, we go over all of the necessary steps needed to start animating objects on your composition utilizing the timeline, which we'll eventually export as we've done with static (nonmoving) objects in the first part of the book. However, before we get into animating objects, we first need to explain the function of the timeline and its components, and how they impact the various objects on the composition.

The following module will explain the purpose and function of the timeline. In addition, we'll go over the various features of the timeline, which are used to animate specific aspects of the objects on our composition. We'll also learn how to use the Timeline menu to control both the timeline and the composition. Commands such as MovieClip and MovieClip Group in the Timeline menu will introduce ways of animating objects independently of other objects on the composition. The purpose of the module is to build a solid understanding of how LiveMotion creates and handles animation. Once you're comfortable with the animation environment in the timeline, animation will be a snap in LiveMotion. Those of you who've used or currently use After Effects, a video-editing application from Adobe, should notice that the timeline in LiveMotion looks almost identical to the one in After Effects. For those who are puzzled by the various aspects and the overall appearance of the timeline, don't stray—as with every other feature of LiveMotion, animation and the timeline will become a friendly (and an extremely addicting) environment, which allows you to be creative and spontaneous.

What Is the Timeline?

The timeline allows you to animate all of the objects you've learned of in the first part of this book. In addition, the timeline is also the control environment for all of your animated objects. As mentioned earlier, the timeline, at first glance, may seem confusing to those of you who've never used the previous version of LiveMotion. However, be assured that by the end of this module every little detail of the timeline will be explained. For those who've worked with the previous version of LiveMotion, the timeline will make you feel right at home—with the exception of a few changes. However, these changes do not impact the process of using the timeline to animate your objects; instead, they're just added features that enhance your productivity.

The Timeline Interface

To access the timeline, use the Timeline menu and choose the Show Timeline Window command. By default, the Timeline window doesn't automatically open for you when a project file is loaded into LiveMotion. A simple combination of keystrokes, CMD-T, will open the Timeline window for your currently opened project.

The Timeline window is divided into two sections, as illustrated in Figure 8-1. The left section contains a list of objects on your composition. Notice the order of your objects. The order reflects which object is located at the topmost layer of the composition, as we've explained in earlier modules. The bottommost object in this section of the timeline is the object located on the bottommost layer on the composition. The right section contains the animation structure for these objects. The concept of animation in LiveMotion works by selecting a specific object in the left section of the Timeline window, and creating animation keyframes (we go over keyframes in just a bit) in the right side of the window. An object selected on your composition is automatically selected in the timeline, and vice versa. Before we actually begin to animate our objects, let's go over the interface in both of these sections in the Timeline window.

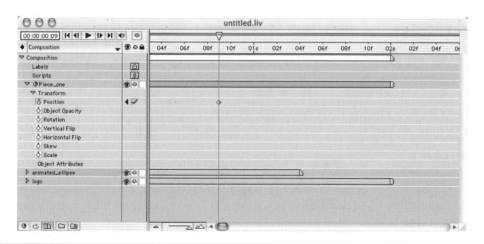

8

Figure 8-1   The timeline

The Playback Controls

Starting from the upper-left corner in the first section of the Timeline window, you'll notice playback controls similar to those found on your VCR. To the left of these controls is the current time at which your current time marker (CTM) is located in the right section of the Timeline window. The CTM will be explained in a later section, "Current Time Market (CTM)." Playback controls allow you to preview your animations within LiveMotion without having to switch back to the Preview mode. However, for better results, switching to Preview mode in order to view your animations is recommended.

The Composition Header

The composition header, located in the left section of the Timeline window right below the playback controls, contains a hierarchy folder structure. Think of your composition header as the main folder in which other folders exist, containing various elements of your composition. All of the objects on your composition appear under this header. The header contains a small arrow located to the left, which when clicked allows you to view these various elements.

Scripts and Labels

With the arrow of the composition header opened, the first two functions inside are your scripts and labels. Their function, however, as well as the process of utilizing them within the Timeline window, will be explained in Modules 12 and 13. For now, we're only concerned with the objects that are followed by these two functions.

The Object Header

Objects on your Composition window appear under the Script and Label functions inside the composition header in the Timeline window. Object headers are your individual objects. Notice the unique name that LiveMotion assigns to your objects as you create them in the Composition window. Names for your objects are made up of their individual attributes. For example, if you create an ellipse and color it red on your Composition window, LiveMotion will name that object Red Ellipse and place it under the composition header in the Timeline window. As the composition header, objects also contain a hierarchy folder structure allowing you to open them using the arrow located to the left. Their individual elements, however, will be explained in the "Objects and the Timeline" section of this module. For now, let's continue describing the interface of the Timeline window.

The Hide, Lock, and Shy Buttons

Each object header under the composition header in the Timeline window contains three buttons to the right. The first button, containing a small eye icon, allows you to toggle show and hide visibility of that object. The button resembles the Eye icon for hiding layers in the Object palette.

The next button over is called the Shy button. This button enables you to temporarily hide its corresponding object. The process, however, takes two steps. First, you'll need to activate the Shy button next to each object that you wish to temporarily hide in the timeline; afterwards, proceed by clicking the Shy Mode button located next to the playback controls. In a nutshell, the Shy button at the top of the Timeline window triggers all of the objects with an activated Shy button and hides them. The object or objects enabled with this option are only hidden in the timeline. To unhide your objects, simply click the Shy Mode button once more and all Shy-enabled objects will be visible to you.

The next button allows you to lock your objects. By locking your objects, you prevent any further changes to that object in the Timeline window and the Composition window. The Lock button is very useful if your composition contains a large amount of objects and you'd like the assurance of not accidentally deleting or unintentionally modifying one of them.

The Loop, MovieClip, Duration Bar, Group, and MovieClip Group Control Buttons

At the very bottom of the first section of the timeline, LiveMotion provides you with access to some easily accessible commands which you find yourself frequently using while working in the Timeline window. All of these commands are also available to you from both the Object and the Timeline menus. We get into the features available to you in the Timeline menu towards the end of this module.

The leftmost button in this section of the timeline is the Loop button, which allows you to create looping animations. However, in order to apply a loop to an animated object, the object itself needs to contain an animation. As with every other feature of the timeline described in this module, use this feature as a reference.

The button to the right of the Loop button allows you to modify your object into a MovieClip. MovieClip objects tend to be objects with various rollover states. In addition, when double-clicked, MovieClip objects contain their own independent timeline, which allows you to create various animations to be played at different states of the rollover process.

8

The button to the right of the MovieClip button allows you to set a selected object's duration bar to equal the duration of the composition's bar. Duration bars are located in the right section of the Timeline window, and we discuss their purpose in a bit.

The button to the right of the Duration Bar button allows you to group any number of objects in your Timeline window. You learned about grouping of objects in previous modules. Any animation in the Timeline window to a grouped object is applied to the entire group as a whole.

The last button in this section is the MovieClip Group button. The button performs the action of the MovieClip button and the Group button as one. Therefore, by applying this effect to any number of objects in your Timeline window, you'll (in addition to grouping them) be providing them with their own independent timeline. The advantage of having objects on their own independent timeline is that it allows you to create animations for these objects that will play independently from the remaining animation contained on the composition's timeline. We'll go over some of these effects and others in the next module.

Time Interval Markers

The Time Interval markers and all of the remaining features covered in this section are located in the right section of the Timeline window. Your timeline markers are measured in frames, which add up to seconds. At the very beginning of Module 1, we discussed the process of creating a new composition. One of the features in the dialog box that displays while creating a new composition is the frame rate preference. Throughout the book, we left this preference in its default state at 12. If you notice, this is the number of frames that add up to a minute in your Timeline window. If you choose to change the number of frames by going to the Composition Settings command under the Edit menu, your Time Interval markers will change appropriately to the frame rate you've chosen.

Current Time Marker

The current time marker, CTM for short, is the thin red line that appears over a specific Time Interval marker in the right section of the Timeline window. The CTM allows you to jump to any specific Time Interval marker by dragging its tab left or right at the very top of the Timeline window. By positioning the CTM to a specific Time Interval marker, you're allowing yourself to edit the animation at that specific frame of your composition. The same follows for independent objects, which contain their own timeline that plays independently from the composition's timeline.

By default, your CTM will always be located at the 00s Time Interval and all of your objects' duration bars will start at that time as well. By placing your CTM at any other interval, all objects created from then on will start at that specific time. Therefore, it's important to be aware of the location of your CTM before creating objects on your Composition window.

Duration Bars

Duration bars are the gray bars that appear in the right section of the Timeline window, next to the objects located in its left section. The composition's duration bar is colored white in order to be able to distinguish it from the other duration bars. The length of the duration bar reflects the length of the animation. The Duration Bar button described earlier allows you to set your selected object's duration bar to match the length of the composition's duration bar.

On the other hand, however, any given object can have a duration bar that is shorter than the composition's duration bar. The object will start and stop playing during your animation relative to where and when it ended on a specific Time Interval marker. In order to stretch or shrink the duration bar of a selected object, use the tabs at each end and drag them either left or right. You may also position an object's duration bar by grabbing the bar at its center and moving it either left or right.

8

The Timeline Scale

The last feature of your timeline is the timeline scale, which appears at the bottom of the Timeline window. The timeline scale allows you to scale the amount of visible frames in your Time Intervals. By increasing the scale, the timeline allows you to see more of the frames in between each second marker. On the other hand, by decreasing the scale, the Timeline window shows fewer frames between each second marker and therefore allows you to see more of the timeline.

1-Minute Drill

● What are duration bars?

● Which key command allows you to quickly open the Timeline window?

● Duration bars represent the length of animation for the object that they correspond to in the Timeline window.

● Use CTRL-T, regardless of whether you're using a Mac or a PC.

Objects and the Timeline

As explained earlier, any objects created on your composition will be named relative to its attributes. In addition, LiveMotion automatically creates a hierarchal folder structure for that object, similar to the one in the composition header shown in Figure 8-2.

The Edit Name Command

By drawing a red square on your Composition window, the Timeline window will name your newly created object Red Square. However, creating several of these types of objects will lead to confusion, as objects with the same attributes will contain the same name. LiveMotion fixes this problem by allowing you to name your objects by selecting the object and pressing the ENTER key on your keyboard. Keep in mind that the Timeline window needs to be the front window when renaming your objects. The name prompt will ask you to type in a name for that given object. However, it's essential that prior to pressing the SPACEBAR key, your Timeline window is the active window and not your Composition window.

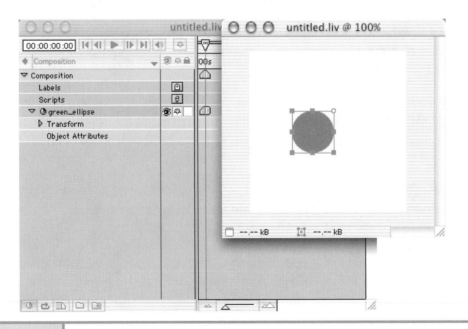

Figure 8-2 An object header in the timeline

The option for naming your objects is also available to you from the Object menu by choosing the Edit Name command. Naming your objects for now represents a way of organizing your composition area and using the Timeline window efficiently. However, naming your objects becomes useful to you once you get into scripting animations, where you call on specific names of objects. Therefore, it is essential that no two or more objects contain the same name. Doing so, ensures that the scripts, which you create in Modules 12 and 13, work properly and call upon appropriate objects on your composition.

? Ask the Expert

Question: My MovieClip object contains two duration bars. The first one appears in the composition and the other one is contained within the object. Which one do I animate?

Answer: In a sense, you are able to animate both of them. The animation contained in the duration bar of the object under the composition will play while the composition is played. The duration bar contained within the object, however, will play independently of the timeline.

Question: What do you mean when you say that the object's duration bar will play independently of the timeline?

Answer: Every animation under the composition is played when your exported file is opened and played. Independent objects, with independent duration bar animations, do not rely on the length of the Composition Duration Bar. Therefore, your independent object's duration bar can be set to loop, or even to play when triggered long after the main composition has stopped playing. You already learned how to create loops with the Loop button in the Timeline window. However, independent animations that are triggered by specific actions such as button rollovers are explained in Modules 12 and 13.

8

Object Transform Components

The hierarchal folder structure of an object displays the object's properties. These properties are subdivided into three sections. The topmost section contains the object's Transform Components, as illustrated in Figure 8-3. In LiveMotion, animation occurs by animating any one of these sections using keyframes, which we get into in a bit. In the following section, we go over the seven components listed under the Transform menu and explain their purpose. While reading their individual descriptions, keep in mind that LiveMotion allows you to use the combination of any number of these components at once. The remaining two sections, "Animate Object Attributes" and "Animate Layers," will be discussed in the next module. The following is a list of Transform Components and the animations they create.

- **Position** Allows you to animate the object's position on the composition. The speed of the object's position change will vary depending on how far apart keyframes are placed for this component. Positioning the object to different areas of the composition is achieved by using the Arrow tool.

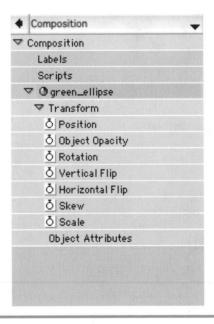

Figure 8-3 Object Transform Components

● **Object opacity**   Allows you to animate the object's opacity using the Opacity palette. The animation either increases or decreases the object's opacity in the process. As with the position component, the speed of the opacity change in the object varies depending on how the object's keyframes are set for this component.

● **Rotation**   Allows you to animate the object's rotation using the Transform palette. The object can rotate either clockwise or counterclockwise in any number of degrees. As you've probably noticed thus far, object rotation occurs over its midpoint, noted as a small blue square (also known as its anchor point). In order for you to be able to rotate an object over its other specified areas, you need to reposition the object's anchor point to that area. To do so, move your mouse over the anchor point located at the center of the object, click and hold the CTRL key, and move your mouse over the area of the object that you would like to move the anchor point to.

● **Vertical flip**   Allows you to vertically flip an object over time. Unlike the other Transform Components, an object using the vertical component doesn't animate over time. Instead, the object vertically flips at the instance the next keyframe is placed. As reference, to flip an object vertically, use the Flip Vertical command in the Transform submenu under the Object menu.

● **Horizontal flip**   Follows the same basic rules as the vertical component, except for the fact that the object animated with this component flips horizontally and not vertically. To horizontally flip an object, use the Flip Horizontal command in the Transform submenu under the Object menu.

● **Skew**   Allows you to animate skewing objects with the help of the Transform Palette. As with the position, object opacity, and rotation components, the speed of the skew will depend on how far or how close the keyframes are set apart from each other.

● **Scale**   Allows you to either increase or decrease an object's size. The speed of the transformation will vary depending on how close or how far the keyframes are set apart for this component.

8

1-Minute Drill

- How would you access the independent timeline for a MovieClip object?
- Where can you find the commands that allow you to flip objects vertically and horizontally?

What Are Keyframes?

While describing the various components of the transform section of an object, we've skipped over a very important factor that allows you to animate objects, keyframes. *Keyframes* are markers along the timeline that signify a change in either the object's Transform Components or Object Attributes, which we get into in Modules 9 and 10. They are single points in time that tell LiveMotion that a change takes place in the object at that specific location. Figure 8-4 displays a screenshot of several keyframes created for an object in the Timeline window.

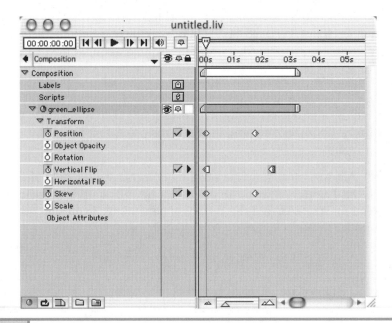

Figure 8-4 Keyframes

- Select the object in the Timeline window and double-click it.
- Use the Transform submenu under the Object menu.

Whether you're animating the scale of an object or its opacity, in order for an object to change over time, at least two keyframes must be placed for that object. The first keyframe represents the object before the change, and the second represents its final output. LiveMotion takes care of the animation in the frames in between these keyframes.

Create Keyframes

The first rule of creating a keyframe is to always be aware of where your CTM is located, as it will determine where the keyframe is placed on your timeline. By default, all of your objects in the timeline are placed at the 00s Time Interval because the CTM is located at that exact marker. By placing the CTM marker at any other Time Interval, every object created on your Composition window from then on will start at that exact time until your CTM is moved.

In order to create keyframes for any type of animation, you first have to click the stopwatch next to the appropriate property under Transform on the timeline. When placing keyframes, it's important to start by placing the first one at the very beginning of the duration bar of your object. Initial keyframes are placed by clicking the button located to the left of the component you're planning to animate. Therefore, if you were to animate the scale attribute of an object, you would click the button to the right of the scale component under the object's transform section. Additional keyframes are placed in the small box that appears to the right of the component. To create your second keyframe, move your CTM to the Time Interval at which you'd like to place your keyframe and once again click the button next to the scale component. After placing the keyframes, the box becomes filled with a check box.

The animation occurs by editing the specified attribute with its corresponding palette at a specific keyframe. Therefore, if you wanted to increase the size of an object over time, you would use the Transform Palette and edit the object's size at the second keyframe.

In addition, you can move back and forth between your placed keyframes without the use of the CTM by clicking the arrows that appear next to the check box. The arrow will display on either the left or the right side of the box only when an additional keyframe is located in that direction.

8

Ask the Expert

Question: How come my Timeline window creates additional keyframes for me after I specifically set the object to contain only two of them in its duration bar?

Answer: Be careful when moving your animated objects, specifically ones with animated position Transform Components. While moving your animated objects on your composition, additional keyframes are being placed in the specific Time Interval that your CTM is located at in your Timeline window.

Question: Is there a way to prevent this from happening?

Answer: Absolutely. The Lock button next to every object in your Timeline window allows you to temporarily lock the specific object. Locked objects can't be further altered or animated until they're unlocked. To unlock a specific locked object, click the Lock button once more.

Motion Paths

The position component of an object displays Motion Paths on the Composition window when two or more keyframes are created for that component. Motion Paths allow you to view the path that the object in question will take during an animation. The option of viewing Motion Paths can be toggled on and off with the Preview Motion Path command under the View menu. The dots that display in the Motion Path represent the consistency, in speed, of the motion. The spacing between the dots of a path will increase if an object takes longer to move from one position on the Composition window to another. On the other hand, the spacing will decrease once the position of the two keyframes is brought closer together in the Timeline window.

The following is an example of an object with three keyframes for its position component. The Motion Paths for the object can be seen in Figure 8-5. The number of frames between the first and the second keyframes on the Timeline window for this object is more than the number of frames between the second and the third keyframes.

1. Create an object on your Composition window, move it to the leftmost portion of your composition, and go over to the Timeline window.

2. Open up the hierarchal folder structure of your newly created object and expand the transform section in order to view its components.

3. Stretch the duration bar of your object up to the 1s Time Interval. Notice how your composition's duration bar is moved up to 1s as well.

4. Click on the stopwatch next to position attribute.

5. Place your first keyframe for your position attribute at the beginning of the object's duration bar.

6. Go over to the 06f Time Interval and create another keyframe for the position component.

7. In your Composition window, move your object to the middle of the composition.

8. Back in the Timeline window, create your third keyframe for your position component at the 1s Time Interval.

9. On your Composition window, move the object to the rightmost portion of the composition.

10. Preview the animation using the Preview mode on your toolbar.

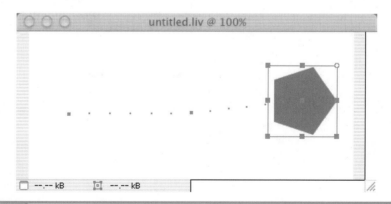

Figure 8-5 | Motion Paths

Besides creating our very first animation, we've also created a speed change for the animated object. We've placed three keyframes for the position components at the left, middle, and right sides of the Composition window. However, the location of these keyframes in the Timeline window differed. Since the number of frames between the first and the second keyframes was smaller than the number between the second and the third keyframes, naturally the object was faster traveling to the center than moving away from it. In addition, if you go back to the Edit mode and take a look at your Composition window, you'll notice the Motion Path of the object. The dots of the path are closer together at first, and later on in the animation are spread further apart.

Even though speed change can be accomplished with three or more keyframes, LiveMotion provides you with easier alternatives for impacting the motion of the object from one keyframe to another by editing the actual keyframe. By right-clicking any given keyframe in your Timeline window, a small menu appears next to the keyframe allowing you to select from five different keyframe types, as shown in Figure 8-6. The following are the menu choices.

● **Hold Keyframe** By choosing the Hold Keyframe option, your keyframe will hold the animation at that specific frame. The icon of the keyframe changes

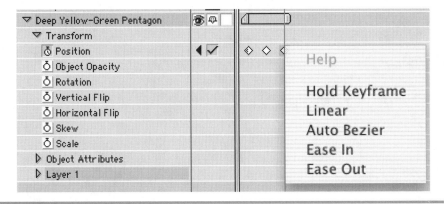

Figure 8-6 Keyframe types

as well, letting you know that the specific keyframe is set to hold. If there's an additional keyframe following a keyframe with a hold option selected, the animation will be suspended between the keyframe with the hold option and the preceding keyframe. Any additional keyframes will remain animated as long as none of them contain a Hold Keyframe option.

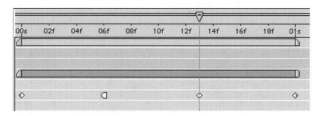

● **Linear**   By setting your keyframe to Linear, the object with that keyframe will move in straight lines.

● **Auto Bezier**   Auto Bezier keyframes move in Bezier curves. The curves generated are similar to those drawn with the Pen tool. Therefore, the Bezier curve will be steeper when the position change at the second keyframe is closer to the position at the first keyframe. On the other hand, objects positioned further away from one another will have less steep Bezier curves.

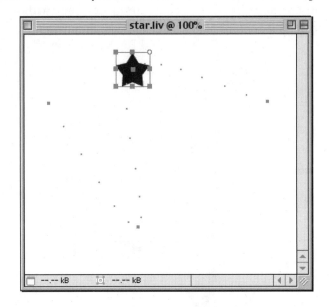

● **Ease In** The Ease In keyframe option will cause the animated object to slow down as it approaches a keyframe set to ease in. Notice the icon change of the actual keyframe.

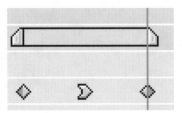

● **Ease Out** The Ease Out keyframe option will cause an animated object to speed up as it approaches a keyframe set to ease out.

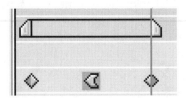

1-Minute Drill

- Which command allows you to toggle on and off the option of viewing Motion Paths on the composition?
- What is the significance of the spacing between the dots in Motion Paths?

Timeline and Object Menus

The Timeline and the Object menus allow you to access helpful commands while animating. While discussing the contents of the Timeline window, many of these commands are exact duplicates of the ones found either at the bottom-left section of the Timeline window, or at its right section. The menus and these commands are simply there for quick and convenient access.

The Timeline Menu

The Timeline menu displays commands that are mainly specific to keyframes, with the exception of the Loop, Implicit Length, and the Clear Animation command, which we go over shortly. Figure 8-7 displays the types of keyframes that LiveMotion enables us to create.

The Timeline/Composition Window   The Timeline/Composition Window allows you to quickly toggle between your Composition and your Timeline window. The command can also be achieved with the APPLE-T keystroke on a Mac, and by pressing CTRL-T on a PC.

Next Keyframe/Previous Keyframe Commands   The following commands allow you to position the CTM to a specific keyframe for a selected object. The Next Keyframe command will jump the CTM to the keyframe located to the right of the CTM. The Previous command will jump the CTM to the left. Be aware that in order to use these commands, your selected object

8

- The View Motion Paths command under the View menu.
- The spacing between the dots in Motion Paths represents the consistency of speed of the animated object. Objects with larger spacing will move slower along the composition than those with smaller spacing.

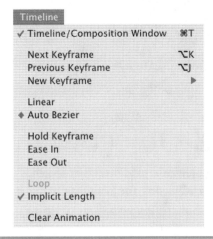

needs to have at least two keyframes. OPTION-J and OPTION-K on Mac, and ALT-J and ALT-K keystrokes on a PC can also be used to quickly jump between keyframes.

The New Keyframe Submenu   The New Keyframe submenu gives you access to creating specific component keyframes in your Timeline window. The submenu allows you to place either a position component keyframe, rotation component keyframe, scale component keyframe, opacity component keyframe, or an anchor point keyframe. However, as noted earlier, make sure that the CTM in the Timeline window is located at the appropriate Time Interval before proceeding with these commands. The following is a list of keystrokes associated with them:

- **Create a position keyframe**   On a PC ALT-SHIFT-P, and CTRL-SHIFT-P on a Mac

- **Create a rotation keyframe**   On a PC ALT-SHIFT-R, and CTRL-SHIFT-R on a Mac

- **Create a scale keyframe**   On a PC ALT-SHIFT-S, and CTRL-SHIFT-S on a Mac

- **Create an opacity keyframe**   On a PC ALT-SHIFT-T, and CTRL-SHIFT-T on a Mac

- **Create an anchor keyframe**   On a PC ALT-SHIFT-A, and CTRL-SHIFT-A on a Mac

We've gone over the placement of keyframes for all of these components except for one: the anchor point. The anchor point component is located in the Object Attributes section of an object. The component allows you to animate the location of an anchor point of a selected object. However, the animation won't be apparent without first animating the rotation component for that object. We go over animating the anchor point as well as the other components of the Object Attributes section of an object in Modules 9, 10, and 13.

Linear/Auto Bezier Commands   The Linear and Auto Bezier commands allow you to set the way an object will move with its animated position component. Switching on the Linear command under the Timeline menu will make all of your Motion Paths straight. All of your animated objects created from then on will move in straight lines along your composition area.

A linear animation can be created in the following manner:

1. Place three position component keyframes in your Timeline window for an object.

2. The first keyframe should place your object in the upper-left section of your Composition window.

3. The second keyframe should place your object in the upper-right section of your Composition window.

4. The final keyframe should place your object at the bottom-right portion of your Composition window.

If your animation is set to Linear under the Timeline menu, your object will move in a straight line from the upper-right portion of your composition to the bottom left.

Switching on the Bezier command under the Timeline menu, on the other hand, will make all of your Motion Paths curved. If the previous example was set to Bezier as opposed to Linear under the Timeline menu, your object would begin moving in a straight line along your composition, then it would arch to the bottom portion as it approached the right portion of the composition.

The Hold Keyframe Command   The Hold Keyframe command either modifies or creates a keyframe to stop its animation. There will be no animation between a hold keyframe and a proceeding keyframe. However, any further keyframes will continue as intended. The benefit of placing a hold keyframe

8

is to verify that your animation won't continue further unless instructed to do so at a later point in time on the Timeline window.

Before placing a hold keyframe or modifying an already placed keyframe to hold an animation, make sure that your CTM is placed at the specific Time Interval. After all, the Hold Keyframe will be created relative to which Time Interval the CTM is located at in your Timeline window.

Ease In/Ease Out Commands   The Ease In and Ease Out commands either create or modify current keyframes to behave like real-life motions. A keyframe modified with an Ease In command will force the animation to slow down as it approaches that specific keyframe and then the animated object will return to normal speed after passing that keyframe. An Ease Out command, on the other hand, will keep the speed of the animated object at normal as it approaches the keyframe, and speed up once having passed the keyframe.

Loop/Implicit Length Commands   The Loop command allows us to set a loop to be played on any animated object. An object with a loop begins playing all over again when its duration bar ends. Therefore, to create short loops out of your animated objects, end the object's duration bar on its final keyframe by dragging its end up to the Time Interval at which the last keyframe is located. As with the MovieClip and the MovieClip Group commands, the Loop command can be also achieved with the Loop button at the bottom of the Timeline window. Objects with a loop will display a small Loop icon next to their name in the Timeline window.

The implicit length simply means that the object will only play once during the animation. This, of course, can be altered with scripting techniques that we learn about in Modules 12 and 13, which are capable of replaying already-played animations at will.

The Clear Animation Command   The Clear Animation command will clear all of the keyframes from a selected object. However, before proceeding with this command, make sure that your CTM in your Timeline window is located at the specific Time Interval that displays your animated object at the state at which you'd like to leave it. In most cases, you'll want to move your CTM to the beginning of the animated object's duration bar prior to clearing its animation. However, the Clear Animation command can be applied at any portion of the object's duration bar. Therefore, if you'd like to clear an animation of an object and want to leave the object as it appears at the end of its duration bar, you would place the CTM at the end and then proceed to clear the animation with the command.

The Object Menu

In previous modules, we covered most of the commands available under the Object menu. The following three commands, however, are specific to animation. As mentioned earlier, these are the very same commands that appear at the bottom-left portion of the Timeline window. Figure 8-8 displays the contents of the Object menu.

The Edit Name Command   The Edit Name command allows you to edit the name of any object either created or brought into LiveMotion. Naming conventions will be extremely important once you begin applying scripts to objects, and will allow you to create advanced interactive animations. Having two objects on your composition with the same name will render the script calling for that particular object useless. In addition, it's also important to start practicing proper naming techniques when naming your object. Try to steer away from spaces between words, and instead use underscores. For example, you would name Green Ellipse, Green_Ellipse. Also, be sure not to use underscores at the beginning of the name. Finally, don't use numbers as the first character of the name.

8

Figure 8-8   The Object menu

Naming also allows you to organize your objects. The Edit Name command lets you name groups of objects created with the Group command. In addition, you can name MovieClips, MovieClip Groups, and even combined objects.

Make MovieClip/MovieClip Group Commands   MovieClip objects are set on an independent timeline, which plays its animation independently of the main composition timeline. Therefore, MovieClip objects are capable of continuing to play long after the main composition timeline has finished playing. Figure 8-9 shows an example of a MovieClip object set on the timeline, displaying its own independent timeline. Notice how the composition header is replaced with the header of the name of the MovieClip object. To go back to the composition timeline, use the arrow located to the left of the header.

Rollover objects are perfect examples of a MovieClip object. The Rollover button continues to function long after the animation set on the main composition timeline has finished playing. In addition, each state of a rollover object contains its own independent timeline, which we play not only independently of the main composition timeline but also independently of one another.

The MovieClip Group command is used when grouping two or more objects, changing them to MovieClips, and finally setting them on the same independent timeline. Figure 8-10 shows an example of a MovieClip Group set on the timeline—the composition header is replaced with the name of the group of the two MovieClips inside it. To get back to the timeline, once again use the arrow located to the left of the header name.

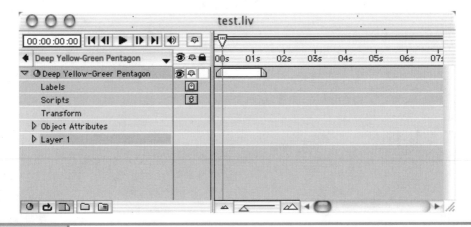

Figure 8-9   MovieClip objects on the timeline

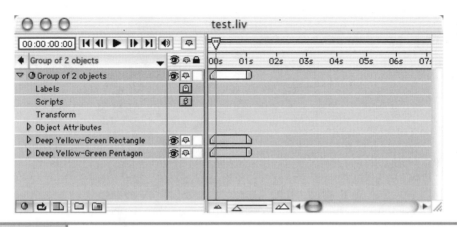

Figure 8-10   A MovieClip Group in the Timeline

Ask the Expert

Question: Can animated objects contain both linear and Bezier keyframes?

Answer: Of course. For example, setting the first and second keyframes of your object's Transform Component as linear and your third as Bezier will animate your object to travel in straight lines between the first and the second keyframes, and to travel in a Bezier curve between the second and the third keyframes.

Question: I'm trying to figure out how to create an animation that will play, stop for a few seconds, and then continue playing. Is there a way to do this?

Answer: The hold keyframe will allow you to perform this type of animation. Place the hold keyframe at the point in time where you'd like you're animation to stop. Afterwards, decide how many frames you'd like the animation to stop for and create an additional keyframe at the point in time where you'd like the animation to resume. In addition, you'll have to create an additional keyframe following the keyframe placed after the hold keyframe in order for the object to continue animating.

Summary

This module's aim was to give you a solid foundation of animation in LiveMotion. We've gone over the entire interface of the Timeline window, which is used to animate your objects on your composition. In addition, we've gone over the Timeline menu, which provides you with some easily accessible commands used in animation.

The next module is filled with projects and examples of animating the three types of objects used in LiveMotion: shape, text, and image. We go over the principles of animating each of these objects, and we learn how to use the Attributes menu of an object in order to animate other aspects of your objects using palettes learned in Part 1 of this book.

☑ *Mastery Check*

1. What's the purpose of the timeline?

A. To animate objects on the composition

B. To name objects on the composition

C. To arrange objects on the composition

D. All of the above

2. What's the difference between the Shy and View buttons in the Timeline window?

A. The View button hides the object on the composition, while the Shy button hides the object on the timeline.

B. The View button hides the object on the timeline, while the Shy button hides the object on the composition.

C. The View button hides the object on the timeline and the composition, while the Shy button hides the object on the timeline.

D. Both the View and Hide buttons hide the object on the timeline.

3. What's the purpose of the current time marker (CTM) in the Timeline window?

A. It shows the current object components in the Timeline window.

B. It marks the current keyframe in the Timeline window.

C. It lets the user know which object is being animated in the Timeline window.

D. It marks the current Time Interval marker in the Timeline window.

8

☑ *Mastery Check*

4. What will happen to an animated object with a duration bar longer than that of the composition?

   A. The object will continue playing even after the composition duration bar ends.

   B. Object duration bars can't be longer than that of the composition.

   C. Object duration bars can't be longer than that of the composition unless their duration bars are independent of the composition.

   D. The exported animation will crash.

5. How many Transform Components does the timeline allow us to edit for each object?

   A. Eight

   B. Seven

   C. Six

   D. Five

6. Which of the following statements is true when defining keyframes?

   I. A keyframe is a point in time that signifies a change in the object at that specific location.

   II. A single keyframe allows us to animate various attributes of an object.

   III. At least three keyframes must be present for an object in order for the object to animate a change between them.

      A. I and II

      B. I

      C. I and III

      D. III

☑ *Mastery Check*

7. Which of the following elements in the Timeline window is used to properly select the location prior to placing a keyframe?

   A. The CTM

   B. The Time Interval marker

   C. The object

   D. The duration bar

8. Which of the following Transform Components of an object are Motion Paths used for?

   A. Rotation

   B. Scale

   C. Position

   D. Skew

9. What is the main difference between MovieClip objects and ordinary objects?

   A. A MovieClip object's animation is independent of the composition. Regular objects are dependent on the composition.

   B. Regular objects are able to contain rollovers, while MovieClips are not.

   C. Regular objects are linear, while MovieClip objects are auto Bezier.

   D. MovieClip objects can't be grouped, while regular objects can.

10. What is the difference between linear and auto Bezier Motion Paths?

   A. Linear Motion Paths follow curved lines. Auto Bezier Motion Paths move in straight lines.

   B. Auto Bezier Motion Paths follow curved lines. Linear Motion Paths move in straight lines.

   C. Linear Motion Paths slow down as they approach a keyframe. Auto Bezier Motion Paths accelerate as they leave the keyframe.

   D. Auto Bezier Motion Paths are composed of three or more keyframes. Linear Motion Paths are composed of three or less keyframes.

8

Module 9

Create Simple Animations

The Goals of this Module

- Learn to animate shape objects
- Learn to animate text objects
- Learn to animate image objects
- Be able to animate object attributes
- Learn about layer animation

Our last module introduced the timeline environment as a way for us to animate objects on the composition. The following module will instruct you how to animate several of the different types of objects you read about in Part 1. Even though the process of animating the three objects you've read about (shapes, text, and images) is the same for each, the suggested technique (as well as some additional features specific to them individually) for each is different.

As stated earlier, the first section of this module covers animating the three objects that LiveMotion allows us to create and import. The second section, however, explains how to animate EPS files containing several layers that are in sequence with each other. Specific commands in LiveMotion not only allow us to import and break down these individual layers, but also to set up their animation in the Timeline window. The second part of this module covers how to import and animate the individual layers of a PSD file created in Photoshop. In addition, we'll also go over animating object attributes, which appear under the object right below the transform section in the Timeline window.

In conclusion, we'll discuss some additional animation techniques that allow you to work efficiently while animating various objects, such as creating aliases of your animated objects as well as copying and pasting animations back and forth between objects.

Animation

Animation in LiveMotion is a lot less complex than it initially appears to be. The best way to describe animation in LiveMotion is to use an example of a flip book. These little books—usually 3.5"×2"—contain anywhere from 50 to 200 pages of either shape, text, or image animation. Each page slightly modifies the object of the previous page, and so on. In LiveMotion, these pages are considered frames. The first page starts at a specific Time Interval, and each additional page continues in moderation of additional Time Intervals. By flipping these books, the person is able to view the animation as a whole. In the same sense, by previewing your animations in LiveMotion, the user is able to view each frame of the animated object in moderation.

Most of the work that goes into animating objects in LiveMotion is performed automatically by the program itself. The user creates keyframes, which inform LiveMotion of the state of that object at that specific Time Interval in the timeline, and LiveMotion fills in the animation in the frames located between these keyframes. As explained in the previous module, in order for the object to perform some sort of animation, the user must create two keyframes at different Time Intervals in the Timeline window. If we were trying to animate a movement of an object, for example, we would create two position keyframes for that object under the transform section of the object. The first keyframe would signify the object's position prior to animation, and the second the object's location after the animation has finished.

The most important rule when it comes to animating in LiveMotion is to always work backwards. This rule is not essential, but working backwards while animating will save you a lot of time. For example, if you created a unique drawing in LiveMotion, and wanted to create an animation of the drawing coming together, it would be a lot easier to create keyframes for the components that you'll animate at the end of the duration bar than it would be to create them in the beginning. To clarify, by creating keyframes at the end of the duration bar, you're already finished with a part of the animation. The keyframes placed for that object tell LiveMotion that this is how we want this drawing to look after a specific amount of time. After doing so, you can go back to the beginning of the duration bar and move and alter the individual objects of the drawing however you like. Remember to only alter the components of the object that you've created keyframes for at the end of the duration bar. For example, if you've only created a position component at the end of the duration bar, and continued by resizing the object at the beginning of the duration bar, the object's size would not be part of the animation since you didn't set the scale component at the end of the duration bar.

Thus far, we've covered the process of animating an object's Transform Components. However, by the end of this module you'll be able to animate other components such as an object's attributes and even its layers. Essentially, any effect applied to an object in LiveMotion can be animated. In addition, almost every object in LiveMotion, whether it's a shape, text, or an imported image, has the ability to contain similar animation effects. However, for the purposes of good taste and file export size, as well as the overall speed performance of your finished project, some animation effects can be applied to specific objects. The following section will cover several animation techniques for the three types of objects that LiveMotion allows us to work with. Keep in mind that these are just suggestions for animation techniques, and that you're not subject to creating them only for the objects specified. In fact, an entirely new book can be written to cover every single type of animation that LiveMotion allows us to create for each of these objects. Since we only have one module to discuss them, we'll stick to just suggestions and examples.

9

Ask the Expert

Question: Why is it helpful to work backwards when animating objects in LiveMotion?

Answer: Working backwards by creating keyframes at the end of an object's duration bar allows you to construct the animation at the beginning of the duration bar.

Question: Can an object's duration bar be shorter than the duration bar of the composition?

Answer: Of course. The object will simply cease playing while the animation of the composition continues to play, including other objects with longer duration bars.

Question: Are objects constrained to starting at the 00s Time Interval or can they start at a later point in time? If so, how would I go about setting them to start at different Time Intervals?

Answer: Objects are not constrained to begin playing at the 00s Time Interval. To make an object play at a different point in time, simply move the CTM to the preferred Time Interval and begin creating your object (as well as its animation). To move an already created object along with its animation to start at a different Time Interval, drag that object's duration bar by its center and move it to a desired point in time in the Timeline window.

Animate Shape Objects

Since shapes are the most diversified objects in LiveMotion, ways of animating them are plentiful. In addition to being able to create rectangular, rounded rectangular, elliptical, and various polygons with shapes, LiveMotion also enables you to combine them using the Combine command for some additional unique shapes, which are just as easy to animate as the shapes that were joined together initially to create them.

In our final project of Module 2 (Project 2-2), we've created two 3D-like balloons. Here's an example of one technique that we can use to animate them:

1. Open our previously created project in Module 2, which we've entitled project2-2.liv, and save it in the LiveMotion Projects folder.

2. Before we begin animating our balloons, let's combine all of the objects that they're composed of on our composition. To do this, select all of the objects belonging to the red balloon and choose Combine, followed by Unite with Color. Follow the same steps for the other balloon.

3. Now open your Timeline window. Name the first balloon **Red Balloon** and the second balloon **Blue Balloon**.

4. Stretch the duration bar of your composition to the 1.5-sec Time Interval. Notice that both of the duration bars are stretched as well.

5. Open the hierarchy folder structure for the red balloon object and the transform section as well.

6. Move the CTM to the 1.5-sec Time Interval and create keyframes for the position, object opacity, and scale components. This will tell LiveMotion that at the 2-sec Time Interval the current object will appear as it does on the composition.

7. Move the CTM to the 00-sec Time Interval and create keyframes for the position, object opacity, and scale components.

8. Make sure that the CTM is still at the 00-sec Time Interval in the Timeline window and go back to your Composition window. Move your red balloon to the upper-right portion of your Composition window. While holding down SHIFT, shrink the balloon to about half its original size, and in the Opacity palette adjust its opacity to 0.

9. Go back to your Timeline window and move the CTM to frame 9, which is located in between the 00-sec and the 1.5-sec Time Interval. Once again, create keyframes for the position, object opacity, and scale components.

10. Make sure that your CTM is still at frame 9 in the Timeline window and go back to the Composition window. Move your red balloon object towards the bottom of the Composition window so that the Motion Path creates a deep arch.

9

11. Follow the same steps for your other balloon, except instead of creating keyframes at frame 9, create them at frame 6. This will ensure that both of the balloons don't move alongside each other and instead move at different speeds.

12. Save your file as Animating shapes.liv in your LiveMotion Projects folder and use the Preview command to view your animation.

Congratulations! You've just created your first animation. If you've followed the steps appropriately, both of the balloons should animate on your composition and move to the final position at different speeds. Figure 9-1 displays the location of all of the keyframes created for this miniproject. If you've noticed, at the ninth frame for the red balloon and the sixth frame for the blue balloon, we unnecessarily created keyframes for the object opacity and scale components. They were unnecessary because we didn't apply any changes to those components at those specific Time Intervals. If you wish, you can go back to those Time Intervals and change both the objects' scale and opacity as desired. Having those keyframes there does not in any way increase the file size of your project or alter the overall animation.

The balloon animation example can be taken even further. If you remember, at the beginning we began by combining all of the objects that make up each balloon. All of those objects appear under the object's hierarchy folder structure. If you wish, you can further animate those individual objects. Since they are combined, however, any animated objects within the overall object will still follow along the animation of the entire object. Therefore, if you animate the string object of the balloon to slightly rotate from left to right, the string object, in addition to performing this animation, would also follow the animation of the red balloon in which it's contained. This should give some insight to how advanced animation can get in LiveMotion. While working on various animations in LiveMotion, take the time to name your objects. Organizing your files by naming them with names that you relate your objects to will ensure proper organization. Practicing this convention at this point will prepare you for even more complex animations—which will contain more objects, each with more within them.

Animate Text Objects

Text animation is one of the most widely used animation types. When it comes to animating text, we're left with two choices: either animate the entire text as a

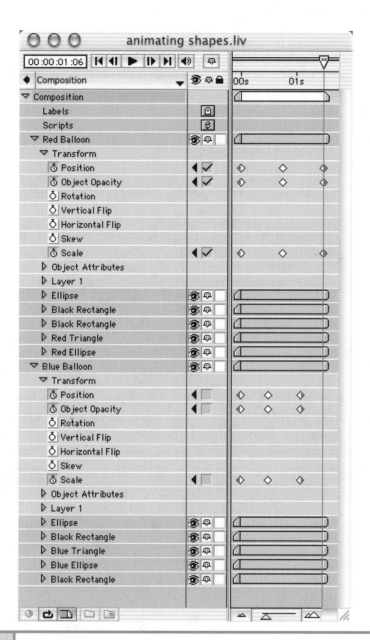

Figure 9-1   Keyframes set up for an animated shape object

whole, or animate each individual character of the text using the Convert Into command under the Object menu.

The following steps outline one technique of animating our previously saved project from Module 4. We will create an animation for the Project4-1 logo.liv file, which you previously saved in the LiveMotion Projects folder.

1. Open the Project4-1 logo.liv file from your LiveMotion Projects folder on your hard drive.

2. Select all of the characters of the word "Motion" on your composition and convert them into a single MovieClip Group.

3. Open your Timeline window and drag the composition duration bar to the 02s Time Interval.

4. Before we start animating the various objects that compose our LiveMotion 2 logo, let's properly name each object. The object at top should be your motion text object. Name that object **Motion Text**. The four objects' rights below are your L, I, V, and E text objects. Name them **L Text**, **I Text**, **V Text**, and **E Text**. The final object is your two-text character text object. Name this object **2 Text**.

5. Now that everything is properly named, let's start by animating the 2 Text object. Create a keyframe for its object opacity component at the 06f Time Interval. Create an additional keyframe for its object opacity component at the 00s Time Interval.

6. Make sure that the CTM is set at 00s, that the 2 Text object is selected, and move on to the Opacity palette. Set the object's opacity to 50.

7. From the Timeline menu, select the Make MovieClip Group command. Afterwards, select Loop from the Timeline menu. You will need to assign a name to the group. Name it **2 Text Loop**.

8. Select the L Text object and create one keyframe for its position component and one for its scale component at the 00s Time Interval. Create the same two keyframes at the 02f Time Interval.

9. Make sure that your CTM is set at the 00s Time Interval, position your L Text object at the center of your Composition window, and stretch it so that it completely covers your composition.

10. Follow steps 8 and 9 for the I Text, V Text, and E Text objects.

11. In order for these four text characters not to animate all at once, let's readjust their duration bars. Leave the L Text object as it is, starting from the 00s Time Interval. Drag the duration bar of the I Text object by its center so that it begins at the 02f Time Interval. Drag the duration bar of the V Text object by its center so that it starts at the 04f Time Interval. Finally, drag the E Text object's duration bar by its center so that it starts at the 06f Time Interval.

12. We're almost done—all that's left is the animation for our Motion MovieClip Group object. Before animating this object, let's drag its duration bar so that it begins at the 06f Time Interval.

13. At the 06f Time Interval, create a keyframe for the Motion MovieClip Group object's position component. Create the other one at the 10f Time Interval.

14. Go back to the 06f Time Interval and drag the Motion MovieClip Group object to the far right so that it's no longer visible on the composition. Make sure to hold down the SHIFT key while dragging so that you only move the object over its X axis.

15. Save your project as **Animating Text.liv**, and save it in your LiveMotion Projects folder. Use the Preview command to view the animation of your text logo.

9

If you properly followed the preceding steps, your logo object animation should begin by having its L, I, V, and E Text objects scale down one by one onto their proper locations on the composition. Afterwards, the Motion MovieClip Group object should quickly scroll down from right to left followed by the animating two-text object flashing repeatedly. The positioning of the duration bars of the animated objects in this mini project is illustrated in Figure 9-2.

If you notice, unlike all of the other objects on your animation, the two-text object is the only one that continues to animate by repeatedly flashing. We've set that object to loop as well as made it a MovieClip group in order for it to contain its own independent timeline; the other objects, however, only play once at the beginning of the animation.

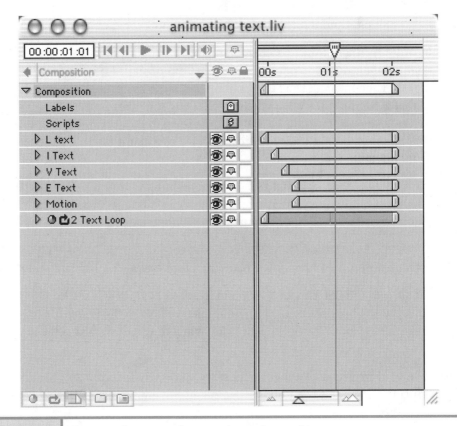

Figure 9-2 Duration bar setup for an animated text object

Ask the Expert

Question: I've noticed that my object contains a lot more keyframes under its duration bar than I originally created. Why?

Answer: Every time you apply a change to the object with regard to the position of the CTM in the Timeline window, a keyframe for the specific change is created under that object's duration bar.

Question: How do I go about changing the locations of my keyframes for a specific object?

Answer: You can move keyframes to any desired Time Interval in your Timeline window by clicking and dragging them.

Question: I've noticed that the animation of my objects stops before reaching a specific keyframe that I've created for that object. Why?

Answer: Even though your objects might contain keyframes outside of their duration bars, these specific keyframes won't play during the animation. Only the keyframes within the constraints of the object's duration bar are played during the animation.

Animate Image Objects

Image animation takes up a lot of space in your final exported file size. If you're planning on exporting your animations to be played on the Internet, try to use as little image animation as possible. Unlike text and shape animations, which tend to be vectors unless they've been modified with specific palettes, all images are raster objects.

The following image animation technique will utilize several Transform Component keyframes. However, if you decide to export this file afterwards, get ready for a shocker. The file size will be significantly larger than the file sizes of our two previously created animations for shape and text objects.

1. Let's begin by creating a new composition with the following dimensions: 300×400.

2. From the Place command, choose the Modue5_image.jpg file.

3. In the Properties palette, select Active Matte, and shrink down the image a bit so that it doesn't cover the entire composition area.

4. Open your Timeline window and move the duration bar of the composition to the 02s Time Interval.

5. At the 02s Time Interval, create keyframes for the position, object opacity, rotation, and scale components.

9

6. Move your CTM back to the 00s Time Interval and once again create keyframes for the position, object opacity, rotation, and scale components.

7. Move your CTM to the 01s Time Interval and enter keyframes for the same components.

8. Move the CTM back to the 00s Time Interval and scale down your image to measure 110×82.

9. Move the image to the bottom-left portion of the composition and set its opacity to 0 in the Opacity palette.

10. Move the CTM to the 01s Time Interval and scale up your image to 194×146.

11. Move the object to the upper-left portion of the composition.

12. In the Transform palette, set the image object's angle to 360.

13. Save your file as **animating images** and use the Preview command to view your animation.

The location and positioning of the keyframes created for this mini project are illustrated in Figure 9-3. Try moving your keyframes around for different effects. For example, if you move the position component keyframe at the 01s Time Interval closer to the 00s Time Interval, the image object will move quicker towards the upper-left portion of your composition. You may also enter either a higher or a lower value for the angle that we've entered for the rotation component keyframe at the 01s Time Interval for a different rotation effect.

1-Minute Drill

● How does LiveMotion decide at what point a looped object begins and finishes so that it may start the process all over again?

● Which palette corresponds to the rotation component?

● An object with a loop begins at the beginning of its duration bar, continues toward the end of its duration bar, and begins playing all over again.
● The Transform palette.

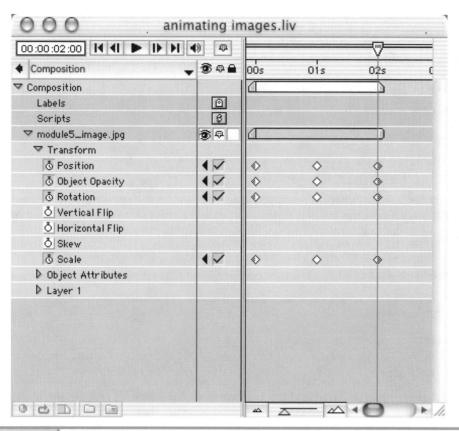

Figure 9-3 | Keyframe setup for an animated image object

Project 9-1: Create a Multiple Object Animation

By now, you should be aware of different techniques of animating various objects in LiveMotion. The following project introduces ways of animating complex objects that we'll create by combining objects together and animating them independently from one another.

In addition to allowing us to combine similar objects together, such as combining a rectangle shape object with an ellipse shape object, LiveMotion also allows us to combine objects such as a text object with a rounded rectangle object. When these objects are combined, the program still allows us to modify the individual objects that are within. The following project will explore such options.

Step-by-Step

1. Create a new composition with the following dimensions: 500×200.

2. Create a red ellipse measuring 147×147.

3. Create a white exclamation point with the Text tool, then set its font to Times Bold and its dimensions to 43×225.

4. Place the exclamation point at the left portion of the circle so that its borders barely touch the borders of the ellipse, and combine it using the Minus Front command under the Combine command in the Object menu.

5. Select your combined object in the Timeline window and set it to a MovieClip Group.

6. Name your combined object **Button** and choose Loop from the Timeline menu.

7. Expand your combined object by toggling the small Arrow icon next to the object's name in the Timeline window, select the ellipse object, and name it **Red_Circle**. Name the exclamation point object **Exclamation_Point**.

8. Select the Red_Circle and the Exclamation_Point objects and set the duration to Implicit/Explicit Length if the button is not pressed in already (this will enable these objects' duration bars to maintain the same length as the duration bar of the main button).

9. Select the entire button and move its duration bar to the 04f Time Interval.

10. Select your Red_Circle object and create a keyframe for its scale component at the 00s Time Interval.

11. Create the same keyframe at the 04f Time Interval.

12. At the 04f Time Interval, scale the size of your Red_Circle object to 150×150.

13. Select your Exclamation_Point object and place keyframes for its position and skew components at the 00s, 02f, and 04f Time Intervals.

14. Move your CTM to the 02f Time Interval and move your Exclamation_Point object to the left side of the circle object while keeping it within the overall circle.

15. In the Transform palette, set the Exclamation_Point object's horizontal skew preference to 3.

16. Move the CTM to the 04f Time Interval and skew the Exclamation_Point object's horizontal skew to -3.

17. Now select your overall Button object, open its transform section, and place a keyframe for its position component at the 00s, 02f, and 04f Time Intervals.

18. Set the CTM back to 02f Time Interval, click the Composition window to make it active and using your up arrow key on your keyboard, move the button object up by clicking the key five times.

19. Go back to your composition timeline by clicking the left arrow next to the button header and save your project as **Project9-1 Advanced button** in your LiveMotion Projects folder.

20. Use the Preview command to view your object's animation.

Project Summary

If you followed the instructions properly, your button object will animate on your composition. In addition, both the red circle of the button and the exclamation point will animate independently of each other both in their own ways. The overall animation will loop back and forth because we set the button to loop. To double-check the positioning of your keyframes in this project, take a look at the keyframe setup in Figure 9-4.

9

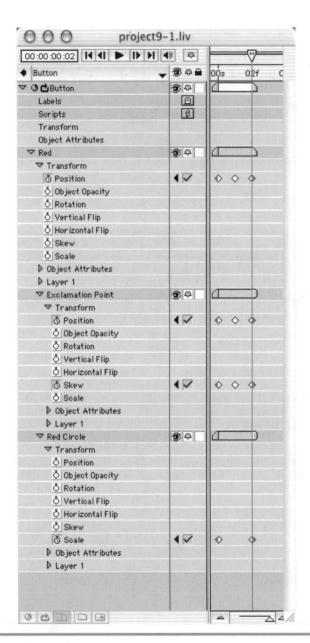

Figure 9-4 A multiple object animation

If you wish, you can further edit your object by either applying several appearance-like effects using any number of palettes, such as the Gradient, Layer, Object, and 3D palettes.

Animate Object Attributes

Thus far, all of our animations were composed by creating keyframes for the object's Transform Components. Right below the transform section of an object is the object attribute section, as shown in Figure 9-5, which contains attributes

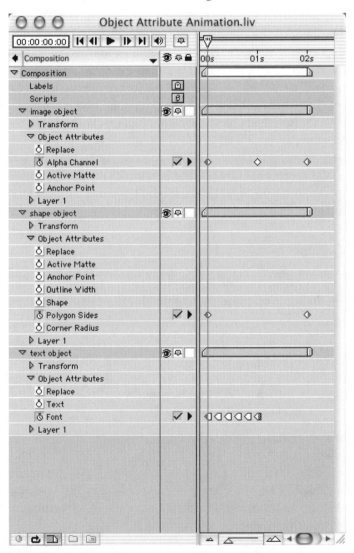

9

Figure 9-5   The object attribute section

that LiveMotion allows us to animate for specific objects. The object attribute section contains individual attributes for each object in LiveMotion. For the sake of not confusing terms in LiveMotion, we'll refer to these components as "attributes."

The process of animating object attributes is done by modifying their effect in the palette that they're associated with. These palettes are the Properties and Transform palettes. All three objects that LiveMotion allows us to either create or import start out with the same types of attributes under their object attribute sections. However, some objects contain attributes that are specific to that object alone. For example, a text object, unlike the other two types of objects, contains text and font attributes, which allow us to animate the actual text of the text object as well as its font over time. There are several other attributes that are specific to that object alone, and you'll discover them as you explore the animation of each.

An object's attributes are animated in the same manner as its Transform Components. We create them by placing keyframes at specific Time Intervals under the object's duration bar. Here's one example of an object attribute animation that is specific to text objects alone:

1. Create a new composition with the following dimensions: 500×400.

2. Create a text object by typing in **LiveMotion** with the Type tool.

3. Open the Timeline window and set the duration bar of the composition to 02s.

4. Create a keyframe for the text attribute at the 00s, 06f, 12f, 18f, 01s, 04f, 01s, and 10f Time Intervals.

5. Move your CTM to each of these keyframes and select an individual font for your text object.

6. Preview your animation with the Preview button.

The animation played will display your text object as it changes its font over time. Creating and placing these keyframes was done in the same manner as with the Transform Components. Here's an example of animating attributes that are specific to shape objects:

1. On the same composition, create a three-sided polygon using the combination of the Properties palette and the Polygon tool. Make sure that the CTM is set at 00s so that your object's duration bar starts at the 00s Time Interval.

2. Open your Timeline window and create a keyframe for the polygon sides attributes at the 00s Time Interval and the 02s Time Interval.

3. At the 02s Time Interval, set the polygon sides to 10.

4. Preview your animation with the Preview button.

The three-sided polygon will animate on your composition by increasing its number of sides until it reaches a total of ten sides. The following attribute was only specific to polygon objects, because other shapes can't be modified in the same manner as text and image objects.

Image objects also contain attributes that are only specific to them. Here's an example of an image attribute animation:

1. Place an image on your composition using the Place command.

2. Scale down the image and set it in an empty spot on your composition. If you need to, move your previously created objects out of the way or delete them.

3. From the Properties palette, choose the No Alpha option for your image object.

4. Create a keyframe for the image object's Alpha Channel attribute at the 00s, 10f, and 01s Time Intervals. While still on that keyframe, go back to the Properties palette and select the Use Alpha Channel option. (Switching back between the alpha options in the Properties palette was necessary. The Alpha Channel attribute would not have shown up if you simply placed an image object on the composition and then rushed to the Timeline window. Some object attributes require you to make a corresponding alteration to the object in order to then be able to edit its attribute in the Timeline window.)

5. Move your CTM to the 10f Time Interval and select the No Alpha option from the Properties palette.

9

6. Save your file as **Object Attribute Animation.liv** in your LiveMotion Projects folder.

7. Use the Preview button to view your animation.

The image object should start out appearing faded out over the white background, grow to normal halfway through the animation, and end by once more fading out. The following attribute is only specific to image objects. For a more drastic animation, try placing image files with Alpha Channels already stored in them.

The following examples of object attribute animation for text, shape, and image objects were only simple demonstrations. Try experimenting by combining Transform Component animations along with object attribute animations for more spectacular animation effects.

Ask the Expert

Question: Why don't some animations gradually change within the boundaries of their keyframes, and instead change only once the CTM reaches the specific keyframe with the change?

Answer: Some components and object attributes—such as the flip horizontal component, for example—only change once the animation reaches that specified keyframe. These keyframes appear differently than others as well. Their icon is a small triangle as opposed to a diamond-like shape of regular keyframes.

Question: What is the difference between Transform Components and object attributes?

Answer: The main difference is that Transform Components are the same for all objects either created or imported into LiveMotion with the exception of sound objects. Object attributes, on the other hand, are specific to each object. A text object, for example, features a text attribute, which allows the user to animate the actual text of that object over time. This specific attribute only corresponds to text objects and is not visible under the object attribute section for other objects.

Animate Layers

Another way to animate your objects in LiveMotion is to animate their individual layers. LiveMotion provides layer animation under the layer section, shown in Figure 9-6—located under the object folder hierarchy, right below the Transform Components and object attributes.

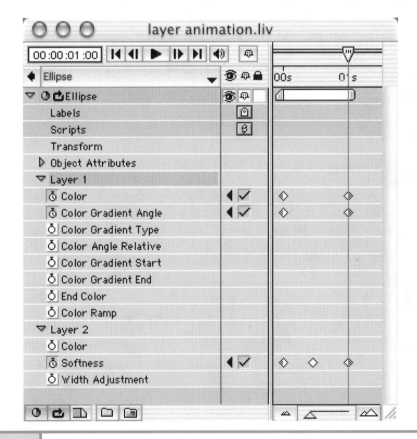

Figure 9-6   An object layer section hierarchy

For the most part, the layer section of an object in the Timeline menu contains a small number of components that LiveMotion allows you to animate. However, by applying various modifications to that specific object, more components begin to appear. These components are relative to the palettes that were used to modify the object. For example, if you applied a linear gradient effect using the Gradient palette, several components would appear under the layer section, which would allow you to animate that specific gradient effect. With these new components, you're able to animate the animation of that specific gradient effect over time. Since LiveMotion allows you to modify your objects using several other palettes, you're able to animate a large number of components under the layer section of an object. In addition, LiveMotion allows you to create these components for each individual layer of an object. Since your objects are able to contain several different layers as well as hold their own unique modifications created by various palettes, the limit of animation provided with this feature is endless.

1. Create a new composition with the following dimensions: 350×300.

2. Draw a large circle using the Ellipse tool.

3. Color your object green with the Color palette, and create a linear gradient effect for that object with the Gradient palette. Your circle object now should contain a blend of green and black color.

4. In your Timeline window, drag the duration bar of your object to the 01s Time Interval, select your object, and open up its folder-like hierarchy, followed by its layer section.

5. Make sure that your CTM is set back at the 00s Time Interval and create a keyframe for its color and color gradient angle components.

6. Move the CTM to the 01s Time Interval and create keyframes once more for its color and color gradient angle components.

7. Make sure that your CTM resides at the 01s Time Interval, and change the color of your object to orange in the Color palette.

8. In the Gradient palette, set the angle of your gradient effect to 360.

9. Select your object in the Timeline window, and make it a MovieClip with either the MovieClip button or by choosing the Make MovieClip command under the Timeline menu.

10. Set your object to loop by pressing the Loop button.

11. Save your project as **Layer Animation.liv** in your LiveMotion Projects folder.

12. Preview the animation of your object by clicking the Preview button in the toolbar.

The following simple animation is probably one of the most unique animations that we've created thus far. The circle object created in this project will animate the angle of its linear gradient effect as well as gradually change its color from green to orange.

We can take the following layer animation even further by creating an additional layer for that object and animating its components. Here's one example:

1. Since we made our previous circle object a MovieClip object, you will need to double-click it in order view its independent timeline.

2. Select your object and create an additional layer for that object with the Object palette.

3. Color your new layer blue with the Color palette.

4. Under its layer section, select Layer 2, which is the default name of the additional layer that you previously created.

5. Move your CTM to the 01s Time Interval and go over to your Layer palette.

6. In the Layer palette, enter **2** for its width preference, and **1** for its softness preference.

7. Now that the softness component appears under the layer section, create a keyframe for the softness component at the 00s, 10f, and 01s Time Intervals.

9

8. Move your CTM to the 10f Time Interval and set the softness preference in the Layer palette to 10.

9. Save your project as **Multiple Layer Animation.liv** in your LiveMotion Projects folder.

10. Use the Preview button to view your new animation.

Notice the effect of your new animation. Both the initial layer of the object as well as the second layer, which we've created in the current project, each animates an independent component during the animation.

As stated earlier, the quantity of animation that we're able to create with the numerous components available to us under the layer section of an object is endless. In addition, as we've demonstrated in the previous project, more than one layer can be animated at the same time. Before proceeding to the next section of this module, experiment animating with some of the other components available to you by modifying your objects with other palettes.

Ask the Expert

Question: How do I distinguish between each layer under the object folder-like hierarchy structure so that I may animate the appropriate one?

Answer: In addition to naming your layers, another way of distinguishing between your layers is to know that the specific layer selected in your Object palette is automatically selected in the Timeline window, and vice versa.

Question: Can I duplicate the animation of one layer so that an additional layer created will adopt all of its animations.

Answer: Yes. To do so, select the layer that you would like to duplicate in the Object palette and click the Duplicate Layer button at the bottom of the palette. The layer duplicated, and in addition to adopting all of the layer's appearance changes, will contain all of its animation.

Project 9-2: Object Layer Animation

In the second part of this module, we covered the process of animating attributes in the object attributes section of an object as well as animating the individual components of a selected layer of an object. Utilizing the Transform Components that we covered in the first section of this module, as well as both the object attributes and layer components introduced to us in the second section, creates some spectacular animation effects. The following project will utilize several object attributes and layer components in the animation. In addition, the animated object will be composed of several layers for the purpose of animating them individually using the components available to us under the layer section of an object.

Step-by-Step

1. Begin by creating a new composition with the following dimensions: 450×300.

2. Create a circular object using the Ellipse tool from the toolbar. The object should measure 137×137.

3. Color your object orange using the Color palette, and create an additional layer for the object using the Object palette.

4. Crop the right side of your shape using the Crop tool, so that only half of your ellipse is shown on the composition.

5. Select the first layer of your object, select Emboss from the 3D palette, and enter the following settings for the effect: **40** for depth, **10** for softness, **100** for lighting, and **135** for angle.

6. Select your second layer in the Object palette, set the Object Layer Opacity preference in the Object palette to **34**, and enter the following settings for the layer in the Layer palette: **-50** for X offset, **3** for width, and **10** for softness.

7. Open your Timeline window and move the composition's duration bar to the 01s Time Interval.

8. Create a keyframe at the 00s Time Interval for its position and rotation components under the object's transform section, and the other two at the 01s Time Interval.

9

9. Move your CTM to the 01s Time Interval and enter **-360** for the angle preference in the Transform palette.

10. Toggle down your object's object attribute section in the Timeline window and create one keyframe for the crop attribute at the 00s Time Interval and another at the 01s Time Interval.

11. Make sure that the CTM is at the 01s Time Interval in the Timeline window and use the Crop tool to restore the previously cropped out part of your ellipse object on the composition.

12. In your Timeline window, toggle down the layer 1 section of your object and create one keyframe for the color component at the 00s Time Interval and another at the 01s Time Interval.

13. Once again, make sure that your CTM is located at the 01s Time Interval and change your object's color from orange to blue in the Color palette.

14. Go back to your Timeline window and toggle down the layer 2 section. Create one keyframe for the offset component at the 00s Time Interval, and another at the 01s Time Interval.

15. Make sure that your CTM remains at the 01s Time Interval, and enter **50** for the X-offset preference in the Layer palette.

16. Save your project as **Project9-2** in your LiveMotion Projects folder.

17. Use the Preview button to view the animation of your shape.

Project Summary

If you followed the steps correctly, your object should start off as a semicircle and eventually morph into a full circle. During the shape change, your object will rotate clockwise and the initial orange color of your shape will change to blue over time. The shadow layer of your shape should move from left to right during the animation. To double-check the positioning of your keyframes created in this project, refer to Figure 9-7.

The animation effect created in this project used at least one component and attribute from each of the sections under the object's folder-like hierarchy structure. Note that some of the components we've animated under each of the layers weren't present prior to our applying the related effect to the object itself. As we discussed earlier, these components don't appear under the object's layer sections until their effects are first applied to the object. During the project, the layer animation effects applied to the object's individual layers were adjusted in their corresponding palettes. Keep that in mind when working

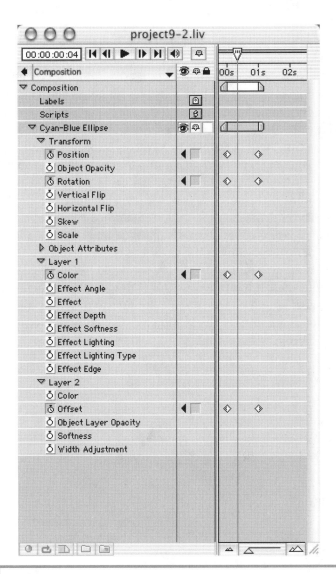

Figure 9-7   An object's layer properties animation

on future projects in future modules. Applying palette effects comes first, and the animation of these effects follows shortly after.

Summary

This module consists of several different types of techniques of animating components and attributes of objects using keyframes in the Timeline window. We've individually gone over animating text, shape, and image objects, and we've discussed their individual animation effects as well as their effect on file size. The module was filled with several mini projects in order to give you hands-on practice, so that you may get a better sense of performing these various techniques on your own.

The next module introduces ways of utilizing advanced techniques in animation. We'll go over animating PSD, EPS, and AI type files that contain a sequence. We will also go over several helpful commands that allow you to cut down on some of the time-consuming tasks and be more consistent. In addition, we'll introduce a unique animation feature available to us, called LiveTabs. You'll learn about their importance as well as how to create them on your own.

Before proceeding to the next module, be sure to test your understanding of all of the rules of animation in LiveMotion by answering the multiple questions in the Mastery Check.

☑ *Mastery Check*

1. Which of the following statements are true?

   I. LiveMotion enables us to animate only objects created in the program.

   II. Working backwards during animation helps the user be more productive.

   III. Shape animation has a bigger impact on file size in comparison to image animation.

   A. I only

   B. II and III

   C. I and II

   D. II only

2. Which two major palettes are the attributes under the object attributes section associated with?

   A. Transform and Gradient palettes

   B. Properties and 3D palettes

   C. Properties and Transform palettes

   D. Layer and Object palettes

3. How many different components and attributes does LiveMotion allow us to animate for any specific object?

   A. Less than 10

   B. 12

   C. 17

   D. More than 20

9

☑ Mastery Check

4. _____ animated objects within a _____ group will follow the animation of the overall object as well.

   A. Individual/MovieClip

   B. Some/object

   C. All/object

   D. Shape/composition

5. Which type of object in LiveMotion allows us to animate more of its attributes under its object attributes section than others?

   A. Shape

   B. Text

   C. Image

   D. All have an equal number of attributes

6. Which of the following statements are false?

   I. At least three keyframes must be created in order to animate an object attribute.

   II. Keyframes allow us to create different states of the object animation.

   III. MovieClip objects can contain loop animations.

   A. I

   B. I and III

   C. II

   D. III

☑ Mastery Check

7. How do layer components differ from both object attributes and Transform Components?

A. Layer components are created by their corresponding palettes.

B. Layer components are specific to each type of object.

C. Layer components need at least three keyframes to function.

D. Layer components correspond to only shape and text objects.

8. How many layers does the timeline allow us to animate?

A. The first and second layer only

B. It varies, depending on what type of object contains them

C. Ten layers at most

D. As many layers as the object contains

9. Which tool in the toolbar helps us move the position of an object's layer so that we may ultimately animate it using specific layer components?

A. The Arrow tool

B. The Layer Offset tool

C. TheCrop tool

D. The Selection tool

10. With which palette are the X offset, Y offset, width, and softness associated?

A. The Object palette

B. The Layer palette

C. TheProperties palette

D. The Transform palette

9

Module 10

10

Advanced Animations and Techniques

The Goals of this Module

- Learn to break down and animate AI and PSD files
- Learn various helpful animation techniques
- Learn how to utilize styles in your animations
- Learn how to use LiveTabs and construct their interface

Module 8 and Module 9 gave you hands-on practice animating various objects in LiveMotion. The following module introduces you to some additional objects that LiveMotion allows you to import and automatically animate using specific commands. These files—mainly AI and PSDs—are capable of containing layers, which LiveMotion is then able to convert into sequences by ordering the layers on the composition. If you're confused at this point, don't stray. These types of animations will be described in full length in just a bit.

We will also cover some helpful animation techniques that'll allow you to be more efficient during the animation process. We'll cover features such as aliases and copy and paste animation commands that'll save you time and the frustration of performing repetitive tasks while animating current and additional objects.

The second section of this module covers two additional helpful features of LiveMotion. Styles, which we've gone over in previous modules, are capable of containing animations. We'll go over some of the benefits of utilizing them within the animation process. The second feature of LiveMotion, which is a new feature for those of you who've used the first version of LiveMotion when it first came out a few years ago, is LiveTabs. LiveTabs make use of LiveMotion's powerful scripting engine to create spectacular effects to the objects on your composition. Here is an even more accurate definition of LiveTabs, taken from Adobe's site: "Extend the application, add tools to the user interface, and create scripted animation without coding experience." Scripting is another new feature of LiveMotion, which we'll cover in the next module.

Animate Imported Files

You've previously learned of ways of utilizing the Place command to bring in various files onto the composition area in LiveMotion. In these previous modules, you've learned of LiveMotion's ability to import native Adobe files such as PSD and AI files. We've discussed using the Convert Into | Objects command to break down layers into individual objects. The following section will discuss using the additional Convert Into | Sequence command found under the Object menu, that'll allow you to break down the individual layers of imported files, as well as animate them.

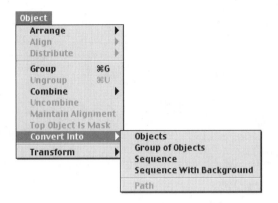

Animate PSD Files

In Module 5, we used the Convert Into | Objects command as well as the Convert Into | Group of Objects command to break down the individual layers of a PSD file. For those of you privileged enough to own a copy of Photoshop 5 or later, you'll be glad to know that these two commands also have the ability to break down the layers within layer sets. To do so, simply apply the Convert Into command once more on an object that contains them. The two additional commands—Sequence and Sequence with Background, under the Convert Into submenu—not only allow us to break down PSD files into their individual layers, but also automatically animate them in the Timeline window.

An imported PSD file converted with the Convert Into | Sequence command will be automatically animated for you with an element index attribute under the Object Attribute section of the converted imported file, as shown in Figure 10-1. Each layer is animated for exactly one frame of time duration. Therefore, an imported PSD file with three layers, for example, will play for exactly three frames of time duration. To stretch the duration of each layer, simply drag the second keyframe for the element index attribute to a further point in time on the timeline.

10

Animate AI Files

Illustrator AI native files are animated very much the same way with the Convert Into | Sequence command as Photoshop native PSD files. The command works with AI files created with versions 7 thru 10 of Adobe Illustrator.

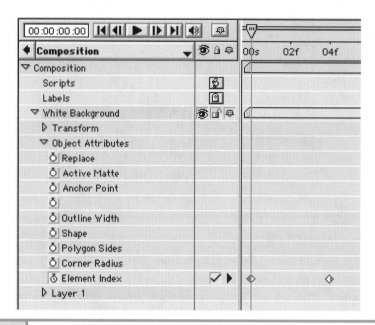

Figure 10-1 An element index attribute

While working with AI files that contain object blends, the Convert Into | Sequence command is also capable of splitting up each of the blends and animating them automatically for you in the Timeline window. Object blends are shape morphs created in Adobe Illustrator by selecting any two objects, followed by applying the Blend command found under the Object menu. Blending objects in Adobe Illustrator only works on vector shapes, either created or imported into the program, and will not work on imported images. Also, the Release to Layers command in Illustrator is only available in versions 9 and later. After successfully creating a blend, choose Ungroup, followed by the Release to Layers command in Illustrator. Save your file as an Adobe Illustrator AI native file and use the Place command followed by the Convert Into | Sequence command in LiveMotion to animate your new shape morph. Figure 10-2 displays an animation example of a blend created in Adobe Illustrator and imported into LiveMotion. For additional information of shape blends, refer to your Adobe Illustrator manual.

Adobe Photoshop and Adobe Illustrator are essential tools for enhancing the way you work in graphic design and photo editing. In fact, they're two of the most widely used applications in these two fields. If you have access or own these two powerful applications, I'd strongly urge you to utilize them along with

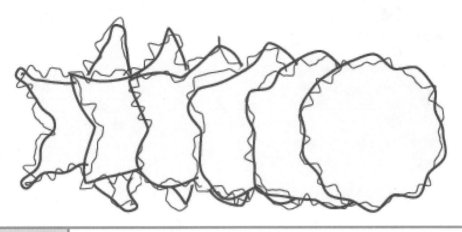

Figure 10-2   An AI blend in LiveMotion

LiveMotion for the most optimal design in your work. As explained in earlier modules, Adobe has incorporated a unique way for all of its applications to not only properly function with one another, but allow the user to make changes to an open file in one Adobe program and simultaneously have that same file imported in another update automatically. This effect is also backward compatible, where the imported file in question would be changed in one Adobe program and have the original Adobe program that created the file simultaneously update it while it's open.

1-Minute Drill

- Which element of both PSD and AI files does LiveMotion allow us to break down and animate?
- What is the difference between the Convert Into | Sequence and the Convert Into | Sequence with Background commands?

Animate AMX Files

Adobe LiveMotion is also fully compatible with AMX (Adobe Motion Exchange) files, which are the native file formats for Adobe After Effects 5.5. AMX files

---

- Layers.
- The Convert Into | Sequence with Background command retains the background layer, if it exists in the file in question during the layer animation.

differ from PSD and AI files because in addition to containing objects and masks within them, they're able to contain keyframes, which are imported from within the file onto LiveMotion's timeline.

The Timeline window in LiveMotion was actually adopted from the timeline in Adobe After Effects. If you've used or are currently using Adobe After Effects, you'll find animating similar. Furthermore, only AMX files created in Adobe After Effects 5.5 will be compatible as far as importing them onto your composition in LiveMotion.

Helpful Animation Techniques

Animating objects in LiveMotion can get quite tedious, especially when you're dealing with several different objects all using the same animation. For example, if you wanted to create a custom text animation effect in which each character of the text performs the same animation, you'd need to edit the animation in

Ask the Expert

Question: I own a copy of Illustrator 5. Will I be able to import AI files created in this version into LiveMotion?

Answer: No. LiveMotion can only import AI files that were created in versions 7 thru 10.

Question: I own a copy of Macromedia Freehand. Can I import Freehand's native file format into LiveMotion?

Answer: No. However, you can choose to export your graphics to EPS format and then import them into LiveMotion.

Question: Can EPS files contain layers?

Answer: Unfortunately, no. EPS files, like JPEG and GIF file formats, are flattened images and graphics. Only PSD and AI file formats are able to contain layers that LiveMotion will allow us to break down and ultimately animate.

each of the characters. The following section will cover some helpful techniques that allow you to be efficient, and that ease many tedious repetitions.

The Paste Object Animation Command

In earlier modules, we learned how to copy objects using the Edit | Copy command, and then apply specific features copied from the object and paste them to others using the Paste Special command. LiveMotion offers us another command—the Paste Object Animation command, found under the Edit menu— which allows us to paste the animation of one object to another. In order to properly paste an animation from one object to another, make sure that the CTM is positioned at the beginning of the duration bar of the object that you're pasting the animation onto. Doing so will allow you to paste the animation accurately onto the object. However, in some cases the animation that gets copied and pasted will only contain the object's Transform Component animation. Animations that contain Object Attributes will not be copied.

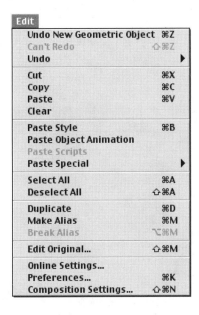

Many designers use this technique when animating the individual text characters that they broke down from a whole text object. Instead of individually animating each piece of text, the Paste Object Animation command allows the user to animate just one individual text character, and then paste the animation to each of the remaining text character objects. For an even more unique effect, we can adjust the duration bars of each of the text characters so that each one starts at a later point in time than the previous character.

Take a look at Figure 10-3, which shows a screen shot of a timeline for individual text character objects. The duration bar for each one of these objects starts and ends ahead of the previous one. This allows each animated character to play individually, followed by the next character, and so on, until all of them play and appear together on the composition.

1-Minute Drill

● What would be a viable reason for the Paste Object Animation command being grayed out after just having copied an object using the Edit | Copy command?

● Can the Paste Object Animation command be applied to layers of an imported file that was broken down using specific Convert Into commands?

The Alias Object Command

The Make Alias command, found under the Edit menu, is yet another helpful technique that allows us to stay consistent and productive while animating in

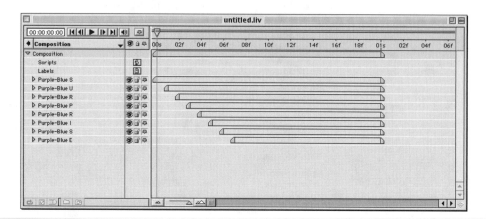

Figure 10-3 The individual text character duration bar setup

● If the object that was copied didn't contain any animation.
● Imported objects as well as any other object in LiveMotion, whether created in the program or outside of the program, can acquire a copied animation with the Paste Object Animation command.

LiveMotion. Unlike the Duplicate command, which we've learned of in earlier modules, the Make Alias command makes it so that the alias created absorbs all of the appearance changes of the object from which it was created. Therefore, if we created an animating ellipse object and used the Make Alias command on that object, the alias would absorb all of the current modifications to that object as well as any future modifications. However, even though an alias will absorb any modifications done by the palettes on the original object, any further animations applied to either the alias or the original will not be reflected on the other. Therefore, when creating aliases, keep in mind that the alias will only absorb the present animations from the original objects; any future animation changes will only reflect on the object on which the animation changes are performed.

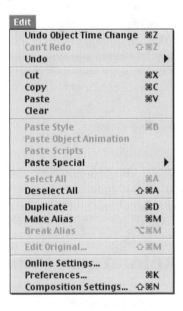

Using aliases in your project can significantly reduce the time it takes you to copy and paste similar objects and then individually modify their appearance. If at any time you wish to break apart an alias from the original object from which it was created, use the Break Alias command—found below the Make Alias command under the Edit menu.

The advantage of using aliases over duplicates is that they significantly reduce the final file size of your exported project. When exporting, LiveMotion recognizes the data from the original object and links that data to the alias without having to duplicate the data for the alias, which would result in a bigger file size.

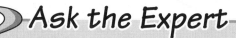

Ask the Expert

Question: Will creating an additional rollover state for either the original or the alias object automatically modify the other?

Answer: Yes, any palette modification will reflect on both ends.

Question: What do I do if I no longer want the alias to receive automatic modifications when the original gets modified?

Answer: You may use the Break Alias command. After doing so, both objects will be treated as individual objects.

Question: I've created an alias of an object that is animated and I've noticed that when I move it, only the position value at the first keyframe changes, not the entire animation.

Answer: In order to move your alias object along with its animation, simply hold down the CTRL-ALT keys if you're on a PC, and the CTRL-APPLE keys if you're using a Mac.

Another interesting feature you'll notice while working with aliases is that even though you are free to move the duration bar of either the original or the alias without having the change reflect back on the other object, resizing the duration bars will always reflect back on either the original or the alias object.

Project 10-1: Animate an Imported PSD File

The following project is aimed at those of you who either own or have access to Adobe Photoshop or Adobe Photoshop elements. If you don't, you can either download a free 30-day demo from Adobe's web site at http://www.adobe.com, or just read on the outline for this project in order to get an idea of how the procedure of animating a PSD file is created in LiveMotion.

Before proceeding with the project, locate several of your favorite photographs and note their locations on your hard drive. We will use these images within Photoshop to create a file composed of several photographs, each contained on a separate layer. If you don't have any photograph images on your hard drive, you may download them online from a variety of web sites.

Step-by-Step

1. In Photoshop, create a file composed of several of your favorite photographs, each placed on a separate layer.

2. Save your Photoshop file as a PSD file in your LiveMotion Projects folder.

3. Back in LiveMotion, create a new composition with the following dimensions: 500×400.

4. Use the Place command to bring in your PSD file on your composition.

5. In your Timeline window, drag the duration bar of the composition to the 03s Time Interval.

6. Select the file and apply the Convert Into | Sequence command.

7. Back in your Timeline window, toggle down the object's folder-like hierarchy structure and open its Object Attributes menu.

8. Select the second element index keyframe and drag it to the 03s Time Interval.

9. Save your file as Project 10-1.liv in your LiveMotion Projects folder and use the Preview command to view your animation.

Project Summary

The animation created will resemble a simple slide show, displaying each photograph in the PSD file for a short duration of time. The length of time that each photograph will play during this slide show animation will vary based on the number of layers you've created back in Photoshop.

The Convert Into | Sequence command applied in step 6 created a new type of Object Attribute in your object, called an element index. By dragging the second keyframe of this attribute, you are able to extend the length of time that each photograph will display during the animation. The specific attribute is specific only to imported files modified with the Break Into | Sequence command and cannot be created within LiveMotion.

10

Animation Styles

In previous modules, we used styles to apply custom-made palette modifications to our objects. In those modules, we noted that styles are also capable of containing animations. To view just styles with animation in the

Styles menu, toggle off every other button except for the Animations button at the bottom of the palette. To apply an animated style to a selected object on the composition, select the animated style from the Styles palette, and click the Apply button to add the animated effect to that object. Since the Styles palette is unable to display the animation of a specified animated style, use the Preview button to view the animation you've just applied.

Once you've applied an animated style to an object, you are free to further edit the animation in the Timeline window. Keep in mind, however, that once you apply an animated style to an object which already contains some type of animation, the style animation will replace that object's current animation.

Create Styles from Animated Objects

As with other styles we've worked with in previous modules, styles created from the objects in the composition can be saved for future use. A saved style is placed in the Styles folder in your LiveMotion folder on your hard drive, as well as within the Styles palette, which allows you to apply that style to any other current or future object you'll either create or import into LiveMotion.

To create your own custom style, create your own unique animation, select the object, and click the New Style button in the Styles palette. You'll be prompted with a pop-up screen asking you which portion of the object you'd like to save as a style, as shown in Figure 10-4. Depending on which effects you applied to your object, some options in the pop-up screen will be grayed out. As with every new style, the very top of this pop-up window asks you to fill in the name for your new style. The Layer check box, when checked, will maintain any information saved within the individual layers of your objects in your new style. By checking the Ignore Color of First Layer option, the style when applied to a different object will not change that object's color. If the object from which you're creating the

Figure 10-4 The Save Style prompt

new style contains any rollover effects or layer component animations, checking the Layer Animation | Rollover option will ensure that your new style contains them within. The Object Animation Rollover check box is the one we're concerned with at this point. When checked, the style will maintain the animation within the overall object. The last check box, when checked, saves any object scripting within your object to your new style. Object scripting and other types of scripting in LiveMotion will be explained in the next module.

Styles become extremely handy in LiveMotion. The files themselves in your Styles folder are significantly smaller in size and can be transferred from one computer to another. Several sites even allow you to download additional styles. We will cover these types of sites in the last module of this book.

10

1-Minute Drill

● How do we create animated styles?

● What is the difference between the Layer Animation | Rollover preference and the Object Animation | Rollover preference?

● Choose an animated object on the composition and click the New Style button in the Styles palette. In the Preference window that appears, be sure to check the Object Animation | Rollover check box and the Layer Animation | Rollover check box if you wish to include additional layer animations within the object to your new style.

● Object Animation | Rollover preference relates to the animated Transform Components of an object, and the Layer Animation | Rollover preference relates to the animated layer components.

LiveTabs

LiveTabs exist in the LiveTab menu. Like styles in the Styles palette, LiveTabs are actual files that reside in your LiveMotion folder. Unlike styles, however, LiveTabs function similarly to palettes in the sense that they allow you to apply specific effects to the objects on your composition from within the LiveTab.

> Align and Distribute
> Basic Color Swatch
> Grid Maker
> Keyboard Codes
> Slide Show Maker
> Star Tool
> TextFX
> Transform Tool
> Web Safe Color Picker

If you open any of the LiveTabs using the Open command, you'll notice that their interface is composed of rollover and text field objects created with the tools found in the toolbar. Beneath these objects, however, is a series of scripts created with LiveMotion's powerful scripting engine that allows you to trigger their effects on the composition once the LiveTab is launched from the LiveTab submenu.

In the following section, you'll not only learn how to use LiveTabs with the objects on your composition, but you'll also go over creating their interface. Since we haven't yet covered LiveMotion's scripting feature, we'll hold off on attaching scripts for the objects in your LiveTab's interface until the next module.

Use LiveTabs

The LiveTab menu consists of several LiveTabs, which Adobe bundled with your LiveMotion program. In addition, like styles, LiveTabs can be found on numerous sites (discussed in the last module of this book). To use them, all you need do is drop them into your LiveTabs folder in your LiveMotion folder on your hard drive.

To launch a LiveTab, simply select one from the LiveTabs submenu found under the Automation menu. Let's use the Align_Distribute LiveTab as an example. Create several objects on your composition and launch the Align_Distribute LiveTab. The buttons within this LiveTab are identical to the ones found in the Align submenu. Their functions are identical as well. Experiment using some of the alignment tools in this LiveTab to adjust the alignment of your object on your composition. Some of the LiveTabs that will be available to you while reading this book will vary from the version being used for this book.

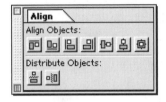

There are numerous varieties of LiveTabs that came with your LiveMotion program. Each of them is different. Try the Startool LiveTab, for example. The LiveTab prompts you to enter a specific dimension for a start, and by clicking the Create button, the LiveTab places a custom-made star shape on your composition. The StarTool LiveTab, unlike the previous one, prompts you to enter specific dimensions and allows you to create your custom star shape without the need of selecting an object. In that sense, LiveTabs differ from both styles and palettes. They offer numerous possibilities for customization.

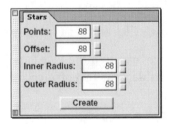

Create a LiveTab Interface

As mentioned earlier, LiveTabs are created in LiveMotion. When launched from the LiveTab menu, LiveMotion plays them as it would a composition triggered in the Preview mode. The main difference between the files that we've created thus far and previewed using the Preview mode is that these files didn't feature buttons that triggered scripting actions. However, creating an interface for LiveTab is quite simple. You've already mastered creating and working with Rollover buttons; therefore, you have the skills needed to create an interface for one. You will apply scripting functions in the next module.

10

When creating a LiveTab, you'll need to select the Live Tab option within the Export palette, as seen in Figure 10-5. Try to keep the dimensions of your LiveTab quite small so that when launched from the LiveTab menu, it takes up relatively little screen space. After creating your new LiveTab composition, you're free to construct any type of interface you desire, composed of every type of object you've learned about thus far. Also, try to stick to vector objects as they significantly reduce the file size of your LiveTabs. Launching LiveTabs that are big in file size will significantly slow down your LiveMotion program.

The following is a simple interface for a custom-made LiveTab, as shown in Figure 10-6. Even though this LiveTab won't have features that allow you to customize any of the objects on the composition, it gives you a better understanding of how LiveTabs work in LiveMotion. At the end of this module, you create a detailed LiveTab interface that you save and for the next module.

1. Begin by creating a new composition: 100×50.

2. In your Export palette, select the Live Tab option.

3. Create an ellipse and animate its scale component in the Timeline window.

4. Set your object as a MovieClip and set it to loop.

5. Save your file as My LiveTab.liv in the LiveTabs folder in your Automation folder, which resides inside your LiveMotion folder on your hard drive.

Figure 10-5　The Export palette LiveTab settings

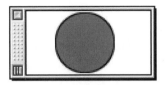

Figure 10-6   The LiveTab interface

Ask the Expert

Question: Why doesn't my LiveTab appear in the LiveTab menu?

Answer: There are two possible reasons for this. First, LiveTabs need to be placed in the LiveTab folder in your LiveMotion folder. Second, it's important to check the LiveTab option in the Export palette.

Question: I've noticed that LiveMotion slows down when loading specific LiveTabs. Why?

Answer: Some LiveTabs are huge. Therefore, it takes LiveMotion a while to display the LiveTab on some computers. If you're working on a Macintosh platform with an OS 9 version or below, try allocating more memory to LiveMotion in its Get Info box. If you're working in MacOS X or on a PC running Windows, consider purchasing more memory if the slowness becomes unbearable. Another major factor is the overall speed of your computer's processor. Be sure to carefully read LiveMotion's system requirements.

Question: Can I edit any of the LiveTabs in the LiveTab folder?

Answer: Yes, of course. In fact, I would strongly urge you to take a look at how they are composed. However, if you plan on modifying them and then saving your changes, remember to use the Save As command in order not to overwrite them. If you do happen to erase them, you may always reinstall them from your LiveMotion 2 CD.

10

In order to display your own LiveTab in the LiveTab menu, you need to save your LiveTab file in that folder. In order for LiveMotion to be able to recognize and display your new LiveTab in the LiveTabs submenu, you need to use the Refresh menu command. After you've done so, select My LiveTab from the LiveTabs submenu. When you launch your new LiveTab, you notice it plays the looping animation you created with your ellipse shape. The LiveTab is pretty much useless, since it doesn't actually trigger any effect on your composition; however, creating one should give you a better understanding of how LiveTabs are created in LiveMotion.

Project 10-2: Create a LiveTab Interface

Previously, you created a simple looping animation that plays when launched from the LiveTab menu. In the following project, we create a LiveTab interface to be further developed in the next module. The interface of your LiveTab will resemble that of a palette. We include information with the palette, noting its purpose for future users.

The interface will also feature a Rollover button, which we further develop in the next module. Its purpose will be to create a duplicate of a selected MovieClip on your composition. Take a look at Figure 10-7 for interface reference. Let's begin.

Step-by-Step

1. Create a new composition with the following dimensions: 165×75.

2. In the Export palette, select the LiveTab option.

3. Using the Pen tool, create a series of points that'll create the shape shown in Figure 10-8. Color the shape a light gray, similar to the color of the palettes.

4. Create a text object, type in **Duplicate**, set the font to Arial Bold, the size to 11, color it dark gray, and place it at the top portion of your shape.

5. Create another text object, type in **Select your MovieClip and click the button below**, set the font to Arial Bold, the size to 11, color it a medium gray, and place it below your previous text object.

6. Create a Rollover button that will ultimately trigger the action to duplicate a selected object on the composition when clicked. Create a rounded rectangle 59×14, and color it a dull yellow.

7. Create another text object, type in **Create**, keep the same font properties as before, and place it at the center of your rounded rectangle object.

Figure 10-7   Creating a LiveTab interface

8. Select both the create text object and the rounded rectangle object and choose Unite with Color from the Combine submenu in the Object menu.

9. In your Rollover palette, create an Over and a Down State for your new combined object.

10. Select the Over State of your rollover object, open your Timeline window, and double-click the MovieClip rollover object.

11. Select the rounded rectangle shape object in the Timeline window, go over to the Color palette, and choose a bright yellow color.

12. Save your file as **LiveTab Interface.liv** and place it in your LiveTab folder in your LiveMotion folder on your hard drive.

13. Execute the Refresh menu command found under the Automation menu and proceed by launching your new LiveTab from the LiveTabs submenu.

Project Summary

LiveMotion launches your newly completed LiveTab in a small window similar to a palette, as shown in Figure 10-8. The Rollover button is completely functional; however, since we haven't yet added a script to the button, it currently performs no action.

We revisit this file in the next module, and apply the appropriate scripting actions so that the button actually creates a duplicate of a selected MovieClip on the composition.

10

Summary

This module was an extension of the previous module in which you covered every aspect of animating your objects in LiveMotion. In this extension of

Figure 10-8   A launched LiveTab

you learned how to import and animate Adobe native files—specifically, how to animate their layers. You also covered some helpful features in LiveMotion, which allow you to be more productive and efficient while animating various objects on the composition. These features—copy and paste animation commands, and Make Alias commands—allow you to save valuable time and reduce a project's exported file size.

In addition, you covered the use of styles with your projects. You learned how they allow you to both save and apply various animations created on the composition. In conclusion, you covered the purpose of LiveTabs in the LiveTabs menu. Even though you weren't yet able to create LiveTabs capable of triggering various effects on the object on a new composition, you learned about their purpose—as well as how they're constructed.

The next module of this book will introduce you to the world of scripting. Scripting is a new addition to LiveMotion for those of you who've used the previous version. In the next module, you use scripts within your animations. You learn how to attach scripts to your objects, and even the timeline. In addition, you learn how to create LiveTabs, which contain scripting actions that allow you to perform specific effects on the objects on your composition.

Before proceeding, however, be sure to answer the questions in the Mastery Check in order to test your knowledge of the new additions to animation learned in this module.

✓ *Mastery Check*

1. Which of the following commands allow us to simultaneously break down and animate the individual layers of either a PSD or AI file?

   I. Convert Into | Objects

   II. Convert Into | Group of Objects

   III. Convert Into | Sequence

   IV. Convert Into | Sequence with Background

      A. I and III

      B. II and III

      C. II and IV

      D. III and IV

2. After breaking down the layers within a PSD file, how would we go about breaking down a subgroup of layers?

      A. Choose the Ungroup command from the Object menu.

      B. Choose Convert Into | Objects once more.

      C. Choose Uncombine from the Object menu.

      D. The action is not allowed.

3. From which Adobe application is LiveMotion's timeline based on?

      A. Adobe Illustrator

      B. Adobe Photoshop

      C. Adobe After Effects

      D. Adobe Premier

10

☑ Mastery Check

4. When using the _____ command to apply a copied animation from an animated object, the animation is created at the _____ of the selected object's duration bar.

A. Style / beginning

B. Paste Animation / location of the CTM

C. Paste Animation / beginning

D. Style / end

5. Which of the following will result from applying an animated style from the Style palette to an already animated object?

A. The previous animation will be replaced with the animation from the style.

B. The style's animation will follow the current animation of the object.

C. Both of the animations will merge into one.

D. LiveMotion will report an error.

6. By checking the Ignore Color of First Layer option, what will result when applying this style to a newly created text or shape object?

A. The object's color will change to the one set in the style.

B. The object's color will merge with the color set in the style.

C. The object's color will remain unchanged.

D. None of the above.

7. Which of the following benefits are true of using alias objects?

I. They significantly reduce the file size of your project when exporting to SWF format.

II. They significantly reduce the file size of your project when exporting to JPEG/GIF format.

III. They allow you to be more productive by reflecting changes made to the original object onto the alias.

☑ *Mastery Check*

      A. I only

      B. I and II

      C. I and III

      D. III only

8. Which of the following interfaces of LiveMotion do LiveTabs resemble?

      A. Styles

      B. Palettes

      C. Styles and palettes

      D. They are distinct from every interface of LiveMotion.

9. In order to create a LiveTab, you need to check the _____ check box when creating a new composition. In order for the LiveTab menu to display your newly created LiveTab, you'll need to first place it in the _____ and _____ LiveMotion.

      A. Make HTML / LiveTab / restart

      B. Make HTML / LiveMotion / shut down

      C. LiveTab / LiveMotion / shut down

      D. LiveTab / LiveTab / restart

10. Which new feature that we haven't yet covered is needed to create a function LiveTab that allows us to apply effects onto the objects in the composition?

      A. Sound

      B. Scripting

      C. Styles with scripts

      D. Behaviors

10

Module 11

Introduction to JavaScript

The Goals of this Module

- Understand how JavaScript is introduced inside HTML documents
- Learn how to create variables and assign them values
- Learn how to create functions
- Understand the variety of JavaScript operators
- Be able to create loops
- Be able to create objects

Understanding both how JavaScript is written and all the techniques used to write it is of vital importance before you read this module, where you learn about scripting in LiveMotion. JavaScript is most often found in the HTML pages you see while you browse your favorite sites on the Internet. Just as with HTML, you don't see the actual code when you view a page that contains JavaScript. Instead, if the JavaScript code is written correctly in the page, the code is executed in the manner it was programmed.

The following module will start your understanding of how JavaScripts are composed. You learn about different types of variables, functions, operators, if else statements, and objects. Understanding all these key elements of JavaScript can help you understand how to compose successful scripts in LiveMotion. This module contains projects to show you how some useful scripts are created. In addition, you have the Mastery Check, the Ask the Expert section, and the 1–Minute Drill to test your knowledge of the information in this module.

While reading, remember, to understand the JavaScript programming language completely and to have the capability to script in LiveMotion, you need to do some additional reading. The last section of this module provides the titles of some useful books for you to consider.

To use and test these JavaScript codes, you can either use a simple text editor such as Wordpad (PC) or Simple Text (Mac) or use a more advanced HTML editor, such as BareBones BBedit. In the next module, you learn how to use these scripts within the Script Editor, which is used to execute them.

Introduction to JavaScript

JavaScript is a programming language used within HTML files on the Web to create many of the effects you come across while browsing, such as button rollovers, popping windows, and many others. If you have any experience with other programming languages such as C, C++, and even Java, you'll find many similarities that will eventually enable you to learn the language more quickly.

Hint

Java and JavaScript are two completely different languages. Java relies on an applet file that's usually located in the same directory. JavaScript, on the other hand, relies on the content of the HTML file and uses it to create its effect.

JavaScript in HTML

JavaScripts in an HTML file are usually placed in its body tags. The following is an example of HTML code that contains a simple script:

```
<HTML>
<BODY>
<SCRIPT language="JavaScript">
document.write("This is my first JavaScript!");
</SCRIPT>
</BODY>
</HTML>
```

When writing a JavaScript in an HTML file, the user first needs to tell the browser that the following piece of code is a script. Therefore, the following piece of code from the previous, tells the file just that:

```
<SCRIPT language="JavaScript">
```

When the code ends in a script, the following tag is added at the end to let the HTML file know the script has ended:

```
</SCRIPT>
```

The actual code of the script is the part that appears between the <SCRIPT> and </SCRIPT tags:

```
document.write("This is my first JavaScript!");
```

The code tells the browser that displays the HTML file to write "This is my first JavaScript!" If you were to write this piece of code in a text editor, save it as a HTML file, and preview it in a browser, this is exactly what you'd see printed on the screen.

In addition, when many programmers write JavaScripts, they add little notes that enable them to access the parts of the code quickly. These notes are called *comments*. Because of the way these comments are written, the browser ignores them and continues executing the rest of the file. The following is an example of the HTML code previously used but, this time, with comments to the user:

```
<HTML>
<BODY>
```

11

```
<SCRIPT language="JavaScript">
// When writing a JavaScript in an HTML file, the user needs to first
// tell the browser that the following piece of code is a script
document.write("This is my first JavaScript!");
//When ending a script, the following tag is added at the end letting
//the HTML file know, that the script is ended
</SCRIPT>
</BODY>
</HTML>
```

The // tags in the previous script are ignored by the browser. Notice each line begins with //. Another way of adding comments is done as follows:

```
<HTML>
<BODY>
<SCRIPT language="JavaScript">
/*
When writing a JavaScript in an HTML file, the user needs to first
tell the browser that the following piece of code is a script
*/
document.write("This is my first JavaScript!");
/*
When ending a script, the following tag is added at the end letting
the HTML file know that the script is ended
*/
</SCRIPT>
</BODY>
</HTML>
```

1-Minute Drill

- What programs can you use to generate HTML files?
- Why do you need to write the <SCRIPT> heads before and after the script?

- To generate HTML files, any text editor application will do as long as the file extension is .HTML or .HTM.
- You need to write the <SCRIPT> heads before and after the script so the web browser can recognize which portion of the code belongs to HTML and which portion is part of the JavaScript code.

JavaScript Components

The following section lists some components of JavaScript. You learn how to use and apply variables; add functions that enable you to write scripts inside of scripts; learn about local and global variables, and understand their difference; and, finally, go over all the JavaScript operators used to calculate and compare variables.

Variables

Variables are used in JavaScript to hold or represent some type of value. You begin by assigning a name to your variable, such as *x*, and then assign a value to it, such as 3. The statement would read *x*=3. The *x* represents the name of your variable and the 3 represents the value of *x* at that given time. The value of your variable *x* will continue to be 3 until you write some type of command to changes that value.

```
x=3;
x=4;
```

Another way to write the following code is by using the var keyword before the variable name, as shown in the following, but this isn't necessary at this point. When you learn about functions, in the section "Functions" in this module, you'll need to add the keyword var before declaring a variable.

```
var x=3;
var x=4;
```

Because the variable *x* was assigned a different value at a later point in the script, its value is changed from 3 to 4.

Assigning values to variables enables you to control the values of other variables in the script. For example, the following code uses the value of one variable to solve another:

```
x=3.79382;
y=78.8734;
z=x+y;
```

11

Here, you see the script defines two variables and assigns them each a value. The third variable z simply says to add the value of x and y.

Variables can also consist of text names. Even though you could have written the last piece of code with // tags that would enable you to define what variable x and variable y stand for, you should use text words for variables, rather than single characters. So, if you want to create a new variable named bill—a value of 345.75—you would write it like this:

```
bill=345.75;
```

The following piece of code represents how you define and use text variables with text values:

```
mycomputer="iBook 500 576 MB RAM";
```

You can now use the variable in a sentence that will be printed in a web browser with the following code:

```
mycomputer="iBook 500 576 MB RAM";
document.write("My current setup is a "+mycomputer);
```

The text will display "My current setup is a iBook 500 576 MB RAM". The +mycomputer outputs the value and adds it on the line. However, because scripting in JavaScript enables you to assign different values to different variables, you can write the following code as follows:

```
intro="My current setup is an ";
mycomputer="iBook 500 ";
extra="with ";
ram="576 MB RAM.";
document.write(intro+mycomputer+extra+ram);
```

The following code is completely made up of variables. When executed in a browser, it appears like this: "My current setup is an iBook 500 with 576 MB RAM." Figure 11-1 illustrates how a browser would display this code when it's appropriately embedded in an HTML file.

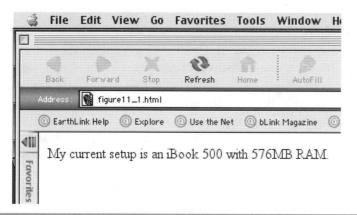

Figure 11-1 Document.write Script executed in a browser

Ask the Expert

Question: Do I always need to use the var keyword when I introduce a new variable in a script?

Answer: No, using the var keyword when you introduce a new variable in a script is optional. Use var when you want to declare a local variable, such as in a function, which you learn about next.

Question: What's the purpose of the ; that follows almost every line in JavaScript?

Answer: The browser reading the script would read each line individually. However, if the ; keys weren't there, the browser would read the statement like so:

```
test1=4;
test2=7;
```

JavaScript would read that line as test1=4test2=7, regardless of whether or not these two variables are defined on separate lines.

11

Functions

Functions in JavaScript are basically smaller scripts within the overall script. Using functions enables you to access them at any point of the script, without needing to rewrite the code within them. Functions provide you with a way to organize parts of the script, as well as give the script itself tasks that must be accomplished within the function. The bigger picture of such a feature is it enables you to create custom effects by having the script execute parts of the function one way and other effects by having the function execute a task another way.

As with variables, functions first need to be declared, and then they need to be defined with some type of code within it. The following is an example of how the beginning and the end of the function are structured in JavaScript:

```
function getamount()
{
//your code goes here
}
```

This function's name is getamount, which is followed by the opening bracket on the next line. The following line contains a code and the last line ends with a close bracket. During the script execution, the code inside the { and the } is executed for the function getamount.

While creating functions such as the following one, try to give them meaningful names that'll enable you to recognize them easily:

```
function print_in_bold()
{
document.write("<B>Hello</B>");
}
```

By giving this function the name print_in_bold, you can easily understand the statement will be printed in boldface. The <B> and the </B> tags inside the document.write code tell the browser to print the statement "Hello" in boldface.

Functions also enable you to bring in variables that were defined in parts outside the function. These variables are placed between the () parentheses that appear after the name of the function. These variables are known as *parameters*. Here's an example of two parameters used. Remember, these variables need to be defined as variables before being entered as parameters to the function. At this point, you need to use the var keyword before the variable name at all times:

```
function getamount (numApples, numBananas) {
    document.write("I bought " + numApples + " apples and " +
numBananas + " bananas.");
}
myApples = 4;
myBananas = 7;
getAmount(myApples, myBananas);
```

When executed, the statement will read: I bought 4 apples and 7 bananas. You defined the variables outside the function, and then used them as parameters inside the function without needing to define them again to use their values in the statement. When using multiple parameters in a function, remember to separate them with commas without any spaces. You can use any number of parameters in a function, as long as you predefine them. Remember, you can also define new variables inside the function.

Functions also enable you to return values generated by the script inside the function to be used in the script outside the function. This feature is known as a *Return statement*. Look at the following script, which uses variables defined within its function and ends by returning a value to be used outside the function:

```
function add_text()
{
var text1="Functions are ";
var text2="easy!";
var added_text=text1+text2;
return added_text;
}
```

The last defined variable in the function—added_text—combines the two values together. The Return statement gathers this value and holds it until it's called on outside the function.

At this point, a good idea is to get a sense of how functions are called in JavaScript. But, before explaining how they're called, it's important to understand when and where to place a function, as well as when and where to call it. You can organize your functions and the code that calls on them in several ways. The main rule, of course, is first to define your functions, and then place the code that calls on them, not the other way around. You can define the function in the body tags of your HTML, and then create a new script in the head tags of the HTML file that will call on the function located in the head tags. You can also simply place the function and the code that calls it on top of one another in the same script.

11

When you begin using some of the JavaScript techniques in LiveMotion's Script Editor, you can place the function and the code that calls on them on specific keyframes along the timeline.

To call a function in JavaScript, all you need to do is write the name of the function in your script. The following is an example of a function, followed by a code that calls for it:

```
Function write_text()
{
document.write("Hello");
}
write_text();
```

The last statement executes the contents of the function. As explained earlier, you can also split this script into two parts in which the function would be contained in the HTML's head tags and the code that calls it would be in the HTML BODY tags. In LiveMotion, you can create a function script on one keyframe, and then create the code that calls it on the Over State of a button. This would enable you to trigger the event by moving over this button. I'm sure you're eager to jump right to scripting now, but first, you need to learn about several other features of JavaScript.

1-Minute Drill

● What are the () set to hold in a function?

● Can the () be left empty or do they always need to contain parameters within them?

Local and Global Variables

Global variables are the variables created outside a function and local variables are those created within a function. When you assign new values to your global variables inside a function, and then call for the result of the redefined value, you need to add var before assigning a new value to the variable inside the function. What this does is change only the local variable in the function and

---

● The () are set to hold parameters in a function.
● If you're not planning on calling up parameters in your function, they can be left empty, like so: (). If you plan to include two or more parameters within the parentheses, you must separate them by a comma.

in no way changes the value of the global variable. The following code listings are two examples. Notice the huge difference the var keyword makes in these two examples:

The incorrect way:

```
var mycomputer=iBook 500";
function my_old_computer()
{
mycomputer="G3 Tower";
document.write("My old computer was a "+mycomputer);
}
my_old_computer();
document.write("My new computer is an "+mycomputer);
//When executed the following statement will read as so:
//My old computer was a G3 Tower
//My new computer is an G3 Tower
```

The correct way:

```
var mycomputer=iBook 500";
function my_old_computer()
{
var mycomputer="G3 Tower";
document.write("My old computer was a "+mycomputer);
}
my_old_computer();
document.write("My new computer is an "+mycomputer);
//When executed the following statement will read as so:
//My old computer was a G3 Tower
//My new computer is an iBook 500
```

The var keyword inside the function makes all the difference. It enables you to change only the variable mycomputer locally, yet retain its value globally through out the script. Remember, though,if you call on this function in the future. You'll get the local values of the variable and not the global values defined outside the function.

Another way of being certain your global variable isn't changed by a function is to use a variable as a function parameter, and then assign a value to the global variable outside the function. The following script—consisting of a function and a global variable—assigns a new variable in its function and sets it to equal the value of the global variable defined outside of the function. Doing so enables you to retain the value of the global variable and have only the value of the new

11

variable inside the function change its value. The code would look like the following:

```
function my_computer(model)
{
        document.write("My old computer was a " + model};
}
simonscomputer = "iBook500";
my_computer(simonscoumpter);
```

When executed, the variable model inside the function gathers the value of the variable simoncompter outside the function, it then goes back into the function, sets a command that tells the browser to display the sentence "My old computer was a iBook 500," and then executes with the last command of the script that triggers the function.

Look at the previous and the following examples of dealing with global and local variables. Understanding how JavaScript treats them as they're executed when the script is run is important.

Operators

At this point, you might be wondering what is the purpose of assigning values to a function. After all, the purpose of scripting in LiveMotion using JavaScript techniques is to have the script generate some type of interactivity within the file. First, the values you assign to functions aren't permanent. For instance, you have the capability to change these values at a later point in the script. By changing values, you can assign special commands that perform some type of action when the value of a variable is x, and another when the value is different from that. The following code adds 1 to the already-defined variable:

```
var amount=500;
Amount=amount+1;
```

When executed, the value of variable amount changes from 500 to 501. JavaScript enables you to use several operators, such as the one you see in the previous script, in which it changes the variable amount to equal itself +1.

Look at Table 11-1, which lists all the operators JavaScript enables you to use.

You can use these operators at any stage of the script either to change or compare the values of your variables. In the case of comparing variables, you

Operator	Definition	Example
+	Adds two or more values.	var amount=7+3 //value is 10
-	Subtracts one value from another.	var amount=7-3 //value is 4
*	Multiplies two or more values together.	var amount=7*3 //value is 21
/	Divides one value by the other.	var amount=8/2 //amount is 4
%	Displays the remainder of the division between one value and the other.	var amount=8%2 //amount is 0
=	Assigns the value to the right of the operator to the variable on the left.	var amount=20 //new value is 20

+=	Adds the value to the right of the operator to the value of the variable itself, and then assigns a new value to the variable.	var amount=20
		var amount+=5
		//or
		var amount =
		amount + 5
		//new value is 25

-=	Subtracts the value to the right of the operator from the variable on the left, and then assigns a new value to the variable.	var amount=20 var amount-=5 //new value is 15
*=	Multiplies the value to the right of the operator by the variable on the left, and then assigns a new value to the variable.	var amount=20 var amount*=2 //new value is 40
/=	Divides the value of the variable by the value to the right of the operator.	var amount=20 var amount/=5 //new value is 4
%=	Divides the value of the variable by the value to the right side of the operator, and then assigns the integer remainder of the division and assigns it to the variable.	var amount =20 var amount%=5 //new value is 0
==	Returns true if the value to the left operator is equal to the one on the right.	var 10==5 //False
!=	Returns true if the value to the left operator is not equal to the one on the right.	var 10!=5 //True
>	Returns true if the value to the left operator is greater than the one on the right.	var 10>5 //True
<	Returns true if the value to the left operator is less than the one on the right.	var 10<10 //False

11

Table 11-1   JavaScript Operators Definitions and Examples

Operator	Definition	Example
>=	Returns true if the value to the left operator is greater than or equal to the one on the right.	var 10>=5 //True
<=	Returns true if the value to the left operator is less than or equal to the one on the right.	var 5<=5 //True
++	Adds a value of 1 to the variable.	var 5++ //new value is 6
--	Subtracts a value of 1 from the variable.	var 5-- //new value is 4

Table 11-1 JavaScript Operators Definitions and Examples *(continued)*

can use *If Else statements,* which enable you to perform specific functions of the script if a statement is true and another if the statement is false. If Else statements are discussed in the next section.

Ask the Expert

Question: What is the difference between the = JavaScript operator and the == operator?

Answer: Both of the = JavaScript operator and the == operator are easily confused, but it's important to note they aren't the same. The = operator is used only when assigning values to variables. The == operator compares the two values on each side and claims they're true.

Question: Can I use parentheses to calculate more than two values?

Answer: Yes, you can use parentheses to calculate more than two values. You need to use parentheses as shown in this example: y=(4+2)-3.

Question: Can I set variables to equal each other?

Answer: Yes, you can set variables to equal each other. Here's an example:

```
x=5;
y=x:
//variable y now equals 5
```

Project 11-1: Create a Function

Earlier, you learned how to use a combination of variables and functions to create scripts within scripts, which enables you not only to be organized, but also to have a variable's values available to you without having to rewrite that part of the script. The following project contains a simple function, which transfers the values of its variable to a statement that gets printed in the document's HTML.

Before proceeding, though, you'll need an HTML editor, such as Macromedia Dreamweaver, Adobe GoLive, or even a simple text editing application such as Text Edit (Mac) or Note Pad (Windows). Do not use Microsoft Word, as it will incorrectly modify the code as you're typing. Enter all the appropriate tags needed to display the document successfully in a web browser. The file should be saved as yourname.HTML. The following is an example of how an HTML file should be constructed.

```
<HTML>
<HEAD>
<TITLE>Project 11-1 Create a Function</TITLE>
</HEAD>
<BODY>
</BODY>
</HTML>
```

Step-by-Step

1. Begin by duplicating the HTML code previously mentioned.

2. Type in the following code between your <BODY> and </BODY> tags (remember to use proper <SCRIPT> tags before and after the script):

```
function get_these_lines(line1,line2)
{
window.alert("I have an "+line1+" and its a "+line2);
}
get_these_lines("ibook","Macintosh");
```

3. Save your file as Project11_1.HTML, place it in your LiveMotion Projects folder, and preview it in a web browser.

4. Your entire piece of code should look like this:

```
<HTML>
<HEAD>
<TITLE>Project 11-1 Create a Function</TITLE>
```

11

```
</HEAD>
<BODY>
<SCRIPT language="JavaScript">
function get_these_lines(line1,line2)
{
window.alert("I have an "+line1+" and it is a "+line2);
}
get_these_lines("iBook","Macintosh");
</SCRIPT>
</BODY>
</HTML>
```

Project Summary

When written properly, the JavaScript code written should prompt an alert box in the web browser in which you're viewing the file with the following statement: "I have an iBook and it is a Macintosh," as shown in Figure 11-2.

If you noticed, the values for the variables in the function were defined outside the function with the following code:

```
get_thse_lines("iBook","Macintosh");
```

The function then uses these values to create the alert text box you see when you preview the file with the following piece of code:

```
window.alert("I have an "+line1+" and it is a "+line2);.
```

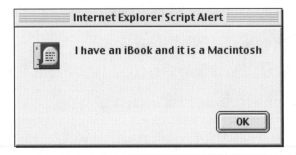

Figure 11-2   Simple function script executed in a browser

Experiment with the code inside. For example, try using more variables or change the way the variables appear. Remember always to use proper punctuation and frequently check your code to see if all the keywords and tags are in place.

Additional JavaScript Expressions

In the following section, you learn about creating an If Else statement block that allows the script to generate a piece of code based on the true or false result of a statement. Understanding how If Else statement blocks are composed allows your scripts to be more versatile by having choices about which action is generated by the script itself. You also learn about creating loops. *Loops* enable you to repeat a certain task several times, without having to type in that specific task the number of times you want it to appear. In addition, the following section also discusses using objects in your scripts. *Objects* enable you to organize data and the data within objects is organized with properties. Using objects within your scripts lets you quickly access properties that correspond to that particular object.

At the end of this module, you learn about some essential additional reading materials needed for you to understand completely how JavaScripts are composed. Because this book only dedicates one of its modules to understanding how JavaScript is written, many additional modules would be needed to cover all the components and features of this programming language.

If Else Statement Blocks

The last seven operators in Table 11-1 of the previous section will be discussed in the following section. As discussed earlier, these operators enable you to write If Else statements. The following is an example:

```
var amount=3;
if (amount==3)
{
window.alert("You win!");
}
else
{
window.alert("You lose!");
}
```

11

In the previous code, the script first creates a value for the variable amount, it then runs an If Else statement by checking to see if the statement in the parentheses (amount==3) is true. The other part of this If Else statement creates a command to be executed if the statement in the parentheses is false. Because the statement is true, the script will display "You win!" in the browser. The rest of the script won't be executed because no instance occurs in the script in which the statement is false.

As you now know, If Else statements are composed of two blocks. The first block is the If block and the second block is the Else block. If Else statements can get even more complex by being nested within one another. For example, you can nest an additional If Else statement inside one of the blocks. The following examples show you how to do that:

```
var havemacintosh="true";
var havecomputer="true";
if (havecomputer=="true")
{
       if (havemacintosh=="true")
       {
       window.alert("I have a Macintosh computer");
       }
       else
       {
       window.alert("I don't have a Macintosh computer");
       }
}
else
{
window.alert("I don't have a computer");
}
```

Notice the indentation of the nested If Else statement inside the If block of the outside If Else statement. This was done to see the code better. At the beginning of the script, two variables are introduced and set to "true." The If Else statement then asks if the havecomputer variable is "true." Because it is true, the script goes on to execute to the nested If Else statement of the If block. If the statement wasn't true, the script would ignore the contents of the nested If statement and go on to execute the Else statement, which would launch an alert window with "I don't have a computer." Inside the If block, the script once again has to choose either to launch the If code or the Else code. Because the variable in that statement is true, however, the script will launch an alert box with the statement "I have a Macintosh Computer," as seen in Figure 11-3.

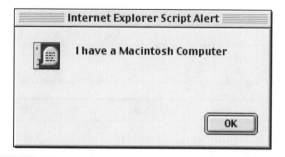

Figure 11-3 Condition statement script executed in a browser

The best way to read an If Else statement is to start from the outside and move toward the middle. After all, the outside If Else statement in the previous example decided whether to run the If Else statement nested in the If block.

1-Minute Drill

● If a statement in the If block isn't true, which portion of the script gets executed?

● Are you limited to nesting only additional If Else statements in the If block?

Create Loops

Creating loops in JavaScript requires you to use statements that derive the number of times a script will loop. The following is an example of a loop structure, which is shown executed successfully in Figure 11-4.

```
for (count=1;count<5;count++)
{
document.write("I'm being looped!<BR>");
}
```

11

Look closely at what this loop is doing. You use the for keyword every time you begin a loop. As with If Else statements, the loop contains a condition inside parentheses, and is followed by the open and close curly braces, which contain a piece of code that will execute a specific number of times, based on

---

● The code that appears in the Else statement script gets executed if a statement in the If block isn't true.

● No, you aren't limited to nesting only additional If Else statements in the If block. You can also add them into the Else block of the If Else statement.

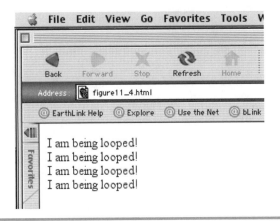

Figure 11-4   Loop script executed in a browser

that condition. Notice the <BR> tag inside the code. This code is part of HTML. It simply tells the browser to skip any repetitive code on the next line. Now, look more closely at the condition to understand how many times the statement will loop. The first statement inside the condition creates a variable named count and sets its value equal to 1. The next statement inside the condition creates a rule that the loop will stop looping when the value of the variable count is no longer less than 5. The final statement of this condition sets the rate at which the variable increases. In this case, the variable count increases by a value of 1. Based on this condition, the sentence "I'm being looped!" is written out—one on top of the other—because of the <BR> tag, which causes the browser to make a carriage return. When the value of the variable reaches 5, it will prove false to the statement count<5 inside the condition and the script ends, leaving you with the following:

```
I'm being looped!
I'm being looped!
I'm being looped!
I'm being looped!
```

If you want to nest the value of your variable as it's being looped, you can also do this. Here's an example:

```
for (count=1;count<5;count++)
{
document.write(count + ". I am being looped!<BR>")
}
```

The only difference between this code and the previous code is the count+. code. What this does is assign a value of the variable count to each piece of the line the loop produces, as shown in Figure 11-5.

Objects

As discussed earlier, objects enable you to organize some commonly used variables. As you learn in the next module, LiveMotion has its own predefined objects. All you have to do is place them in your scripts in the Script Editor. All of this is explained in detail in Module 12.

In JavaScript, objects are created from similar variables. The following is an example of an object for the variable computer, which contains its own variables, known as parameters, which are RAM, hard_drive, and processor:

```
var computer = new Object ();
computer.RAM = 256;
computer.hardDrive = 80;
computer.processor = "P4"
```

What you see here is the object named computer taking in three parameters: RAM, hard_drive, and processor. Objects are extremely useful in scripting. Your final project for this module provides you with the steps needed to create a script that first creates a constructor function, followed by an instance, and then instructs the browser to use the value in a sentence.

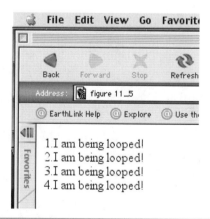

| **Figure 11-5** | Another loop script executed in a browser |

11

Reading Requirements for Beginners

As mentioned in the beginning of this module, the following short JavaScript tutorial is in no way complete. To prepare fully for the scripting involved in LiveMotion's Script Editor, you need to brush up on your JavaScript skills with some additional reading. Consider looking at, *JavaScript: A Beginner's Guide,* by John Pollock (ISBN: 0-07-213140-3, McGraw Hill/Osborne, 2001). Another book I highly recommend is *ActionScript: The Definitive Guide* by Colin Moock. Also, you might want to look at some ActionScript books written for Macromedia Flash. *ActionScript* is what LiveMotion uses to create scripts that use JavaScripts. As you soon learn in the next module, many of the rules for writing JavaScript codes in LiveMotion are bent. For example, introducing a JavaScript with the following code—<SCRIPT language="JavaScript">—is no longer needed.

Ask the Expert

Question: How can I successfully combine a loop with an If Else statement?

Answer: The following is an example of how to combine a loop successfully with an If Else statement:

```
for (counter=1;counter<11;counter++)
{
if (counter==5)
  {
  document.write("This is the halfway point for the loop!<BR>")
  }
  else
  {
  document.write("I'm being looped!<BR>")
  }
}
```

The example used a loop to generate a different statement when the value of the variable counter reaches 5. Before and after reaching 5, the counter variable continues to loop until it ends, when it reaches a value of 11.

Project 11-2: Create and Use Objects

You've learned so far that as functions, objects enable you to organize the content of your scripts. With objects, you can call out specific variable values within them and use them to produce some type of a response when they're previewed in a browser. The following is a simple example of an object constructor function and an instance that calls up its values. This project is composed of two scripts. The first script is composed of the object constructor function and its instance. The second script is placed in the HTML's BODY tags and provides the browser with instructions needed to display the variables of the object in two different sentence structures.

Step-by-Step

1. Begin by creating your first script in the HTML's <HEAD> tags. Type in the following script (as in the previous project, remember to include proper <SCRIPT> tags at the beginning and the end of the script):

```
var new_drawing = [ trees:"green", sky:"blue", house:"brick" }
var old_drawing = { trees:"dark-green", sky:"light-blue", house:"wooden"
```

2. Now that you've created your object constructor function and its instance, let's create a script that will call some of the object's values in a sentence structure to be displayed when the HTML is loaded in a web browser. Type in the following code between the <body> tags of your HTML:

```
document.write ("My old drawing contained "+old_drawing.trees+" trees,
"+old_drawing.sky+" sky, and "+old_drawing.house+" house.<BR>");
document.write("My new drawing contains "+new_drawing.trees+" trees,
"+new_drawing.sky+" sky, and "+new_drawing.house+" house.<BR>");
```

3. Wrap up and save your file as Project11_2.HTML, place it in your LiveMotion Projects folder, and preview it in a web browser.

4. The entire piece of code in your HTML document should look like the following:

```
<HTML>
<HEAD>
<TITLE>Project 11-2 Create and Use Objects</TITLE>
<SCRIPT language="JavaScript">
var new_drawing = { trees:"green", sky:"blue", house:"brick" }
var old_drawing = { trees:"dark-green", sky:"light-blue", house:"wooden"
}
</SCRIPT>
</HEAD>
```

11

```
<BODY>
<SCRIPT language="JavaScript">
document.write("My old drawing contained "+old_drawing.trees+" trees,
"+old_drawing.sky+" sky, and "+old_drawing.house+" house.<BR>");
document.write("My new drawing contains "+new_drawing.trees+" trees,
"+new_drawing.sky+" sky, and "+new_drawing.house+" house.<BR>");
</SCRIPT>
</BODY>
</HTML>
```

Project Summary

Congratulations! You've just created an object with which you could send out specific values to variables used to produce two different types of sentence structures. Figure 11-6 shows what your browser should display when previewing your HTML file in a web browser. Here's the rundown of the steps. In the first step, you created two objects: new_drawing and old_drawing. Both of these objects have these attributes: tree, sky, and house. You assigned the attributes to the objects using a literal syntax. This is called an *object literal,* which assigns property/value pairs to the attributes in a colon-separated list. So, this object literal

```
var new_drawing = { trees:"green", sky:"blue", house:"brick" }
```

could also have been written like this:

```
var new_drawing = new Object();
new_drawing.trees = "green";
new_drawing.sky = "blue";
new_drawing.house = "brick";
```

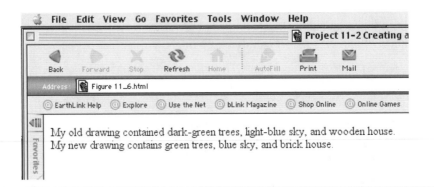

Figure 11-6   JavaScript object script executed in a browser

As you can see, the literal syntax does the same thing, but requires less typing. And less typing is better than more typing. In the final step, you used document.write to display the text and object attribute values.

Before going on to the Mastery Check, try reprogramming some of the code. For example, try adding another instance, which contains different adjectives of the variables inside the object. Remember to add another sentence structure in the second script that will call up these values.

Summary

I hope this module helped to sharpen your JavaScript skills. Even though you've only learned the basics of creating script with JavaScript, you should feel more comfortable in the scripting environment, which is introduced in the next module. Combining both a full introduction to JavaScripting and a LiveMotion 2 tutorial would make this book over 1,000 pages, but the information provided in this module should jumpstart your understanding of the scripting environment in which you'll soon start working.

Before proceeding to the next module, be sure to complete the Mastery Check, as well as review the 1-Minute Drills and the Ask the Expert sections, which quiz you on the terms and features of JavaScript you learned in this module.

As mentioned earlier, the next module covers the scripting environment used in LiveMotion to generate custom animation effects on your objects, the composition, and the timeline. In addition, for those of you who've used behaviors in the previous version of LiveMotion, you'll learn how to access them easily within the scripting environment and how to use them as you did before. For those of you new to the LiveMotion community, behaviors were used as a substitute for the scripting environment. You'll be glad to know that while behaviors are no longer available in the current version of the program, they're new and improved, and more versatile as scriptable commands in LiveMotion's scripting environment.

11

✓ *Mastery Check*

1. Which of the following codes represents the appropriate tags for introducing JavaScript to HTML?

A. <script>
   </script>

B. <script language="JavaScript">
   </script>

C. <SCRIPT language=JavaScript>
   </SCRIPT>

D. All of the above

2. Which of the following statements is/are true?

I. Scripts can only be placed in the HTML's <BODY> tags

II. Scripts can only be placed in the HTML's <HEAD> tags

III. More than one script can exist in a single HTML page

   A. I and III

   B. III

   C. II

   D. I and II

3. What is the significance of variables in JavaScript?

   A. They're capable of containing numeric values

   B. They're capable of containing alphanumeric values

   C. They're used by functions and objects

   D. All of the above

☑Mastery Check

4. _____ variables are the variables created outside a function and _____ variables are created within a function.

   A. Local/global

   B. Global/local

   C. Function/object

   D. Function/loop

5. The ____ JavaScript operator adds the value to the right of the operator to the one on the left. The _____ JavaScript operator subtracts the value to the right of the operator from the one on the left and sets the variable to that amount.

   A. +/+=

   B. +/-

   C. +/+=

   D. +/-=

6. Which of the following is the appropriate method of writing a function?

   A. function test()
   ```
       {
       //code here;
       }
   ```

   B. function test()
   ```
       {
       //code here
       }
   ```

   C. function test;
   ```
       {
       //code here;
       }
   ```

   D. function test()
   ```
           //code here;
           }
   ```

11

✓ Mastery Check

7. Which of the following statements is true about If Else statements?

I. They enable you to execute different codes depending on the true or false result of their condition

II. They can be nested within each other

III. They use If The' and Else Then keywords to generate different parts of a code set in each of these blocks

A. I

B. I and II

C. I and III

D. III

8. Which of the following keywords is used to create a loop?

A. loop

B. for

C. set

D. amount

9. In the following example of a condition in a loop (count=1;count<5;count+=2), what is the purpose of the last variable: count+=1?

A. It sets the variable's value to 2

B. It represents the rate at which the loop will run

C. It sets a condition that the loop will loop at least once

D. It sets a condition that the loop must loop two or more times

☑ Mastery Check

10. Which term is used to describe the initial part of an object in which you introduce various parameters and assign them values?

A. Instance parameter

B. Instance

C. Constructor function

D. Construction parameter

Part 3

Web and Multimedia Design

Module 12

Scripting in LiveMotion

The Goals of this Module

- Understand LiveMotion's Script Editor
- Learn how to add scripts to Rollover States
- Learn how to add scripts to the Event Handlers
- Learn how to script the timeline

S cripting was one of the most highly requested features for LiveMotion by its community of users back when the first version was released a few years ago. Many users were reluctant to give up their copies of Macromedia's Flash, which already had these powerful scripting capabilities that let users create interactive animation effects, as well as the capability for its exported files to interact with other files, such as databases. The only advantage of LiveMotion over Flash was its incredible ease of use, plus Adobe's reputation for creating the world's most widely used applications in the graphic design and multimedia fields. Adobe read all your feature requests posted on the Forum pages on its web site and implemented many of them into the current version—a powerful, user-friendly scripting engine is one of its main features.

Scripting is a way for an exported file in LiveMotion to interact with the objects inside of it, as well as pull information from outside sources, such as databases. LiveMotion's scripting is written in the form of a series of ActionScripts, which are supported by all web browsers. Although writing scripts in LiveMotion does require some of knowledge of how JavaScripts are written, the interface of the *Script Editor,* which is used to write scripts in LiveMotion, is extremely user-friendly and enables you to access all the commands available while scripting. Because you already learned some of the JavaScript basics, you'll be able to jumpstart directly into LiveMotion's interface of its powerful Script Editor, since ActionScripting is based on the fundamentals of JavaScript.

By understanding how to use the interface of the Script Editor explained in this module, you learn how to add scripts to the project's Handlers, Rollover Object's States, as well as how to add scripts to the timeline using labels. You learn how to place these labels on your timeline for your scripts created in the Script Editor to point your exported Flash animations easily to a specific Time Interval. In addition, the use of labels enables you to execute specific scripts located along different portions of the timeline.

Access the Script Editor

You have many convenient ways to access the Script Editor, which you'll use to write script for both your objects and the timeline. Figure 12-1 displays its interface. If you're working with MovieClip Object States, for example, you can easily access the Editor by clicking the Edit State Script Icon button at the bottom of your Rollover palette, relative to the state you're planning on adding the script to. The Script Editor would take you directly to that State in its Editor and enable you to place your script in its appropriate location.

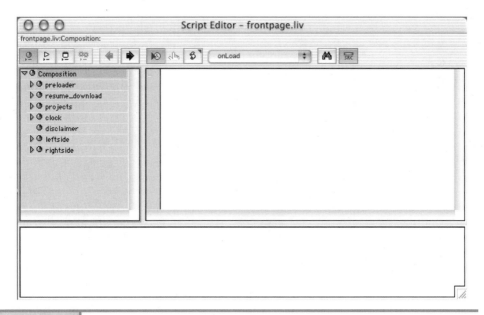

Figure 12-1 The Script Editor

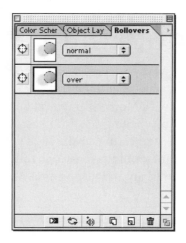

On the other hand, if you want to add a script to a specific Time Interval on the timeline, or even a keyframe, you can easily do so by first positioning your CTM (Current Time Marker) to that Time Interval/keyframe, and then clicking the Script Icon button in the Timeline window. As before, LiveMotion would take you directly to the location inside the Script Editor where you can write a script for that Time Interval or keyframe.

You like to familiarize yourself with the interface of the Script Editor first, and then discuss all of the features inside where you'll add scripts to the timeline, Handlers, and your objects. The easiest way to access the Script Editor—as well as go to its default location—is to launch it from the Script menu, by selecting Script Editor.

Script Editor Interface

After launching the Script Editor from the Script menu in LiveMotion, you'll be greeted by the Script Editor's interface which is composed of three windows

Ask the Expert

Question: Do I have to close the Script Editor every time I want to select another object to write a script for?

Answer: No need for that. You can simply move the Script Editor to the site, select the object on your composition you want to work with, and the Script Editor will automatically update itself.

Question: Why do scripts appear on the Timeline window when I didn't enter any into the Script Editor after creating them?

Answer: Every time you create a script on your timeline, a Script icon appears. In a way, LiveMotion treats the script as a placeholder and enables you to return to it at a later point.

Question: Can I delete these Script icons?

Answer: Of course. Do so just as you've done with keyframes. Simply select the Script icon and click the DELETE key on your keyboard.

and a menu bar at the top filled with various buttons as shown in Figure 12-1. The buttons in the menu bar help us control the left and the right side windows. The bottom window provides us with brief descriptions of objects selected in the left window. If you're confused at this point, don't worry. We'll tackle these different portions of the interface independently while explaining how they interact with one another.

Handlers, State, and Keyframe Scripts

As just explained, the menu bar in the Script Editor provides us with several buttons that trigger both the left side window as well as triggering the different types of scripting techniques entered in the right side window. Lets get started by first going over the buttons located at the center of the top menu bar. By default, your Script Editor displays the location in which you're able to create Handler Scripts. You'll notice that the Handler Scripts button is pressed in. Handler scripts will allow you to create scripts for various actions performed by either you, or by your exported file. For example, we can create a script for the OnEnterFrame Handler, which would allow us to create some type of actions once the CTM in your Timeline reached a specific Time Interval on your

Composition. The drop down menu, just a few buttons ahead of your Handler Scripts button allows you to select a specific Handler from the list and create a script for it. Notice that the OnEnterFrame Handler is just one of many which are available to you. Once a Handler is selected, you're ready to start typing a script for that Handler in the right side window.

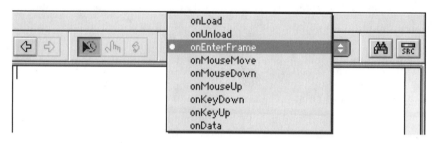

Object and the Composition are both capable of containing Handler scripts. In order to create a Handler Script for the Composition, make sure that no object is selected on your Composition and proceed to the Script Editor. However, if an object is selected, the Handler Script entered in the Script Editor, will reflect on only that object alone.

The button to the right of the Handler Script button is the State Script button. At the present time, the button might be grayed out and inaccessible depending on whether or not your Composition contains any rollover objects. After all, creating a script for a rollover objects does require the rollover object to exist on the Composition. Use the techniques learned in Module 6 to create a simple rollover on your Composition with four states: Normal, Over, Down, and Out. Make sure to alter each state in order for each one to differentiate from one another. When you're finished, make sure that your rollover is selected and go back to the Script Editor. The State Script button should now be accessible; click on it. Once clicked, the drop down menu to the right updates and allows you to jump right to the State that you wish to create a script for.

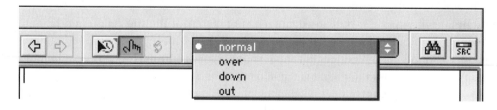

Note

When working with State scripts, the rollover button for which you're creating the script must be selected before proceeding to the Script Editor. If no rollover object is selected, the State script button in the Script editor will remain grayed out.

Previously we've mentioned that an easy way to access this specific location in the Script Editor is to click on the Edit Script State icon button in your Rollover palette, relative to which state you plan on scripting. As with Handler Scripts, the area in which you'll type in scripts for the States of your button takes place in the right side window. Ways of creating script for your rollover object's states will be explained in just a bit.

The last button in this category, just to the left of the State Script button is the Keyframe Script button. The button is most likely grayed out because your current Timeline doesn't contain any Keyframe Scripts. Previously we mentioned that an easy way to access this location in the Script Editor is to position your CTM in the Timeline to the Time Interval that you wish to create a script for and click on the script icon button in the Timeline window. Doing so, we'll automatically launch you into the appropriate location in the Script Editor at which you'll be able to write a script for. You'll now notice that the drop down menu to the right of the button now displays a specific time at which you've created your first Keyframe Script. If you create any additional keyframes in the future, all of them will be accessible from that drop down menu by simply selecting them.

As with Handler Scripts and State Scripts, both the Composition as well as MovieClip objects, are capable of containing their own Keyframe scripts. It's all relative to in which location you place the Script in as well as whether or not a MovieClip Object is selected or not. As with the other two types of scripting explained earlier, ways of creating Timeline scripts will be explained in the second section of this Module.

12

The arrow button next to the three buttons that we've just gone over allow you to travel from script to script. For example, lets say that we've just created a script for an object's Over State and proceeded to create another script by going to the Keyframe Script section and create a script at a specific Time Interval. To easily get back to the location in which we've created our previous script, we can simply use the back button. Basically, the actions of these buttons resemble those found in a browser, which allow you to travel to the pages that you've previously visited as well as go to the pages that you were on prior to hitting the back button. These two buttons are there as a convenience.

The buttons to the right are some other useful buttons in the Script Editor. The first button is the Find button and it allows you to find and/or replace any portion of a script entered in any location of your Script Editor. Figure 12-2 illustrates the window that pops up when the button is triggered. The second button, the Syntax Highlighting button located next to the Find button, allows you to trigger the use of color code in your scripts on and off. Turning this feature on will allow LiveMotion to color code each piece of the script in the scripting section of the Script Editor. If you choose to turn it off, the script will resume a black text. I'd strongly suggest leaving this feature on. Working on complicated scripts can be overwhelming in the process of not only writing an effective script, but also keeping the syntax and proper punctuation in tact. Turning the Syntax Highlight button on will allow you to more easily pinpoint the portions of your script in which perhaps a bracket or a colon might be missing.

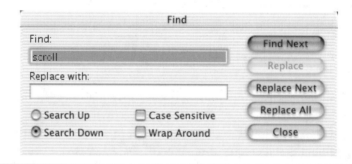

Figure 12-2 Find and Syntax Highlighting Buttons

1-Minute Drill

- What is an easy way to access the Script Editor when creating State Scripts?
- Once inside the Script Editor, how would you go about switching between the three different types of Player Scripts?

The Library Window

In order to discuss the next set of buttons in the top menu bar of the Script editor, we'll need to explain how they trigger the content of the left side window, which is used as a library. In short, the buttons at left of the menu bar, control the content of the left window. By default, the left most button is selected, and the contents of the left window display its properties. That button is known as the MovieClip Navigator. It displays a hierarchy of all of your MovieClip and MovieClip Group objects on your Composition in the left window as shown in Figure 12-3, which displays several MovieClip objects by listing their names. Selecting this rollover MovieClip from the left window allows us work with just that button. When selected, all of the State, Handler, and Keyframe Scripts entered into the Script Editor will be relative to that object alone. In order to switch back to working with just the Composition, double click on the Composition in the MovieClip Navigator section of the Script Editor. This provides us with an easy way to select a specific object in the Script Editor without needing to leave the Script Editor in order to select an object on the Composition.

You might not have noticed, but while creating you're rollover, LiveMotion simultaneously created the script that creates this effect in the Script Editor. To see this script, with your rollover MovieClip selected, go to the drop down menu of your Handler scripts section. Notice that many of the Handlers from the drop down menu have a star next to them. This announces that the specific

---

- In the Rollover Palette with the Edit State Script button.
- Use the three Player Script buttons at the top menu bar of the Script Editor.

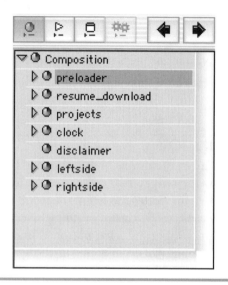

Figure 12-3 Script Editor's Library Section

Handler contains a script. For example, go to the OnButtonPress Handler, which is one of the Handlers that contains a star next to it and notice the code written by LiveMotion: 'this.lmSetCurrentState("over");'. The code tells LiveMotion that when the button is pressed, the button's state changes to its 'Over' state. In the previous module, it was explained that the keyword signifies that the script is accessing an Object in the script. In this case, LiveMotion comes with an already preexisting definition of its own object we can easily access from the Script Editor. We'll get into that in just a bit. For now, notice that the object that the script is calling is the 'lmCurrentState' object which is an already preidentified and reserved object name in LiveMotion. Try accessing some of the other Handlers marked by the star, which were automatically created for the object by LiveMotion when you applied its rollover effect.

```
•   onLoad
    onUnload
    onEnterFrame
    onMouseMove
    onMouseDown
    onMouseUp
    onKeyDown
    onKeyUp
    onData
*   onButtonPress
*   onButtonRelease
    onButtonReleaseOutside
*   onButtonRollOver
*   onButtonRollOut
    onButtonDragOver
*   onButtonDragOut
```

The next button in the menu bar at the top triggers the Scripting Syntax
Helper library in the left window, also known as the DOM (Document Object
Model). The Helper library displays Object methods and properties that are
available to you as you script, as shown in Figure 12-4. You can use any of
these methods/properties to further modify your MovieClip objects. To get a
short definition of each of these Object methods and Properties, all you have
to do is select them. The definition will appear in the bottom window of your
Script Editor. In order to use them, first select either a specific Handler, State,
or keyframe location for your Object, and then double click on that Object
method/property and it will appear in the right window, which is the location
of where you'll be entering your scripts in just a few moments.

Notice that the Object methods and Properties in the Helper Library are
organized into categories. Each category is followed by a short description
of its purpose. Since by default, the left side window is too small to display
both the category name and its description, you'll need to move your mouse
between the left and the right window, and click and drag the bar that separates
them to the right until you're able to see the name in full length. The same applies
for the bottom window that displays the definition of each Object method and
Property selected in the Helper Library. To stretch it, move your mouse between
the top two windows and the bottom one, and drag the bar that separates them
either down or up.

12

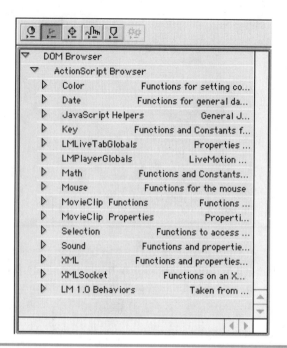

Figure 12-4   Script Editor's Scripting Syntax Helper Library

The next button at left of the menu bar of the Script Editor, called the Composition Browser. When triggered, it displays all of the objects on your Composition, which you can choose to target by a script of another object. For example, if we created a remote rollover triggering another button's specific state, the code for both objects would appear in this section. In addition, you can use this section to create additional scripts that will target other objects in other ways as well. To begin a script that will target a specific object on your Composition, double click on that object, followed by the code that will create some type of effect. Figure 12-5 displays several sample MovieClips.

In addition, the Composition browser displays all of the states of an object available to you on the Composition that the Script Editor will allow you to trigger during the script. As before, to get started on creating such scripts, double click on the state that you'd like your script to trigger followed by the script that will create the effect being triggered. Finally, the Composition browser section also displays all of the lables on your Composition as well as

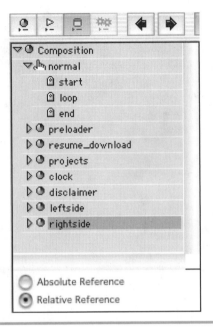

Figure 12-5   Script Editor's Composition Browser

those found in both MovieClip and MovieClip Group objects that reside on your Composition. As before, to trigger a specific label during your script, select it in the left window, and double click it to add it to you script in the right window. Unfortunately, we haven't yet gone over the creation and use of labels in our Timeline, therefore, at the present, no labels will be available to you at in the Composition Browser. However, we'll go over labels later on in this Module. After knowing how to create and use them, you'll be able to use the contents of the Composition Browser to trigger the Labels you desire in your scripts.

The final button at the top menu bar of your Script Editor is the Automation Syntax Helper Library. Currently the button is grayed out. In order to access it you'll need to check on the LiveTab option in your Export settings for the current Composition. The library that it displays in the left window when triggered is used for creating scripts that will control other Compositions. Figure12-6 displays its interface. As with the Syntax Helper library, the Automation Syntax Helper, contains various Object models and properties that are available to use while we script. Similarly, all of the Object models and properties are contained in categories followed by a brief description that appear next to them. Additionally,

12

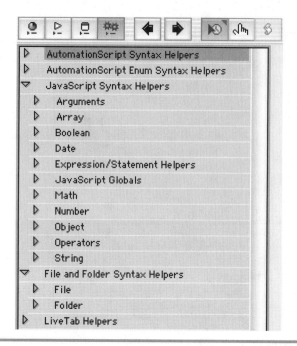

Figure 12-6 Script Editor's Automation Scripting Syntax Helper Library

each Object model and function also contains its own description that is seen in the bottom window of the Script Editor.

We've previously learned that LiveTabs are the features of LiveMotion that are created by a user for the purpose of creating and modifying various object on our Composition. We will use the contents of the Automation Scripting Sytax Helper Library, to create such LiveTabs in the next module in which we'll go over additional features of the Scripting interface of LiveMotion.

Scripting Area

You previously noted that the right window of the Script Editor, as shown in Figure 12-1, is reserved for entering scripts. Remember, the scripts are relative both to the object selected on your composition and the type of scripts you're creating: Handler, State, or Keyframe. The menu bar provides you with several useful buttons that are available to you while you're creating scripts. For

Ask the Expert

Question: I'm trying to read the description of a category inside the Scripting Sytax Helper Library, but the window is too small. What can I do?

Answer: Position your mouse in between the left-side and the right-side window, and then drag the line separating these two windows as far to the right as possible until you can see the full description.

Question: How do I use the content in the Library window?

Answer: Simply double-click one of the methods or properties, and it'll appear in your Scripting window. Remember, though, the Script Editor won't write the script for you, so you'll have to position and punctuate this content appropriately.

example, the two arrow buttons are similar to the arrows in any browser that you use to browse the Web. The Back button lets you return to the area you've previously been working on and the Forward button enables you to skip ahead.

Project 12-1: Simple Handler Script (Draggable Object)

Now that you've been introduced to the Script Editor's interface and have a basic understanding of how the various portions of the interface interact with one another, let's create a simple script using Handler Scripting. In the following project, you create script for the specific Event Handler of an object that lets you drag it to any portion of the composition once the animation is exported and viewed in a web browser.

By now, I'm sure you've come across many types of web sites that use the feature of an object that a user can drag across the screen. For example, many designers use them on their sites as a way to let the user know about any recent changes to the site—more specifically, Site News. The capability of dragging this object across the screen is convenient for the visitor. For example, if the object is in the way of another object or a piece of text, the visitor can simply drag it out of the way.

12

Step-by-Step

1. Begin by creating a new composition with the dimensions 500×300.

2. Create a Site News template containing sample information. Create a dark blue rectangular object measuring 144×86.

3. Create two additional layers for this object. Make the first layer dark gray, with its width set to 1 in the Layer palette. Set the second layer opacity to 38 with a Smooth preference in the Layer palette set to 9.

4. Create an even darker blue rectangular object measuring 146×17. Place it so its top two corners match with the top two corners of the previous rectangular object.

5. Create a white text object and type in **Site News**. Use a font of your choice, but make sure your text object fits between the boundaries of the second rectangular object.

6. Create the second white text object. Use a smaller font and type in **10.15 New images added**. On the next line type in **10.01 Friend section just added**.

7. Place this text object within the boundaries of the first drawn rectangular object. Use your judgment for its actual alignment and placement underneath the Site News text object.

8. Select all your objects and convert them into a MovieClip Group by selecting the command from the Object menu.

9. Open your timeline and create a name for the object without any spaces. When calling up objects during the scripting phase, proper punctuation of the objects must be in place. Objects with spaced names won't function. Calling your object site_news, for example, is acceptable.

10. Let's start scripting now. Open your Script Editor, make sure the MovieClip Navigator is opened in the left-side window, and proceed by clicking your MovieClip object from this library.

11. Once again, make sure the Handler Scripts button is triggered and select the onMouseDown Handler from the right-side, drop-down menu.

12. Type in the following piece of script in the right-side window:
```
this.startDrag(true);
```

13. Now, select the OnMouseUp Handler from the drop-down menu and proceed by entering this code in the right-side window:
`this.stopDrag();`

14. Close the Script Editor, save your file as Project 12-1.liv in your LiveMotion Projects folder, and preview it in a browser.

Project Summary

Figure 12-7 displays the object attached to the cursor and the object left alone. When clicked and dragged, the object follows your mouse cursor. The code you entered for the Handler OnMouseDown calls the predefined method StartDrag from the Scripting Syntax Helper Library in the Script Editor. This method is located under the MovieClip Functions category. The keyword "this" calls on that object and assigns it to your current MovieClip. In addition, the StopDrag method is called on in the OnMouseDown Handler, with the keyword "this" calling it up in the script.

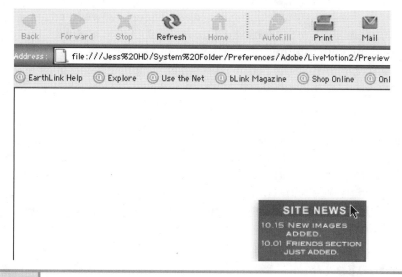

Figure 12-7   Draggable object project

12

Player Scripting

As you learned from Project 12-1, the Script Editor doesn't need to define JavaScript <Script> tags the way you'd need to define it if you were creating a script in an HTML file outside LiveMotion. Instead, it lets you automatically get to the point by calling out a predefined object from the Scripting Syntax Helper Library and assigns it to a MovieClip object on your composition.

When beginning to comprehend the way scripting is performed in the Script Editor, the Scripting Syntax Helper Library will assist you in letting you copy and paste several predefined object scripts set to affect the objects on your composition. The bottom window of the Script Editor provides a short description of the Object Script and enables you to get a sense of the Object's Script effect when applied or set to be applied to an object on your composition.

When dealing with objects on your composition, the Script Editor is only capable of creating scripts for MovieClip and MovieClip Group objects. (You can also create scripts for the main composition, which is done by launching the Script Editor without having an object selected, or simply choose the Composition from the MovieClip Navigator.) Therefore, when creating a script for an object, make sure you convert it to a MovieClip or a MovieClip Group if you're working with multiple objects, as you did in the previous project, before creating a script for it in the Script Editor. The scripting techniques— Handlers, States, and Timeline/Keyframe scripting—are known as *Player Scripts*. The reason is this: when they're exported, the Player Scripts manipulate the player (the Flash plug-in in your web browser that enable you to view SWF files) and allow the file to perform the tasks the scripts within it are programmed to do. Another type of scripting the Script Editor is capable of doing is Automation Scripting, which was briefly discussed during the explanation of the Automation DOM Library function. You learned that Automation Scripting enables you to create scripts capable of controlling other compositions and their objects, namely by creating LiveTabs. Automation Scripting is discussed in the next module.

1-Minute Drill

- What's the purpose of the bottom window in the Script Editor?
- What modification needs to be applied to an object before using it in a script or creating a script within it?

- It displays the description of any object function selected in the Library window.
- An object needs to be modified as a MovieClip before using it in a script or creating a script within it.

Create Event Handler Scripts

Event Handler Scripts are a result of either a user action or a predefined system event. The Script Editor enables you to write scripts for 16 different types of Event Handlers. In your previous project, you used two of them: OnMouseDown and the OnMouseUp events, which are both a result of a user action. The *Mouse Down Handler* is the result of a user clicking his mouse button on the MovieClip object, which results in the script for that Handler being executed. The *OnMouseUp Handler* is a result of the user releasing her mouse button from the MovieClip, which results in that Handler's Script being executed.

Some of the system-based Handler events are a result of a system event. For example, the *OnLoad* event is executed when the MovieClip to which the script is associated with first loads. In addition, the *OnUnload* event is executed when the object is removed from its parent object or the top level of the composition known as _root. You learn more about loading and unloading additional SWF files on top of currently playing files in the next module. Table 12-1 displays each Event Handler accessible from the Script Editor and its effect on a MovieClip object.

Just as you can use the Position Component to animate MovieClip objects on your composition, you can also program specific Event Handlers to do this automatically for you, based on either a user action or a system-based event. When entered for the OnMouseMove Handler of the MovieClip object, the following script will animate its position:

```
this._x+=3;
this._y+=2;
```

When previewed in a browser, the object moves diagonally across the screen, more specifically, down 3 pixels and to the right 3 pixels. This action is triggered by the mouse pointer. In addition, the event suspends when the mouse pointer is still, and then returns to move, once the mouse pointer is moved again. The _x object property is called on in the first line of the script and modified to add 3 to the object's horizontal position, so when executed, the object's horizontal attribute is increased by a value of 3. In this case, the 3 stands for 3 pixels, so the object is animated to the right by 3 pixels. The second line of code uses the _y object property to modify the object's vertical attribute. In this case, it's modified by the value of 2, so the object is animated down 2 pixels by this portion of the script. Because the event is triggered every time the user moves her mouse cursor, the MovieClip object continues animating down and right, until the user stops moving her mouse cursor. This results in the MovieClip maintaining its last modified location by the script.

12

Event Handler	Effect on a MovieClip
OnLoad	Executes when the MovieClip object is loaded in the SWF file. A useful place to declare or initialize variables or to introduce a function that will be accessed at a later point.
OnUnload	Executes when either the MovieClip is removed from its parent object or the _root, which stands for main composition's timeline.
OnEnterFrame	Executes as each frame in the object's timeline is played.
OnMouseMove	Executes when the MovieClip is loaded and the user moves the mouse pointer.
OnMouseDown	Executes when the user presses down his mouse button over the MovieClip.
OnMouseUp	Executes when the mouse button is pressed.
OnKeyDown	Executes when a specific keyboard key is pressed after the MovieClip is loaded on the composition.
OnData	Executes when data is received in a loadVariables or loadMovie action. When specified with a loadVariables action, the data event occurs only once, when the last variable is loaded. When specified with a loadMovie action, the data event occurs repeatedly, as each section of data is retrieved.
OnButtonPress	Similar to the OnMouseDown event, the script executes when the user presses down her mouse button over the MovieClip.
OnButtonRelease	Executes when the button pressed over the MovieClip is released.
OnButtonReleaseOutside	Executes when the user releases his mouse button outside the MovieClip; while no longer directly over the MovieClip.
OnButtonRollover	Executes when the user's mouse pointer passes directly over the MovieClip.
OnButtonRollout	Executes when the user's mouse pointer leaves the MovieClip.
OnButtonDragOver	Executes when the user passes over the MovieClip with her mouse button pressed down.
OnButtonDragOut	Executes after the user passes over the MovieClip with his mouse button pressed down and follows to pass over and away from the MovieClip.

Table 12-1 Event Handlers and Their Functions

When writing scripts for Event Handlers, having some type of action to enable the animation to resume back to its initial state is useful. In this case, you'll create a script that would return your MovieClip object back to the position where it started. After all, if you move your mouse pointer for a specific amount of time, the MovieClip itself soon goes out of the composition's dimensions. When it's entered for the MovieClip object's OnMouseDown Event Handler, the following script will reposition it, so it's located 150 pixels down from the top of the composition and 200 pixels from the left side of the composition. If your composition's dimensions are set to 400×300, the following script would reposition the MovieClip to the center. Here's the script:

```
this._x=200;
this._y=150;
```

Once again, the _x and the _y object attributes are accessed and modified. In this case, however, they're set to equal the value to the right of their operators, allowing the OnMouseDown event to position your object 200 pixels from the right and 150 pixels from the top. From now on, every time the user moves his mouse cursor, he can reposition the MovieClip to the center by pressing down his mouse button.

Create and Use Labels

To explain the useful features of writing Keyframe Scripts, you first need to learn about the use of labels in your projects. *Labels* allow Keyframe Scripts (and any other types of Player Scripts, for that matter) to position the CTM in your timeline to specific Time Intervals.

Creating labels is quite easy. In your Timeline window, select a specific Time Interval where you want to create a label and proceed by clicking the Label button. After clicking the button, you're prompted to assign a name for that label. Be sure to use simple names, as well as names that don't contain any type of spacing. For example, this is an incorrect name assigned to a label—"label 1"—but, the following example is correct—"label_1". As explained earlier, spaced words sabotage your scripts and, in turn, the script won't function correctly. When created, the Label icon will appear along with the name of the label, to the right of the Label button on your timeline, as shown in Figure 12-8. When creating your own projects, you're free to create as many labels as you want. Be sure not to assign the same name for any two labels, though, because doing so will confuse the scripts you learn about shortly, which access those specific labels.

The location of where you place your label is also important. In a way, by creating a label, you're creating a bookmark to which you want to return in the

12

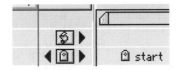

Figure 12-8 Label icon on the timeline

near future. For example, if you want to access a specific state of an animated object at a specific Time Interval at a later point, you can create a label at that specific Time Interval. Later, you can compose a script to trigger the animation to return to that specific Time Interval. The script will call on that specific label, allowing the animation to pinpoint that specific Time Interval.

The following are the appropriate ways to call specific labels in the Script Editor, assuming the label in question is named "label_1":

```
gotoAndPlay("label_1");
```

When executed, the following script will move the CTM in the composition's timeline to that specific label and continue playing the animation. In addition, you can also create scripts that tell the CTM to go to a specific label, and then stop the animation. Here's a way to compose that script:

```
gotoAndStop("label_1");
```

When executed this time, the CTM will simply go to that specific label and stop the animation of your composition. To access these two types of scripts easily, open the Scripting Syntax Helper Library in the Script Editor, and toggle down the LMPlayer Globals category. Afterward, double-click either the "gotoAndStop(Label)" or the "gotoAndPlay(label)" predefined objects. Doing so will trigger the Script Editor to copy and paste them automatically in your Scripting window. Make sure to replace the label in the parentheses of the script, however, with the name of your label, along with the quotation marks around the label name, inside the two parentheses.

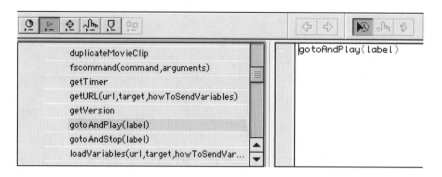

Remember, you can also create labels in the independent timelines of your MovieClip and your MovieClip Group objects. As explained in previous modules, these timelines play independently of the main timeline of your composition. Creating and triggering labels in these timelines only affects those specific MovieClip objects to which they're associated and the timeline on your composition will continue to play unaffected. When writing scripts that will trigger labels on the composition, as well as those inside MovieClips, however, you need to specify the locations of the labels located on the composition with the keyword _root. Placing the _root keyword before the script that calls on a label instructs the player that the label being triggered is located on the composition. Here's how the script would look.

```
_root.gotoAndPlay("label_1");
```

The _root keyword also enables the player to access the label on the composition if the script is executed from within an independent timeline of a MovieClip object. Leaving out the _root keyword in that situation would confuse the player in trying to find the label in question. Because of the way the script is written, the player would search for the label only on that specific independent timeline of the MovieClip object and the script wouldn't execute.

When creating scripts that will trigger labels within a MovieClip, on the other hand, you need to use the following syntax:

```
MovieClip.gotoAndPlay("label_1");
```

You now need to replace the MovieClip command with the name of the MovieClip from which you're accessing the label. If the name of your MovieClip is red_rectangle and the name of your label is "start," for example, the script that tells the CTM to go to that specific label within that MovieClip and continue playing the animation of the MovieClip looks like the following:

```
red_rectangle.gotoAndPlay("start");
```

Once again, note the name of the MovieClip object. No spaces exist. In addition, this explains the reason for creating unique names for the objects you create on the composition, which you learned about in earlier modules. Not only do they quickly enable you to pinpoint the appropriate objects when writing scripts, they also allow the scripts to function properly when the names of the objects are written correctly with no spaces in between them.

Create Keyframe Scripts

Keyframe Scripts appear along the timeline, as shown in Figure 12-9. If you're creating these types of scripts with the independent timeline of your MovieClip objects, however, the scripts will appear only along those timelines. Creating and assigning locations for your Keyframe Scripts is as easy as creating labels. To create a Keyframe Script at a specific Time Interval on your timeline, position your CTM to the Time Interval where you want to set the script and click the Scripts button in the Timeline window. When triggered, the Scripts button opens the Script Editor and automatically assigns the location of the script. For example, if you positioned the CTM to the 02s Time Interval and then clicked the Scripts button inside the timeline, the Script Editor would display that Time Interval and enable you to enter a script for it. Likewise, a Script icon appears at the Time Interval where you created the script, to the left of the Script button in your timeline.

To access your Keyframe scripts easily, you have two choices. You can either double-click the Keyframe Script icon at a specific Time Interval or you can use the drop-down menu in the Script Editor to jump through each Time Interval where you created a Keyframe Script. Remember, even if you don't enter a script once you've created a Keyframe Script, the Script icon, as well as the Script Editor's drop-down menu, will display the icon of the script and the specific Time Intervals.

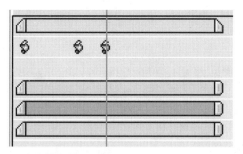

Figure 12-9	Keyframe Script on timeline

Keyframe Scripts, unlike Event Handlers, aren't based on a user action, unless other scripts exist on your composition that trigger your Keyframe Scripts. Keyframe Scripts are executed once the CTM passes over the Time Interval where they're located. For example, once the animation of your composition came to an end, creating a Keyframe Script at the end of your composition's duration bar would trigger the player to execute it. Similarly, Keyframe Scripts created within your MovieClip object follow the same rule. Creating a Keyframe Script within the independent timeline of your MovieClip object would be only be executed once the CTM on that timeline passed over the Time Interval where the Keyframe Script is located.

When working with Keyframe Scripts—both on your composition's timeline and on those on the independent timelines of your MovieClip objects—accessing them within the Script Editor can get a bit tricky. The easiest way to do this is to double-click them in your Timeline window. Once opened, the drop-down menu in your Script Editor only enables you to access all the scripts based on that specific timeline. To switch timelines, you need either to double-click the MovieClip object from which you want to access its scripts set on its timeline or to double-click the particular Keyframe Script. Regardless of how you go about switching between timelines, the Script Editor's drop-down menu only displays the Keyframe Scripts set on that timeline. In a way, this is for your own convenience.

The following miniproject uses the same script used for your Event Handlers, which enabled you to modify the position of your MovieClip object. This time, however, the script uses Keyframe Scripts that execute it, and it's no longer controlled by the user. In addition, the script also makes use of a label that

12

allows it to jump from one Time Interval to another and repeat the script. Here are the steps:

1. Create a new composition and set its dimensions to 400×400.

2. Create a new square object and select MovieClip command in the Object menu.

3. Enter the following location for the object in the Transform palette: X=40 and Y=40.

4. In your Timeline window, select your object and name it **Box**.

5. Drag the composition's duration bar to the 01s Time Interval and create two labels. Create the first label at the 00s Time Interval and name it **one**. Create the second label at the 06f Time Interval and name it **two**. (You can also use numerical values for labels, but scripts tend to be more stable with alphanumeric names.)

6. Create your first Keyframe Script at the 00s Time Interval and leave it empty for now. Simply close the Script Editor when it pops up.

7. Now, create Keyframe Scripts at 06f and 01s time intervals.

8. Now that you've created the locations of your scripts, let's start coding. Double-click the Script icon located at the 00s Time Interval and enter the following code:

```
_root.Box._x=40
_root.Box._y=40;
```

9. From the drop-down menu in the Script Editor, select the next Time Interval 00:00:00:06 and enter the following script:

```
_root.Box._x+=20;
_root.Box._y+=20;
```

10. Now, select the last Time Interval from the drop-down menu in the Script Editor 00:00:01:00 and enter the following If and Else statement:

```
if (_root.Box._x>=300&&_root.Box._y>=300)
{
gotoAndPlay("one");
}
else
```

```
{
_root.gotoAndPlay("two");
}
```

11. Close the Script Editor, save your file as Keyframe Script.liv, and place it in your LiveMotion Projects folder.

12. Click the Preview button in the toolbar to view your new scripted animation.

The box should travel right and down diagonally on your composition. Before going out of bounds, however, the object returns to where it started, and continues to move down and right diagonally. The animated object will do these steps infinitely.

Here's a rundown of the scripts you entered. The first script assigns values to the _x and the _y variables, which represent the position of the object. The second script modifies their X and Y positions by increasing them by 20 pixels. The final script is an If and Else statement. It states that if the X and Y positions of the object are greater or equal to 300, the player will position the CTM to your first label located at the exact point where your first script is and starts playing the animation from the beginning. Furthermore, the Else statement tells the player that if the X and Y positions aren't greater or equal to 200, the player positions the CTM to the second label located at the same Time Interval as your second script. Because the object increases its X and Y position every time the second script is executed, the object continues to animate until it constrained by the If Else statement in the last Keyframe Script that instructs it to start all over.

You should now understand the difference between Handler Scripts and Keyframe Scripts. Even though Keyframe Scripts aren't based on a user action, using conditions such as If Else statements enables you to give the MovieClip a set of rules it must obey. With the help of labels, the rules are easily provided to the player.

Create State Scripts

Adding scripts to Object's States, unlike Handler Scripting, enables you to write scripts to the Normal, Over, Down, and Out States, as well as to any custom States created in that rollover. These States are completely independent of the timeline, so all the scripts in the States of a button object are accessible at all times (unless, of course, the object's duration bar is ended before the composition's

12

duration bar). These scripts are only executed when the mouse button is directly over the corresponding object.

All the objects created or imported to the composition have, by default, a Normal State. Rollovers, on the other hand, contain additional States that make them intractable with the user. When you create State Scripts, however, applying them to the Over, Down, Out, and Custom States of a button object makes more sense. After all, creating a State Script for an object's Normal State would, in turn, activate it once the object is loaded or whenever the object was returned to its Normal State.

Accessing the appropriate location in the Script Editor for entering State Script for an object is quite simple. To start, create a simple object on the composition. In the Rollover palette, create an Over, Down, and Out State for that object. Any object modified with the Rollover palette automatically becomes a MovieClip object, so there's no longer a need to convert a Rollover object to a MovieClip. To create a State Script for your Rollover object in the Rollover palette, select a State and click the Edit State Script button located at the bottom of the palette. When clicked, the script editor launches and provides you with the appropriate location for entering your script. Once in the Script Editor, you can use the drop-down menu to switch back and forth between all the States created for that object. In addition, a Script icon appears next to the State for which you entered a script. The Event Handlers of a Rollover object are updated as well, once additional states are added to an object. For example, LiveMotion automatically enters the following script for the OnButtonPress Event Handler once a Down State is created for an object:

```
this.lmSetCurrentState("down");
```

Because the Down State executes the same type of user action as the onButtonPress Event Handler, LiveMotion enters this script to relate these two types of user actions to each other. As explained earlier, the keyword refers to the object's self and tells the player to display the Down State of the object.

State Scripts are extremely expendable. Because they ultimately rely on User Interaction with the object, State Scripts can be programmed to interact with other scripts, such as Handlers and Keyframe Scripts. In addition, State Scripts can also trigger remote animated objects. The final project of this module instructs you on how to do so and you create an animation that uses a State Script.

Project 12-2: Control Animated Objects

In the following project, you use a Scripted Rollover button that triggers an animated object to replicate itself. You write this clip to the Over State of your button. In the Out State, you instruct the player to remove your duplicate object.

Step-by-Step

1. Create a new composition with the following dimensions: 500×400.

2. Create a small elliptical shape and animate its position component, so it moves from one side of the composition to the other. Simultaneously, animate its scale component, so the shape grows as it approaches the center of the composition, and then shrinks again.

3. Now, select your object and select the Make MovieClip Group command under the Object menu. Also, click the Loop button at the bottom of the timeline.

4. Make sure your object is still selected and choose the Edit Name command found under the Object menu. Enter **animatedobject**. The name is case-sensitive, so be sure to enter it exactly the way it's written.

5. Create a new object by drawing a small rectangle and place it at the bottom of the composition. This is your Rollover button that will trigger an additional effect to your animation.

6. Rename this object control.

7. Select the object, and then create an Over and an Out State for it in the State palette.

8. In the State palette, select the Over State and click the Edit State Script button. Enter the following script:

```
duplicateMovieClip("_root.animatedobject", "animatedobject2", "3");
_root.animatedobject2._alpha=50;
_root.animatedobject2._width=100;
_root.animatedobject2._height=100;
```

9. Now, while still in the Script Editor, select the Out State from the drop-down menu and enter the following script:

```
removeMovieClip("_root.animatedobject2");
```

10. That's it, you're done! Save your project as Project12-2, and then save it in your LiveMotion Projects folder.

12

Project Summary

When you preview your new animation, you'll notice that by going over the Rollover button at the bottom of the composition, a scaled up and transparent version of the animated object appears and animates along with its parent. Once you move your mouse away from the Rollover button, the scaled-up object disappears. Here's what happens in the Over and Out States. In the Over State, the following part of the script

```
duplicateMovieClip("_root.animatedobject", "animatedobject2", "3");
```

creates an exact duplicate of your animated object named animatedobject, place it on the main Timeline _root, and name it animatedobject2. The other three lines of the script

```
_root.animatedobject2._alpha=50;
_root.animatedobject2._width=100;
_root.animatedobject2._height=100;
```

change the opacity of the new object to 50, and increase its height and width to 100. In the Out state

```
removeMovieClip("_root.animatedobject2");
```

the duplicate gets removed by pointing to its direct path.

Summary

This module provided you with an extensive overview of the Script Editor's interface and all its features. You learned how to access the Library window located in the left-side window of the Editor to provide you with commonly used Player Scripts, target-specific MovieClips on the composition, target labels, and target MovieClip States. In addition, you learned how to use the Script Editor to compile Player Scripts. You learned that Player Scripts consist of Event Handler, Keyframe, and State Scripts.

Once you understood how the three types of Player Scripts are written, you learned some basic scripts executed by an Event Handler Script, a Keyframe Script, and State Script.

In the next module, you learn about some additional features provided by LiveMotion's scripting interface. You learn how to access some already compiled scripts available to you from the Script menu and how to use the Debugger to test the performance of a compiled script. In addition, you learn how to compile some additional scripts that were available in the previous version of LiveMotion and were categorized as Behaviors. You also learn how to use another form of scripting know as Automation Scripting, which is used to script objects that trigger various effects on other compositions. In this module, you learned how LiveTabs, like palettes, are used to trigger various effects on the objects on the composition. LiveTabs use Automation Scripts, which trigger these effects. You learn how to construct Automation Scripts in the next module, along with the rest of the features of LiveMotion's scripting environment.

12

☑ *Mastery Check*

1. Player Scripts are composed from which of the following scripts?

    A. Object Scripts, State Scripts, and Keyframe Scripts

    B. State Scripts, Keyframe Scripts, and Handler Scripts

    C. Object Scripts, Rollover Scripts, and Handler Scripts

    D. Rollover Scripts, State Scripts, and Keyframe Scripts

2. In which window of the Script Editor are scripts entered?

    A. The left-side window

    B. The right-side window

    C. The bottom window

    D. The menu bar

3. The _____ icon lets you know if a specific State or an Event Handler contains a script.

    A. Star

    B. Exclamation Point

    C. Bullet

    D. All of the above

4. Some Event Handlers and all States are _____-based events.

    A. User

    B. System

    C. Object

    D. Player

☑ *Mastery Check*

5. How are Keyframe Scripts executed during an animation?

    A. When another script instructs the player to play the frame at which the Keyframe is located.

    B. When another script points the player to play the label located at the same Time Interval.

    C. Once the player passes over the Time Interval where they're located.

    D. All of the above.

6. Which of the following combinations of an Event Handler and an Object State are executed by the same type of a user action?

    A. OnMouseDown/Down State

    B. OnMouseDown/Over State

    C. OnButtonRelease/Normal State

    D. OnButtonDragOver/Over State

7. Which of the following is/are a system-based Handler Event/s?

    I. OnLoad

    II. OnData

    III. OnKeydown

        A. I and II

        B. I and III

        C. II

        D. III

12

☑ *Mastery Check*

8. When you enter scripts into the scripting window of the Script Editor, when are the <script language="JavaScript"> and </script> tags learned in the previous module needed?

    A. When writing Keyframe Scripts

    B. When writing Event Handler Scripts

    C. When writing State Scripts

    D. Never

9. When a label is created, where does it appear?

    A. On the timeline

    B. In the object's Rollover State

    C. In the script editor

    D. All of the above

10. Which of the following scripts is the appropriate way to call up a label named "1" that's located on the timeline of the composition?

    A. gotoAndPlay("2")

    B. _root.gotoAndPlay('2')

    C. _root.gotoAndPlay("2");

    D. _root.gotoandplay("2");

Module 13

Advanced Features of Scripting

The Goals of this Module

- Learn the features of the Script and Automation menus
- Understand the importance of the Debugger
- Learn how to use the scripting environment to create Behaviors
- Understand automation scripting
- Learn how automation scripts are used in LiveTabs

Modules 11 and 12 paved the way for you to understand how JavaScript is utilized in the Script Editor to control the player by creating player scripts. In this module, we'll wrap up the scripting environment of LiveMotion 2 by discussing the construction of automation scripts, which are used to control other compositions you've seen being utilized in LiveTabs. In addition, at the end of the module, you'll be ready to create a LiveTab of our own.

You will also learn about several other features of the scripting environment such as the Script menu. We'll go over the Debugger, which allows you to test the stability of your scripts, as well as go over applying ready-made scripts to your MovieClip objects. For those of you who are LiveMotion 1 veterans, we'll go over the creation of Behaviors scripts, which although missing from their prior location, are still a part of LiveMotion's scripting environment in the form of individual scripts.

LiveMotion 1 Users

For those of you with experience using the first version of LiveMotion, you'll notice that a lot of things changed in the second version. The main change, of course, is LiveMotion's ability to script the player and the composition. Users of LiveMotion 1 were limited to using Behaviors, which when set up correctly would trigger the player and the project's composition. However, Behaviors were limited to just a fraction of what the scripting engine of LiveMotion 2 is capable of performing.

What Happened to Behaviors?

Even though Behaviors are no longer part of the initial interface of LiveMotion 2, users can still access them within the Script Editor. All of the Behaviors are located in the Scripting Syntax Helper library section of the Script Editor. As with the ActionScript and JavaScript Syntax Helper libraries, to place a LiveMotion 1 Behavior in your Scripting window, select and double-click on the Behavior and it'll appear in that window in the form of a script. LiveMotion 2 provides you with a short description of the Behavior selected in the bottom window of the Script Editor.

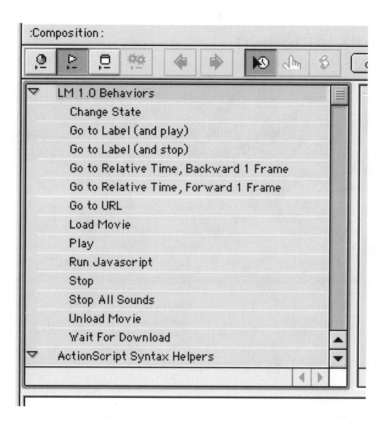

While working with LiveMotion1 Behaviors in the Script Editor of LiveMotion 2, keep in mind that they're simply there to allow you to compose your Behaviors and other scripts within the Script Editor. Adobe created this section for LiveMotion 1 users in order to allow them to make a smooth transition between LiveMotion 1 and LiveMotion 2. All of the Behaviors in the LiveMotion 1 Behaviors section of the Scripting Syntax Helper library can be found in the ActionScript Syntax Helper library, and you'll find yourself abandoning the LiveMotion 1 Behavior section as you familiarize yourself with the way that they're written as ActionScripts.

13

Behaviors Rundown

Table 13-1 lists the 11 types of Behaviors from LiveMotion1. It shows you how they're composed in the Script Editor, displays a sample script utilizing that specific Behavior, and lists the description of the effect of the sample script. The description of the sample script will be marked with the "//" keys. You've previously learned in the JavaScript module of this book that the "//" keywords are ignored during the execution of the script and simply serve to allow you to read the function of the script.

The Wait for Download Behavior was probably one of the most popular and widely used Behaviors in the previous version of LiveMotion. The Behavior

LiveMotion 1 Behavior	Script in LiveMotion 2	Example Script and its Description

Stop	movieclip.stop();	blue_dot.stop();
		//When triggered, it stops the
		//movie clip's timeline.

Play	movieclip.play();	blue_dot.play();
		//When triggered, it plays the
		//movie clip's timeline.

Change State	movieclip.lmSetCurrentState (stateName);	blue_dot.lmSetCurrentState('Down');
		//when triggered, movie-clip object
		//named 'blue_dot' will change its
		//rollover state to 'down'.

Go to Relative Time	movieclip.prevFrame();
	and
	movieclip.nextFrame();
		blue_dot.prevFrame();
		//when triggered, the timeline will go
		//back one frame and stop for the
		//movie-clip named 'blue_dot'.

Go to Label	movieclip.gotoAndPlay(label);
	and
	movieclip.gotoAndStop(label);
		blue_dot.gotoAndStop('start');
		//when triggered, the player will go
		//label named 'start' and stop the
		//animation of the object 'blue_dot'.

Go to URL	getURL(url, window);	getURL(http://www.livemotionstudio.com, _blank);
		//when executed, 'livemotionstudio.com'
		// will load the URL in a new browser
		// window.

Run JavaScript	getURL(javascript: code);	getUrl(javascript: alert('under construction'));
		//when executed, this behavior will pop
		//up a small dialogue window displaying
		//'under construction'.

Table 13-1 Behaviors into Scripts Guidelines

LiveMotion 1 Behavior	Script in LiveMotion 2	Example Script and its Description

Load Movie	loadMovieNum(url, levelNum);	loadMovieNum(http://www.test.com/ test.swf, 2);
		 //when triggered file named 'test.swf'
		 //will load on top of the currently
		 //playing file, on level 2.

Unload Movie	unloadMovieNum(levelNum);	object1.unloadMove();
		 //when triggered, it removes a movie
		 //clip named 'object1' that was
		 //loaded with the loadMovie method

Wait for Download	if (this._framesloaded < lmFrameOfLabel(finishLabel))
	 {
	 this.gotoAndPlay(repeatLabel);
	 }
		if (this._framesloaded < lmFrameOfLabel('end'))
		 {
		    this.gotoAndPlay('start');
		 }
		 //every time this script is executed,
		 //the player will go back to the label
		 //named 'start' and play again. The
		 //only way this script will be bypassed
		 //is if when the label named 'end' is
		 //loaded along with its frame.

Stop all Sounds	stopAllSounds();	stopAllSounds();
		 //when triggered, all sounds in your
		 //file will be turned off.

Table 13-1   Behaviors into Scripts Guidelines (*Continued*)

allows you to create what is called "preloader," which allows you to create an animating object that will continue to animate until a specified frame is loaded from your file. The upcoming project in this module instructs you how to go about creating one. In addition, we'll go over using another useful Behavior that allows you to load additional files over currently playing ones without actually replacing the currently playing file only overlapping it with a loaded one.

1-Minute Drill

● Where are LiveMotion 1 Behaviors located in LiveMotion 2?

● How do you use Behaviors in LiveMotion 2?

13

● Inside the Script Editor in the Scripting Syntax Helper library.
● Double-click on them and format them in the Scripting window of the Script Editor.

Script Menu

You've previously learned that the Script menu provides you with quick access to the Script Editor by selecting it in that menu. In addition, the menu also allows you to control the Debugger. A Debugger is used to test the contents of the scripts in your project. The Script menu lets you choose to either launch the Debugger screen when an error occurs in the script or to launch it whenever a script is executed. In addition, the Script menu allows you to turn this feature off by simply selecting Don't Debug.

Debugger

The Debugger is only used when a file is being previewed inside the program. To launch the Debugger in order to view its interface, select the Debug at Start option in the Script Editor and click on the Preview button in the toolbar. Figure 13-1 features the interface of the Debugger window once it is launched in LiveMotion.

Like the Script Editor, the Debugger is composed of three windows and a menu bar containing buttons that allow you to control the contents of the scripts in your project. The left-side window displays the portion of the script that the Debugger is testing. The bottom window, known as the Source window, contains the script that the Debugger is testing. The Variable window alerts you whenever a problem occurs in your script. For example, the problem might be as simple as forgetting to close a bracket. However, on some occasions the integrity of your script and the way its written might not be proper, and the right-side window will alert you to the problem. The left-side window is known as the Call Stack window, and its purpose is to highlight the piece of code in your script that the Debugger is questioning. The piece of script is accompanied by a red arrow pointing to it.

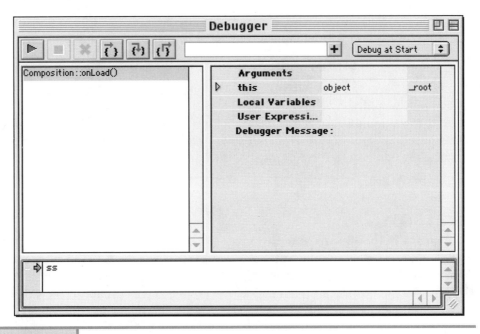

Figure 13-1 Debugger window

Now let's go over the buttons that allow you to control the Debugger. The first button is the Play button, its purpose is to allow the Debugger to begin testing your scripts. The next button over is known as the Break button. This button allows you to select a break point in your script at which the Debugger will pause when the script is being tested. The next button is known as the Kill button. When triggered, all testing done by the Debugger will end and the Debugger window will close. The remaining buttons—Step, Step In, and Step Out—allow you to control the flow of the execution.

Automation Menu

The Automation menu contains several useful features. It allows you to launch LiveTabs from your LiveTab folder in your LiveMotion folder, load LiveTabs that were not present in that folder prior to you launching the program, launch

13

automation scripts, and even apply several already-compiled scripts to the MovieClip objects on your composition.

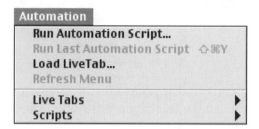

LiveTabs

To open any of the already-compiled LiveTabs, which were shipped with your version of LiveMotion, use the Automation menu to select the LiveTab submenu and choose the LiveTab that you'd like to open. All LiveTabs work the same way as your palettes. This means that to apply their effect to your composition, simply select an object and enter specific characteristics for it in the LiveTabs from which you're applying the effect.

The Automation menu also features a way to bring in LiveTabs that haven't yet been saved into your LiveTab folder prior to launching the program. The Load LiveTab option allows you to import a saved LiveTab from anywhere on your hard drive and make it appear both on your screen and in the LiveTab submenu of the Automation menu. The option is extremely convenient after you've created a LiveTab and want to test it. This process doesn't require you to quit and restart LiveMotion in order for the newly created LiveTab to be available to you.

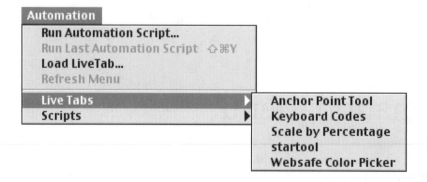

We'll go over the process of creating automation scripts that will be required to create LiveTabs that apply specific tasks to your MovieClip objects on your composition. For now, use the LiveTabs that are available to your from the LiveTabs submenu and familiarize yourself with their functions.

Scripts

The Script submenu is another convenient feature of LiveMotion located in the Automation menu, which allows you to apply custom effects to all types of objects on your composition. The Script menu displays several already-compiled scripts that are available to you at all times while you work on your projects in LiveMotion. As with LiveTabs, however, these scripts require a MovieClip object in order for the effect to function properly.

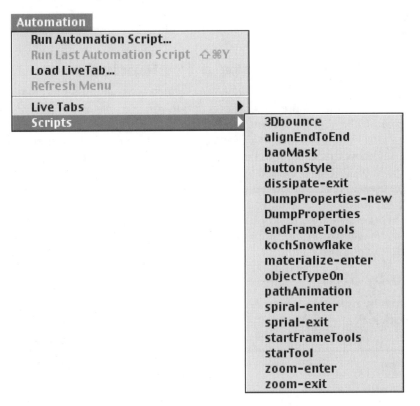

13

The scripts are compiled using automation scripting techniques. As you've just learned, automation scripting is used to create interactive LiveTabs that function the same way as palettes. The Automation menu also allows you to bring in automation scripts that are located anywhere on your hard drive with the Run Automation command. As with LiveTabs, the option is convenient when you have just created an automation script and want to test it. In addition, the Run Last Automation command is also available under the Automation menu, which allows you to run a previously opened automation script after just having run a new one.

1-Minute Drill

● How would you go about importing a script into LiveMotion?

● How would you go about importing a LiveTab into LiveMotion?

Project 13-1: Create a Preloader

Preloaders are one of the most widely used effects when it comes to creating interactive SWF files. A preloader allows you to run a simple or complex animation that plays while your file is being loaded in a browser. Oftentimes your files might take several minutes to load in a user's browser, and a preloader is there to let that user know that the page they are viewing is functioning properly and that they need to wait for it to load in order to view it. In another way, a preloader can be used to create suspense for the animation they are about to view.

In the following project, you will use the script that is available to you under the LM 1 Behaviors section of the Scripting Syntax Helper Library in the Script Editor. We will customize this piece of code in order for the preloader to properly function with our file.

Step-by-Step

1. Begin by opening up your Animating Text project, which you created in Module 9.

● With the Automation menu, by choosing Run Automation Script and then selecting a script from your hard drive with a .js file extension.

● By choosing the Load LiveTab command, found under the Automation menu, and choosing a LiveTab that you'd like to load.

2. Open up your Timeline window, stretch the Duration Bar of the composition to an additional one-third of a second, and select and group all of your objects.

3. Move the duration bar by its middle to begin at the 04f time interval and ungroup your objects.

4. Move your CTM back to the 00s time interval and create a simple looping animation. This animation will be used to repeatedly play until the rest of your objects are loaded in the browser.

5. Make sure to convert your animation to a MovieClip and set it to loop. Additionally, make its duration bar end at the 04f time interval. The 04f Time Interval should also be the same interval at which the rest of your objects begin playing.

6. Move your CTM back to the 00s Time Interval, create a new label at that location, and name it **start**.

7. Move your CTM now to the 04f time interval, create another label, and name it **loop**.

8. Create your last label at the end of the duration bar of your last object by moving your CTM to it and naming that label **end**.

9. Now go back to the 04f time interval and create a new keyframe script.

10. In the Script Editor that opens, toggle on the Scripting Syntax Helper library and toggle down the LM 1 Behaviors category.

11. Select the Wait for Download Behavior and double-click on it. The code is placed in your Scripting window.

12. Replace "finishlabel" with **"end"** (make sure to use quotes), and replace "repeatlabel" with **"start"** (again, remember to use quotes).

13. Save your file as **Project13-1**, and place it in your LiveMotion Projects folder.

14. In order to properly test the preloader, you'll need to upload the file tour web site and test it with a slow connection. Doing so will allow you to view your preloader animation repeatedly looping until the rest of your file has been loaded. After the rest of the object loads, the preloader will disappear and your animated text effect will begin animating.

13

Project Summary

Figure 13-2 displays a screen shot of how the labels should be placed and organized in your Timeline window. When creating preloaders, try to keep them small in size. After all, it's pointless to have to wait for the preloader to load.

Automation Scripting

Automation scripting is no different then player scripting, which you learned of in the previous module. However, unlike player scripting, automation scripts are capable of controlling objects on other compositions while you work in LiveMotion. The following section will introduce you to applying these already-compiled automation scripts to your MovieClip objects on your composition as well as using automation scripting techniques to create an interactive LiveTab out of the interface that you created in Module 11.

Apply Automation Scripts

The Automation menu allows you to both apply already-compiled automation scripts and apply automation scripts that you've created, by importing them into LiveMotion.

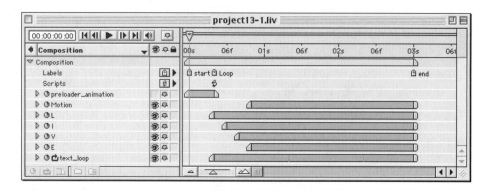

Figure 13-2   Label setup for preloader object

The following is an example of an object having been modified by one of the automation scripts that are available to you from the Script submenu of the Automation menu:

1. Create a small ellipse and place it in the center of your composition.

2. Choose a desired color for the object from the Color palette.

3. From the Scripts submenu under the Automation menu, select and apply the Effect – Spiral Enter script.

4. Use the Preview mode to view the effect on your object.

Experiment with some of the other scripts available in the Scripts submenu. Each of them offers its own unique effects when applied to object on the composition. If you wish to modify any of these scripts, simply go over to the Scripts folder, found in the Automation folder inside of your LiveMotion 2 folder.

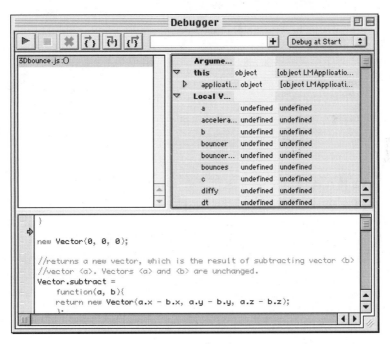

Ask the Expert

Question: What is the difference between automation scripting and LiveTabs?

Answer: Both of them are basically the same. However, LiveTabs, unlike automation scripts, provide you with a visual interface and allow the user to enter specific characteristics for the automation script that the LiveTab will trigger.

Question: Can I import additional automation scripts into LiveMotion?

Answer: Of course. In fact, by the time you read this, several hundred different automation scripts will be traded back and forth between LiveMotion 2 users. Your best source for more information on this topic would be to visit the LiveMotion 2 forums found on Adobe.com.

Apply Scripts from the Styles Palette

The Style palette provides another section where you can apply various scripts onto your MovieClip objects on your composition. The process of applying these scripts from the palette is the same as applying styles that contain animations, layers, and rollovers. Simply select a MovieClip object and apply a specific script style form the Style palette.

Script Window

Automation scripts are written in the Script window, which can be launched with the New Script command under the File menu. As shown in Figure 13-3, the Script window resembles the Script Editor's interface; however, unlike the Script Editor, the Script window allows you to save your script with a .js file extension. The .js file extension (JavaScript), is read and executed by LiveMotion once it's imported with the Run Automation Script command under the Automation menu.

The interface of the Script window is composed of three windows and a menu bar. As with the Script Editor, the left window displays various libraries

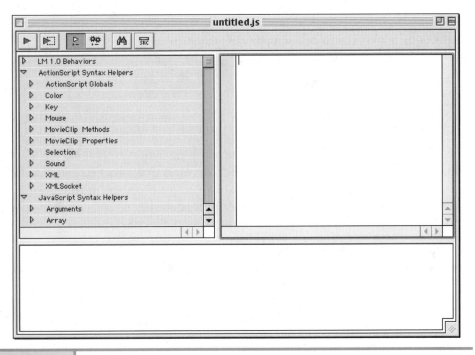

Figure 13-3   Script window

that you can refer to while composing your scripts, the right-side window is the area where your script is written, and the bottom window displays a short description of script techniques selected from the left window, which displays it in its library.

The menu bar, however, is little different than the menu bar of the Script Editor. In fact, the interface is a combination of the interface of the Debugger and the Script Editor. The leftmost button, known as the Run Script button, allows you to execute the script in the right-side window. The next button, the Run Selected Script button, allows you to select a portion of your script and run it in the Scripting window. The next two buttons display your Player Scripting and Automation Scripting libraries. Finally, the Find and the Syntax Highlight buttons perform the same functions as the ones found in the Script Editor. The Find button allows you to find and replace specific portions of your script and

13

the Syntax Highlight button allows you to toggle on and off the colors in your scripts, which are used to distinguish various portions of the script.

To view the Automation Script library, click on the Automation Script button in the Scripting window. At a first glance at the Automation Script library, some of its contents resemble the contents of the Scripting Syntax Helper library. Each automation script is organized into specific categories that target certain features of the object. The following is an example of an automation script, which we'll use in our LiveTab interface project created in Module 10:

```
var comp = application.currentComposition;
for (i=0;i<comp.selection.length;i++) {
  comp.selection[i].duplicate();
  comp.selection[i].position.x += 15;
  comp.selection[i].position.y += 15;
}
```

The first piece of code tells LiveMotion that the code will be targeting the current composition. The second piece of code sets up a statement using the keyword For. When it passes its arguments in the parentheses, it executes the statement in its third line telling the program to duplicate the selected object. Additionally, lines 4 and 5 get executed as well. In the forth line, the script instructs the player to place the duplicate 15 pixels to the right of the original. In the fifth line, the script instructs the player to place the duplicate 15 pixels down from the original.

Since LiveMotion allows us to create, open, and trigger our own automation scripts, we can save this script as a 'script' and place it in the Scripts sub menu of the Automation menu, so that we have it at our disposal. Here are the instructions:

1. First, enter the previous code into the Scripting window of LiveMotion by selecting New Script from the File menu and typing in the code into the right-side window..

2. Save the file into your LiveMotion Projects folder and name it **duplicate_script**.

3. Close down the Scripting window and create a new composition with a simple object.

4. Select the object and from the Automation menu select the Run Automation Script command, and choose your saved script from your LiveMotion Projects folder.

You'll notice that your object is now accompanied by an exact duplicate. As mentioned earlier, we'll use this code again in our project at the end of the module.

Ask the Expert

Question: Why do automation scripts use the var comp keyword at the beginning of their script?

Answer: As you've learned in Module 11, "var" stands for variable. In the previous sample automation script, the variable named Comp was assigned to the predefined object named application.CurrentComposition.

Question: Where can I learn more about JavaScript?

Answer: There are tons of books out there to teach you step by step the basics and the advanced features of JavaScript. However, if you're planning on using JavaScript in conjunction with LiveMotion, you should be looking for books on ActionScripting. Check your favorite bookstores for this type of book.

Question: Can I find more information on ActionScripting online?

Answer: Of course. Keep in mind that ActionScripting has been out for a while. After all, it was introduced back when Macromedia introduced version 4 of Flash. The last module of this book will provide you with several useful web sites in which you can find specific contents including ActionScripting.

13

Project 13-2 Automation Scripting a LiveTab

Since you were previously able to create, launch, and apply an automation script to an object on your composition, creating a LiveTab that will allow you to perform the same function will be a snap. In fact, the only difference between LiveTabs and automation scripts is that LiveTabs provide you with a visual interface. In addition, you can use LiveTabs to enter specific variables that will trigger various effects on the object on your composition. Be sure to experiment with some of the LiveTabs that shipped with your version of LiveMotion for these options.

Step-by-Step

1. Begin by opening up your previously created project in Module 10, called LiveTab Interface and saved in your LiveMotion Projects folder.

2. Select the down state of the Bottom button that will trigger the automation script on other compositions and type the following script into the Script Editor for that State:

```
var comp = application.currentComposition;
varcomp=application.currentComposition;
for (i=0;i<comp.selection.length;i++) {
  comp.selection[i].duplicate();
  comp.selection[i].position.x += 15;
  comp.selection[i].position.y += 15;
}
```

3. Close down the Script Editor and save your file as **Duplicate Object** in your LiveMotion Projects folder.

4. In your Automation menu, select the Load LiveTab command and choose the Duplicate Object file.

5. Create a new composition with a simple object.

6. Select that object and click on the button from the LiveTab to trigger the automation script onto the object.

Project Summary

You can use this LiveTab now to duplicate just about any object on your composition. Figure 13-4 displays the LiveTab next to a composition in which an object was just duplicated. However, you can trigger the same effect with both the Copy and Paste commands, as well as the Duplicate command found under the Object menu. This short tutorial should give you some insight into the convenience and usefulness of automation scripting and LiveTabs.

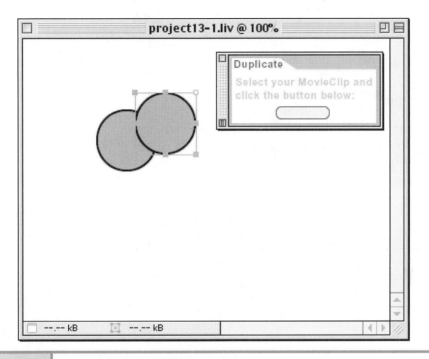

Figure 13-4   Creating and scripting a LiveTab

Summary

This module wraps up the introduction to the scripting feature of LiveMotion. As the program becomes more and more widely used and adopted by both previous LiveMotion 1 users and those who are both new and veterans of creating flash animations utilizing scripts to control the flow of animation, you'll discover many of the features of LiveMotion 2 (such as LiveTabs and automation scripts being shared with the LiveMotion community). Opening and using the LiveTabs and Automation Scripts in your program is as easy as launching them from the Automation menu. For those of you who are still not comfortable with creating your own scripts, brushing up your understanding of how JavaScripts and ActionScripts are composed is a necessity if you'd like to further develop your animation in LiveMotion. However, various automation scripts and LiveTabs are available, and you have all of them at your disposal.

13

In the next module, we'll go over the use of sound in your projects. We'll cover the use of sound in your rollovers as well as creating longer sounds that will play during the entire length of your projects. The use of sound can also weigh heavily on the file size of your projects. However, since you're now capable of creating preloaders that will loop while your projects load in a web browser, you can worry less about this problem.

In addition, the next module will also show you how to use the Load Movie Script to import external music files into the currently playing SWF file in a browser. Doing so will allow you to create music jukeboxes in which the user has the ability to decide which music file they'd like to listen to.

☑ *Mastery Check*

1. Where can you find LiveMotion 1 Behaviors in LiveMotion 2?

   A. In the Rollover palette

   B. In the Scripting Syntax Helper library

   C. In the composition browser

   D. In the Automation Scripting Helper library

2. Which type of Behavior is the following script associated with?

```
blue_dot.lmSetCurrentState(Down);
```

   A. Change State

   B. Load Movie

   C. Wait for Download

   D. Go to Relative Time

3. What is the purpose of the very first label placed on the timeline when creating a Wait for Download script?

   A. It allows the script to know how much of the file has loaded.

   B. It allows the script to know when to end the looping animation of the preloader.

   C. It allows the script to go ahead to the last label at which the looping process of a preloader begins.

   D. It allows the script to go back to it and replay the animation.

4. What's the purpose of a preloader?

   A. It instructs the browser to increase the speed at which to load the file.

   B. It loops a continuous animation that plays until the file finishes loading in a web browser.

   C. It loads the animation of the file by first playing the last frame and continuing to do so until the animation reaches the first.

   D. All of the above.

13

☑ Mastery Check

5. What's the purpose of the Debugger?

A. To test the integrity of the scripts in your projects.

B. To help you see which part of the script you're having problems with.

C. It prompts you with specific error messages every time there's an error in your script.

D. All of the above.

6. From which menu are you able to run and open scripts?

A. Script menu

B. Automation menu

C. Edit menu

D. Object menu

7. Player scripting controls the _____, while Automation scripting controls other _____.

A. Player/players

B. Player/compositions

C. Composition/scripts

D. Composition/player

8. Which of the following sections of LiveMotion allow you to trigger scripts on the object on your compositions?

I. Scripts submenu

II. Script menu

III. Styles palette

IV. LiveTabs

☑ Mastery Check

A. I, II, and III

B. I, III, and IV

C. I II, and IV

D. I, II, IV

9. How does the Script window differentiate from the Script Editor?

A. It allows us to create automation scripts.

B. It allows us to save its scripts into a JavaScript format.

C. None of the above.

D. All of the above.

10. Which of the following is true about LiveTabs?

I. They use automation scripts.

II. They are similar to palettes.

III. They can be loaded at any time into LiveMotion.

A. I and II

B. I and III

C. II and III

D. All of the above

13

Module 14

Music and Sound

The Goals of this Module

- Learn how to use the Sound palette
- Know how to attach sound to object states
- Be able to play sound during an animation
- Know how to import sound as an object on your composition
- Learn how to control sound: Play, Stop, Loop, Volume, Pan, and so forth
- Learn how to attach sounds to exported animated SWF files

LiveMotion uses two types of sounds. The first kind is the type of sound you attach to an object's State. When done so, the attached sound is executed/played when the user interacts with that specific object by triggering the specific State where the sound is attached. These types of sounds are known as Event Sounds. The second type of sound is the type you import in to LiveMotion using the Place command. In this module, you learn what types of file formats LiveMotion enables you to import on to your composition. Additionally, when a sound is imported in such manner, it appears on your timeline and resembles any other object in your Timeline window. A sound object has its own object header, as well as its own duration bar, whose length is stretched relative to the duration of the music file. This module discusses both of these types of sound files and provides you with a means to manipulate and control them during the editing process, as well as during the interaction that occurs when a user interacts with the exported piece.

As with the Library and Style palettes, you learn how to use the Sound palette, which stores small sound files that can be applied to Object States at any time. You also learn about using the Export palette to control how the sounds on the composition get exported. In conclusion, the final project of this module provides a way for you to create a music jukebox from which users can select the type of background music they'd like to listen to when viewing your exported animated file. In the project, you use the Load Movie Behavior Scripts you learned about in the previous module to create such an effect.

Sound Palette

At first glance, the Sound palette resembles the Styles, Texture, and the Library palette. In fact, these four types of palettes share the same purpose: all are used to store various files users can either interact with or attach to the objects on their composition. As with the other three palettes, the Sound palette enables you to control how the sound files inside are displayed. The small triangle in the top-right corner of the palette enables you select from three different types of views: Swatches, Preview, and Name. The buttons at the bottom of the palette are used to control the sounds within. The first button starting at the left enables you to preview a selected sound file by letting you listen to it. To hear a specific sound file, simply select it and click this Play button to hear the sound.

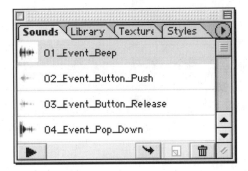

The next button over is the Apply button. When triggered, a selected sound in the Sound Library is applied to the selected State of an object on the composition. Remember, if you apply a sound to a newly created object for which you haven't yet created addition States, the sound file attached will be played automatically once the object is loaded. The sound file will only play once because it executes from the object's Normal State.

Attach Sounds to Object States

To make the sound file trigger by a user action, you first need to create additional States for that object, and then apply the sound file. The following is an example:

1. Begin by creating a simple shape on your composition.

2. Select the object and create a Down State for the object in the Rollover palette.

3. Make sure the Down State is selected, and then click the Apply button in the Sound palette after you select a specific sound.

4. Use the Preview mode to test your new interactive button.

14

When clicked, the button will play the specified sound file you attached to it from the Sound palette. As long as the object stays loaded in your composition during the animation, the object will always trigger that sound when a user clicks the object.

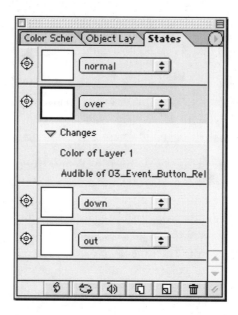

In addition, you can apply more sounds for the object by creating other States. For example, you can have one sound play for the object's Over State, another for its Down State, and yet another for its Out State. In addition, you can also apply sounds to the object's Custom States. These types of states are triggered by remote rollovers. For more information on remote rollovers, review Module 6.

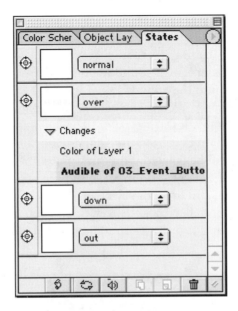

Deleting unwanted sound from your Object States is quite simple. Select the specific State of an object from which you want to remove a sound file, toggle on the small triangle that displays all the alterations done for that State in the Rollover palette, select the sound file, and then click the Delete icon at the bottom of the Rollover palette. The sound for that state is now gone. Another way to remove sound from an object's State is to select and double-click that object's state in the timeline, and then proceed by removing the attached sound object, which is located inside.

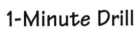

1-Minute Drill

● How do you attach sounds to Rollover buttons?

● What's one method of deleting sounds from Rollover buttons?

● What's the other method?

● Select a specific State in the States palette and click the Add Sound button.
● Toggle on the small triangle in the specific state, which opens a hierarchy of all the effects made to that Object State. Then, simply select the sound in the hierarchy and click the Delete icon at the bottom of the palette.
● Double-click the specific state that contains the sound object in the Timeline window, and then remove that sound object.

14

Custom Audio Library

The Sound palette also enables you to import your own sound files and place them in the palette for later use. A sound file brought into the Sound palette is automatically placed into the Sounds folder in your LiveMotion folder on your hard drive. When you click the DELETE button in the Sound palette, LiveMotion prompts you with the message: "Really delete this file? Deleting this file permanently removes it from the Sounds directory on your disk." If you click yes, the file will be deleted. You can bring sound files in to the Sound palette in two ways: either drag and drop a sound file on to the Library palette from anywhere on your hard drive or select an already imported sound file from your Timeline window, and then click the New Sound button in the Library palette. You learn about importing your own sound files into the Sound palette next.

Ask the Expert

Question: Ever since I began adding my own sounds to the Sound Library, I've noticed LiveMotion takes longer to load. Why?

Answer: The more sounds you bring in to the Sound Library, the longer LiveMotion takes to read through all those sounds on startup. You can either delete some of the sounds you no longer use from the Sounds folder or purchase more RAM for your computer.

Question: How does RAM speed up the process?

Answer: All your programs require random access memory (RAM) to run. Programs use this memory as a buffer. When the buffer is close to being full, programs tend to slow down and react more slowly to user action.

Question: How do I know how much RAM and what type of RAM to purchase for my computer?

Answer: Your best bet is to contact your computer's manufacturer and ask its representative. You might also search for this type of information online in user forums or public chats relative to this topic, or even on your computer manufacturer's web site.

Work with Imported Sounds

Importing sounds into LiveMotion works the same way as importing images. To import a sound file, use the Place command, select a sound file from anywhere on your hard drive, and click OK. The sound file and its duration bar appear inside your Timeline window, as shown in Figure 14-1, but you want to see the file physically on your composition. LiveMotion treats the imported sound file just as it does any other object in the Timeline window.

Unlike other types of objects created or imported into LiveMotion, imported sound files don't contain any Transform components. They do, however, offer two types of object attributes: Volume and Pan. These object attributes can be controlled from the Properties palette once the sound file is selected in the Timeline window. As with different types of objects, you'll notice the Properties palette is completely different. The Pan enables you to control the output from the left and the right speaker of the computer. By creating keyframes for this Object attribute, you can animate a sound file's Pan.

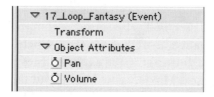

The Volume setting enables you to control the volume of the sound playing. As with the Pan Object attribute, you can also animate the Volume attribute on

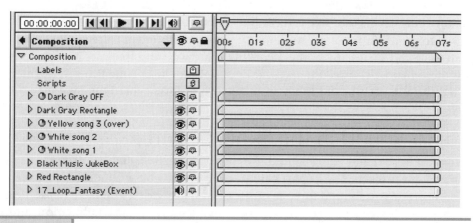

Figure 14-1 Timeline view of an imported sound object

14

the timeline. You'll also notice the drop-down menu at the bottom of the Properties palette offers three options: Solo Event Sound, Even Sound, and Streaming Sound. By default, all sound files brought into LiveMotion are Event Sounds. The difference between the Event Sound and the Event Solo Sound options relates more toward sounds used in object States. For example, a State with an Event Sound plays every time a user triggers that specific State, whereas an Event Solo Sound only plays once. The remaining option, Streaming Sound, is quite useful for sounds that have been imported into LiveMotion. Streaming Sound is played while the file is loading, so a user waiting for a file to load can listen to the sound while it's loading and needn't wait until everything has completely loaded. Using the Streaming Sound option can significantly reduce the quality of the sound being streamed, however. Experiment with both Event Sounds and Streaming Sounds and choose the type that best fits your needs.

Audio Formats

LiveMotion enables you to import a variety of file formats. These formats include AIFF, AVI, WAV, MIDI, and MP3. LiveMotion takes in all these formats and, when the file is exported as a SWF, the sound is compressed as an MP3 for the most optimum sound quality, as well as file size. When you work with sound files that are hefty in size, however, your exported files will be quite huge. In the upcoming section "Load Movie," you learn about the Load Movie Script Behaviors you'll use to load sound on to your playing SWFs to split your projects into multiple parts, where each loads individually, based on the user's action.

You can get audio for your projects in literally thousands of places but be aware of any copyright laws that protect any of the sounds you plan to use. Your best bet for being on the safe side is recording audio yourself. The simplest way to do this is to get a computer microphone (if your computer isn't already equipped with one) and to use any of the recording shareware and freeware applications out there that let you record and save sound files. QuickTime Pro is only one of many available. Try doing a search for such programs on **download.com**.

Adjust Sound in the Export Palette

After you import and adjust sound files in your timeline, and before you export your projects, the Export palette can provide you with multiple ways of compressing the sound in your projects. In many cases, you have to sacrifice quality for file size and vice versa. Experiment using various combinations until you're satisfied with both.

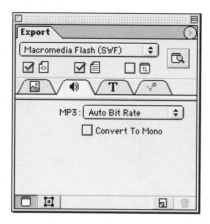

The two compression choices the Export palette provides you with are Auto bit rate and an option to convert the sound file into mono. In many cases where you're using human voice sounds, it's best to check off the Mono option because it won't impact the quality of the sound that much. However, it will significantly reduce the file size of the sound file within the exported SWF.

Project 14-1: Play Music in the Project's Background

In the following project, you import and adjust a sound file, so it will play alongside the animated objects already created and animated in the timeline. You use a previous file from a previous project and attach a sound file to it. Before proceeding with this project, get an MP3 or any other music sound file you want to use. You can also use any of the sound files that were included with LiveMotion 2. You'll find them in the Sounds folder, located in the LiveMotion 2 folder on your hard drive.

Step-by-Step

1. Begin by opening up the Animating Text.liv project you created back in Module 9.

2. Go to the Timeline window. Make sure the CTM is set to the 00 time interval, and then import a music sound file by using the Place command found under the File menu. If you're importing any of the music sound files that came included with LiveMotion 2, be sure only to import those with the word "loop" in them. These files are edited in such way that when they're set to loop, they do it flawlessly.

3. Now you have to adjust the duration bar of the composition header in your Timeline window to match the length of the duration bar of your imported music sound file.

4. To make your new sound file loop infinitely, first you need to select the sound object in the Timeline window, convert the object into a MovieClip Group, and then set it to loop.

5. You can now save your file as Project 14-1.liv in your LiveMotion Projects folder and preview it in the Preview mode.

Project Summary

When you preview your new file, the sound file is looped infinitely. If you want it to loop only a set amount of times, open the MovieClip Group you created for it, stretch the duration bar of the file to the length you want the file to loop, and be sure to uncheck the Loop button.

You can also play around with the other features of music objects. For example, you can animate the Pan Object attribute or create custom volume effects in which the volume of the file's sound objects rises in the beginning, and then lowers once the file is ending.

Control Sounds

Animating the two Object attributes of an imported sound object isn't the only way to control it. You also have your powerful scripting engine at your disposal. For example, you can instruct the file to begin and end playing at a specified keyframe or assign this action to a specific Rollover button's state. You also have the capability to loop sounds either infinitely or for a set amount of time. You learned about that option in your previous project.

Finally, one of the most convenient scripts available to you is the Load Movie Script. With the *Load Movie Script,* you can attach an exported SWF file that contains sound files set to begin playing when they're launched and attach them to an already playing SWF file. You learn about the Load Movie Script in the upcoming section "Load Movie." In addition, the last project of this module uses such script to provide a way for you to create a custom jukebox from which users are given a selection of music files they're in control of launching while they view your animated SWF file.

Loop Sounds

As you previously learned, looping music sounds works the same way as looping animating objects. For example, if you want to loop a sound infinitely, set it as a MovieClip Group, and then set it to loop. In many cases, though, you may want to have the sound file loop only for a specified number of times. This can also be done quite easily. If you've noticed, whenever you import a sound file into LiveMotion, the program automatically sets its duration bar as long as the length of the sound file itself. Now, if you want to have the sound file end early, you can simply drag the right end of its duration bar to the left. Or, to have it start playing at a later time, all you must do is drag the left end of its duration bar to the right. To have the object loop for a specific number of times, all you have to do is drag the right end of its duration bar to the right as far as desired. The dark gray lines that begin to appear on the duration bar itself tell you when the sound file ends and when it begins playing again. With this information, you can predict and adjust the number of loops you want to set your sound file to play.

Stop and Play

Another way to control your music sound files is to write simple scripts for them, which enable you to control when they start and when they stop. For example, the following script, when placed as a Keyframe Script on the 00 time interval inside a MovieClip Group that contains a sound file, instructs the player to suspend playing the sound file:

```
movieclip.stop();
```

Of course, you have to replace the MovieClip with the name of the sound file. In addition, the reason you placed this Keyframe Script inside a MovieClip Group is to prevent the rest of the files in the project from suspending to play. After all, you only want to suspend the sound, and not the rest of the animation. Because the MovieClip Group plays independently of the rest of the animated objects in the project, the Stop Behaviors Script will only have an impact on the sound file.

Now that you've created a Stop Behavior Keyframe Script, you need to create a Play Script that enables you to trigger the sound file to begin playing. As with the Stop Keyframe Script, you can make the Play Script a Keyframe

Script, but having this action controlled by the user would probably be much more useful for you. Therefore, the Play Script would be more useful to you on a specific State of a Rollover object. This is also done easily. Simply enter this script on the Down State of a Rollover object:

```
movieclip.play();
```

Once again, the Movie Clip keyword needs be replaced with the name of the sound file. In addition, you can also attach the Stop Script to another Rollover Button State. Doing so, enables you to give the user control of when to start and stop playing the sound file.

Control Volume and Pan with Event Handlers

The Script Editor enables you to create script that controls both the volume and the Pan of specified sound objects. The following miniproject takes you through controlling the volume of a specified sound object playing in the background.

1. Begin by either placing one of the Sound loops found in the Sounds palette or importing one of your own. You can find plenty of free looped music sounds at **Flashkit.com**.

2. Convert your Sound loop into a MovieClip Group and set it to loop.

3. Rename the MCG to mymusic.

4. Type in **volume** using the Type tool and, next to it, create three small square shapes. These squares will act as the button to control the volume of the mymusic object.

5. Select all the shapes and convert them into MovieClips.

6. Select the first shape, launch the Script Editor, and go into the OnButtonPress Event Handler.

7. Type in the following script into the right-side window of the Script Editor:

```
music=newSound(_root.mymymusic);
music.setVolume("100");
```

8. Select the next button and type in exactly the same script, except change the value of 100 in the second line to 50.

9. Select the last object and change the value to 0.

10. Preview your composition in a browser

When you click the three buttons, the volume of the sound playing automatically changes. Here's what's happening in the script. In the first line, you create a new sound object—located on -root named mymusic—and you define the variable as "music." In the second line, you set the variable to run the function setVolume, which sets the volume to the value in the parentheses. The value can be anywhere between 0 and 100. 100 equals Full Volume and 0 equals Mute.

A similar method can be used when controlling the Pan of a playing sound object. Pan enables you to control the sound coming from the left and right speakers of the computer. In the following example, you work with your previous project.

1. Select the text object volume and rename it to Pan using the Type tool.

2. Select the first MC (MovieClip) button, go to the Script Editor, and select the OnButtonPress Event Handler.

3. Replace the contents of the previously entered script with the following:

```
pan=newSound(_root.mymusic);
pan.setPan(-100);
```

4. In the next button, replace the script, except enter the value of 0 in the parentheses of the second line.

5. In the last button, replace the script with your updated one and enter the value of 100 in the parentheses of the second line.

6. Preview your composition in a browser.

As with the Volume project, clicking the third button executes the script inside. The first button sets the Pan to –100, which sets the Pan to play from your left speaker. The second button sets the Pan to 0, which sets the Pan to

14

play from both your speakers. The last button sets the pan to 100, which sets the Pan to play from your right speaker. The script executed is similar to the Volume Script, except you use the setPan function to set the Pan of the sound file named mymusic In addition, the value in the parentheses can be anywhere between −100 and 100.

Load Movie

One of my favorite Behavior Scripts in LiveMotion is the *Load Movie Script,* which enables you either to replace or attach additional SWF files on top of those already playing. Not only does this give you the freedom to truncate your files into several pieces, but it also gives the user the freedom to control which files to attach. For example, because sound can have a huge impact on the file size of an exported SWF file, you can choose to load them, rather than call them within the file. The Load Movie Script gives you such an option. The following miniproject is a reflection of such an effect. It involves the creation

?Ask the Expert

Question: After exporting and previewing my file that contains both animation and a background music file, I noticed that after the animated object finishes animating, my sound file also stops. How come?

Answer: This could happen for multiple reasons. The most likely reason is the duration bar of your sound file is longer than the duration bar of your composition. You can either stretch the composition's duration bar to the length of the sound files or create a MovieClip Group of the sound file.

Question: How would creating a MovieClip Group from the sound file help me?

Answer: Because MovieClip Groups contain timelines that play independently from the composition's timeline and the objects on it, creating a MovieClip Group from a sound file would let your sound file play independently of the rest of your composition. Even after your composition's timeline commenced playing, therefore, the sound file's duration bar would continue playing until it ended.

of two SWF files that are triggered to join together with the Load Movie Behavior Script by a user action:

1. Let's begin by creating your first file. Create a new document with the following dimensions: 500×300.

2. Using the Place command, import a sound file. As noted previously, you can use any of the ones found in the Sounds folder or import one of your own.

3. Now select the sound file, make it a MovieClip Group, and set it to loop.

4. Finish by saving your file as music1.liv and exporting it as music1.swf into your LiveMotion Projects folder.

You use this file by calling it up in the following file:

1. Again, create a new document with the same dimensions and create a simple text object by typing **Play**.

2. You can further develop this object by combining it with a shape object to make it into a more real life-like button.

3. Now, go to the States palette and create an Over, a Down, and an Out State for this button.

4. For the Over State, be sure to alter the button in some way, so when users interact with it, they'll know the button is used to perform some type of task.

5. Select the Down State and click the New Script button next to it in the States palette.

6. Enter the following script into the scripting window of the Script Editor that was triggered when you clicked the New Script button in the States palette:

```
LoadMovieNum("music1.swf:, "2");
```

7. Close the Script Editor, create another text object, and combine it with a shape object that will represent your Stop button.

14

8. As before, create three additional states for the button and be sure to alter the Over State.

9. Select the Down State of the Stop button and click the New Script button that, once again, will bring up the Script Editor.

10. Enter the following script:

```
UnloadMovieNum("2");
```

11. Close the Script Editor, save your file as loadmusic1.liv, and export it as loadmusic1.swf into your LiveMotion Projects folder.

12. To preview your file, launch it in a web browser. Clicking your Play button will trigger your music1.swf file to attach and play to your currently playing movie. Clicking the Stop button triggers the Unload Movie Script and unattaches the file, which suspends the music from playing.

The significance of the 2 in the first and second script is that LiveMotion treats it as a level on which to load the movie. The initial file that loads the music file will always be on level 0. By loading the music file on level 2, you let yourself load additional movies on levels between 0–99 without overwriting your music. The second script simply tells the player to unload the movie playing on level 2.

1-Minute Drill

● What happens if you load a movie on the same level as an already-playing movie?

● Which level is higher, level 45 or level 78?

● What happens if you load a movie on level 45 while another is playing on level 78?

● The newly loaded movie replaces the movie that's already playing.
● Level 78
● Any object that came with the movie loaded on level 78 would overlap those loaded along with the movie on level 45.

Project 14-2: Create a Music Jukebox

In your previous miniproject, you created two buttons that enabled you to trigger on and trigger off a music file that got loaded and attached to your currently playing movie with a simple script. In the following project, you use the same technique but, this time, you provide the user with a few more choices. Doing so enables you to create a minijukebox, from which users can select the type of music they want to listen to while they view the rest of your animations.

Step-by-Step

1. Because you've already created one type of music file in your previous miniproject, let's begin by creating a second one. Following the same steps as before, use the Place command to import a music file either from one of your own or one from the Sounds folder inside your LiveMotion folder. Set it as a MovieClip Group, and then set it to loop.

2. Follow Step 1 until you have exactly three different looping music files exported as music1.swf, music2.swf, and music3.swf (its important to leave these three looping music files in the same location on your hard drive as the file you'll create shortly that will call on them and attach them with the notion that they're located in the same directory. The same applies when you upload these files to your site).

3. Now create the file that, as in your previous miniproject, will load these movies based on a user action. Begin by creating a new composition with the same dimensions you used for your previous files.

4. Start by creating a simple text object by typing **Music JukeBox** using the Type tool.

5. Next to it, create a small text object by typing **OFF** using the Type tool.

6. Now create a thin horizontal line that stretches below both of these objects. Underneath this line, create a small rectangle to be used as a menu bar from which a user can select a song to play.

7. Create three buttons inside the rectangular menu bar you just created. In Figure 14-2, song 1, song 2, and song 3 text buttons were used.

8. Select the three menu bar choices and the OFF text object, and then create an Over, a Down, and an Out State for them in the States palette. Be sure to distinguish the Over State by changing the appearance of the object at that State.

14

9. Select the Down State of the first menu bar choice—song 1—and click the New Script button in the States palette.

10. In the Script Editor, enter the following script:

```
LoadMovieNum("music1.swf", "3");
```

11. Do the same for the song 2 Menu Bar button and the song 3 Menu Bar button, but be sure to alter the script for each of them, where button 2 would be calling up music2.swf, as opposed to music1.swf.

12. Now go to the OFF button, select the Down State for that object, and click the New Script button. In the Script Editor, enter the following script:

```
UnloadMovieNum("3");
```

13. After doing this, save your file as Project 14-2 in your LiveMotion Projects folder, export your file to the same location where you saved your three music SWF files, and preview it in your browser.

Project Summary

Your new jukebox animation now has the capability to let a user select from three different music sounds they want to hear. Figure 14-2 displays its simple interface. Each time a different option is chosen from the menu bar, the previously playing movie is replaced with the new one. In addition, until it's triggered again, the OFF button not only enables you to unload any of these music files playing on level 3, it also lets you turn off the music completely.

Be sure to experiment by creating a more complex interface for your new jukebox. For example, try including some animation. In addition, you can also create a preloader for each of the song files you created. Doing so lets the users see a looping animation while they wait for their selected song to play.

Music JukeBox   OFF

song 1
song 2
song 3

| Figure 14-2 | Music jukebox interface |

Summary

Adding music to your animation adds a bit of flavor to your projects. Remember, when you work with audio, be sure to respect any copyright infringements that protect the file you're working with. As you learned earlier, plenty of sites are out there that offer free music loops, which can be imported to and used in LiveMotion. These types of loops are often referred to as Royalty Free Loops. In the final module of this book, you learn about several techniques used to design a smooth navigational interface you can use. In addition, you use additional palettes, such as the Color Scheme palette, to create a sense of consistency in your work. The palette enables you to match and save all the colors you'll use to design these interfaces.

In addition, you go beyond simply using the Load Movie Script to attach music files. You learn about its capability to attach objects on top of objects.

14

☑ *Mastery Check*

1. Which of the following palettes does the Sound palette resemble?

   A. State palette

   B. Library palette

   C. Properties palette

   D. Transform palette

2. Which palette lets you alter the two types of Object attributes for an imported sound in the Timeline window?

   A. Transform palette

   B. Object palette

   C. Properties palette

   D. Sound palette

3. Which of the following isn't an Object attribute of an imported sound file?

   A. Pan

   B. Pitch

   C. Volume

   D. All of the above

4. Which of the following options lets your sound files play alongside an animation?

   A. Streaming Sound

   B. Event Sound

   C. Event Solo Sound

   D. State Sound

✓ Mastery Check

5. What's the effect performed by the Pan Object attribute?

  A. It enables you to set from which speaker the sound is coming from.

  B. It enables you to adjust the 3-D stereo of the sound.

  C. It enables you to set the quality of the sound.

  D. It enables you to set the pace at which volume increases and decreases.

6. What's the significance of the 65 in the following script?

```
UnloadMovieNum("65");
```

  A. It tells the player the movie will unload in 65 seconds.

  B. It tells the player the movie named 65 is to be unloaded.

  C. It tells the player that on the 65th click of a mouse, a movie is to be unloaded.

  D. It tells the player to unload the movie on level number 65.

7. What will happen to a file that contains a Stop Script located on the 00s time interval on the timeline that contains the music file, along with other animated files?

  A. When the file loads in a browser, the imported music file won't begin playing, but another object will.

  B. Neither the music file nor other files will begin playing.

  C. LiveMotion won't let you export the file.

  D. The player and the browser will ignore the script and begin playing both the sound file and the rest of the animated objects.

14

☑ Mastery Check

8. Which of the following methods are the correct steps to take to create a Stop Script for a music file when you don't want it to start playing when the file loads in a browser?

I. Move the duration bar of the sound file to a further time interval

II. Create a MovieClip Group from the sound file

III. Shrink the duration bar of the sound file

   A. l and II

   B. I and III

   C. II

   D. III

9. Which of the following is the appropriate way to create a script that will trigger a sound file named music1 to begin playing?

   A. music1.play();

   B. play.music1.();

   C. music1.play()

   D. music1.play;

10. On which level is the initial-playing SWF file located, in reference to other SWF files loaded on top of it?

   A. 99

   B. 1

   C. 0

   D. 10

Module 15

Smooth Design

The Goals of this Module

- Learn several different types of menu techniques
- Learn how to set the position for your loaded SWF files
- Be able to use the Color Scheme palette
- Learn about consistency when designing a web site from LiveMotion
- Learn about various ways of exporting your text
- Know about various free resources available to you on various web sites
- Know about various LiveMotion sites from which to draw inspiration

Every single project that we've discussed and created in the book was set on the idea of creating a single page filled with a static graphic, a simple animation, or an advanced one that utilized some sort of scripting. In this module, we'll concentrate more on utilizing LiveMotion to create a series of pages that are linked together. We'll discuss various ways to create navigational menus that enable the user to easily find their way around your site. We'll also discuss using the Load Movie Script behavior within these navigation menus, to allow ourselves to easily attach SWF files on top of one another.

We'll also go over using the Color Scheme palette, which comes equipped with several premade schemes containing a range of colors that are either analogous or complementary to one another. The use of color is extremely important in design and you'll find this palette very handy when it comes to working with color.

As with color, font type and style are also important in designing your web site. In Module 4, we covered the use of text in design and its ability to have a significant impact on the message that your project is trying to get across. In this module, we'll go over using and exporting clean fonts that are anti-aliased and will display properly on all types of computers that will be previewing your work.

In conclusion, we'll go over several different types of sites that may be able to assist you while working in LiveMotion. These sites will range from ones that offer you an abundant amount of free resources such as ActionScripts to ones that will inspire you. At the end of the module, in the final project you'll create a simple three page navigation utilizing all of the techniques that you've learned.

Interface, Navigation, and Transition Between Pages

When designing a web site, consistency in transition between pages is important. Therefore, when creating a navigation menu on the various pages of your site, keep them in the same location on all pages so that the visitors will be able to quickly familiarize themselves with the structure of the site. You should also keep their appearance the same; doing so enables the visitor to distinguish the navigational area from the rest of the content of the page.

In the previous module, we briefly utilized the Load Movie Script to attach a movie on top of one that was already playing. A navigational section of your site can utilize a similar technique.

Staying consistent when working with navigational menus also applies when designing an interface for your web site. If you load a navigational menu on the left side of the page, keep it on the left side of the page for all of your pages. If you happen to preview images from your gallery page on the right side of your screen, do so for all of your images. A good interface allows your visitors to quickly familiarize themselves with your web site. How many times have you visited a site on which the content was so scattered all over that you finally gave up? However, not everyone shares this opinion, and sometimes it takes being unorganized to stick out from the crowd. After all, you wouldn't want your site to resemble Yahoo! Therefore, take these suggestions for what they are— just suggestions.

Create Navigation Menus

Navigation menus come in all shapes and forms. The most popular and most widely used type of menu is a folder tab style, like those found in your palette windows. There are numerous sites that utilize them: amazon.com, Apple.com, and bn.com are just a few of them. They're structured to resemble folders stacked on top of one another. The idea behind using this type of a navigational system is to in some way or another change the appearance of the tab the visitor is currently viewing. For example, take a look at Figure 15-1, which displays a simple navigational menu utilizing the folder tab appearance. Notice how the appearance of the tab called Home differs from the others. The idea behind this type of folder tab navigation menu is to darken the color of the tab the visitor is viewing. Therefore, the "home page" tab is darker than the other tabs.

In following miniproject, you'll design a three-page web site consisting of the folder tab navigational menu system. This navigation menu will be the same as the one found in Figure 15-1. When you're finished designing it, you'll export all of the files into one location on your hard drive, and then preview them in

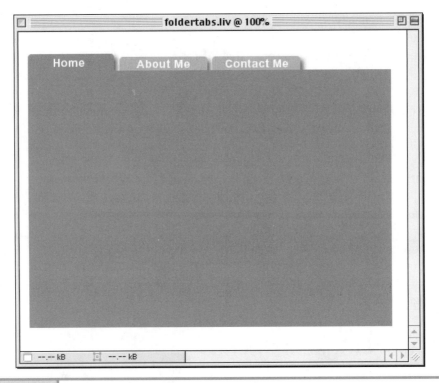

Figure 15-1 Folder tab appearance

your browser. All of the content on the composition will be exported into the JPEG file format:

1. Begin by creating a new composition with the following dimensions: 500×400.

2. Create three rounded rectangles, each measuring 123×35.

3. Select all of your rounded rectangle objects and apply the drop shadow effect from the Styles palette.

4. Color the first one a dark gray tone, and the remaining two a lighter gray tone.

5. Position the first rounded rectangle to the following location (use the Transform palette to assist you): X: 11 Y: 27. Position the second to X: 131 Y: 31, and the third to X: 250 Y: 31. (Note that the second and the third rounded objects are positioned at the same Y attribute. The idea behind this appearance is to display the home folder tab slightly higher than the remaining ones, which will (in addition to color) let the viewers of this navigational menu know that they're currently on the home page of the site.)

6. Create three text objects, the first called **Home**, the second **About Me**, and the third **Contact Me**. Now place and center each of them into the rounded rectangles that you've just created.

7. Create a large rectangle measuring 468×322, and position it to the following location: X: 12 Y: 49.

8. We'll need to now apply links to our folder tabs. Select the first rounded rectangle and go over to the web palette. Enter the following page: **home.html**. Select the second rounded rectangle and enter the following page: **about.html**. Finally, select the last rectangle, and enter the following page into the web palette: **contact.html**.

9. We're done with our first page, so let's first save it in our LiveMotion Projects folder as **FolderTab1.liv**.

10. Create a new folder in your LiveMotion Projects folder and call it **Folder_Tab_Navigation**. Choose Export Settings from the File menu and choose the Auto Layout Option. Choose JPEG as the file type, and export your composition with the Export As command. Save your HTML file as **Home.html** into Folder_Tab_Navigation.

11. Go back to your composition, select your first rounded rectangle along with its text object, and move it down so that it aligns with the others.

12. Select the second rounded rectangle object along with its text object and position it at Y: 27.

13. Color the second rounded rectangle the same color as the first rounded rectangle.

15

14. Use either the Eyedropper tool or the Color palette and color the first rounded rectangle the same as the third rounded rectangle. (We've pretty much made it so that the first folder tab and the second folder tab switched their appearance.)

15. As before, save your file as **FolderTab2.liv** in your LiveMotion Projects folder.

16. Export your file using the Export As command and save it as **aboutme.html** into your Folder_Tab_Navigation folder.

17. Go back to the composition once more and this time switch the appearance between the last rounded rectangle and the second rounded rectangle. Remember to also switch their positions so that the last rounded rectangle is slightly higher than the others.

18. After doing so, save your file as **FolderTab3.liv** in your LiveMotion Projects folder, and export it as **about.html** into your Folder_Tab_Navigation folder.

19. Launch and preview the home.html file that you previously exported in your Internet Browser.

The navigation menu that you've just created lets you easily switch back and forth between three pages. The folder tab corresponds to the page you are on. If you wish, you might further develop this project by providing some sort of information on each of these pages.

1-Minute Drill

- Why is it important to stay consistent when designing both the interface and a navigational menu for a site?
- Where are images saved to after exporting a file with either the JPEG or GIF option set in the Export palette?

Utilize the Load Movie Script

Unlike the previous method, the Load Movie Script allows you to load SWF files on top of your current SWF file rather than just taking you to a new page. Another benefit of using the Load Movie Script is that it allows you to retain

---

- To allow your visitors to quickly orient themselves around on your site
- Into the images folder, which is one directory lower than the HTML file

the information from the previous SWF file, even after an additional SWF file is loaded on top. An example of this effect is to imagine a piece of paper containing a drawing of a house in the bottom-left corner and a tree in the bottom-right corner. Now, imagine placing a similar piece of paper that is transparent except for one area. In the bottom-left corner of this transparent sheet of paper is a drawing of a tree. Placing the transparent sheet of paper over the other sheet will replace the drawing of the house in the bottom-left corner with the drawing of the tree. However, the drawing of the other tree located in the bottom-right corner of the first sheet of paper still appears, because no drawings on the second sheet of paper overlap or block it.

The Load Movie Script techniques are not only convenient because they allow you to either replace or retain specific objects from the previous playing SWF file, but they also allow you to significantly reduce your project's individual file sizes. For example, if you wanted to display a specific image on each page of your site, you can easily do so by utilizing the Load Movie Script in addition to leaving that part of the page transparent in any additional SWF files that you'll be loading on top of one another.

Making files transparent and solid in some areas is a lot simpler than it sounds. By default, every location on your exported SWF that does not contain an object on it is transparent. Therefore, if no object exists in the upper-left corner of your project, that area will be transparent when exported. Sometimes, however, blocking an object with another object doesn't do the job right. For example, blocking out an object that is bigger than the one that we are trying to replace it with will result in parts of the bigger objects remaining to be apparent even after the smaller object appears on top of it. The best method to resolve this problem is to use an additional object to help you replace the previous one. For example, in the following scenario, you can use a rectangle object colored the same color as the background that measures relatively the same as the previous large object and place it a level lower, behind the smaller object on the second SWF file. Now when the second SWF file with the smaller object loads on top of the first SWF file with the larger object, the rectangle object will overlap the larger object, and since the smaller object of the second SWF file is a level higher than the rectangle object, it will be the only one visible.

Positioning

Using the Load Movie Script the way it is composed requires you to always load an SWF file that measures the same as the one that you're planning to replace it with. The reason for this is that SWF files, when loaded on top of one another, are automatically aligned to the upper-left corner. Therefore, if you were trying to attach an SWF file that is smaller, it would automatically position itself to the upper-left corner of the SWF file that is being replaced. On the other hand, if you were trying to attach an SWF that is larger than the one already playing, it would get cut off.

Unfortunately, there's no way to fix the issue of the larger file attached over a smaller file being cut off; however, we can do something about controlling at which position our attached SWF files appear. The following is an example of the Load Move Script that attaches the file named contactus.swf at a specific location:

```
movieclip.loadMovieNum("contactus.swf", "2");
```

When triggered, the SWF named contactus.swf loads into the upper-left corner of the object named MovieClip. The MovieClip object can be any object on your SWF. Be sure to pick one that is located at the position that you'd like to load your new SWF file onto. However, let's say you would like to load your new SWF file at the center of the MovieClip object located on the first SWF. To do so, you would need to readjust the anchor point of your MovieClip object. The anchor point, by default, is always located at the upper-left corner—that's why movies always load onto that location. However, you can easily change that. Simply use COMMAND-CTRL-CLICK at the upper-left corner of your MovieClip and drag the anchor point that appears to the center of the object. Now, when you load the movie on top of this particular object, it'll load at its center rather than align itself to the upper-left portion. Another way of positioning your anchor points is to use the Transform LiveTab submenu, located under the Automation menu. The Transform LiveTab enables you to select from nine preset locations for the selected object.

Color Scheme Palette

Colors play an important part in a good design. The color scheme allows you to work with both analogous colors and complementary colors. Take a look at the Color Scheme palette as well as your Color palette. By selecting a color from the Color palette, the color wheel in the Color Scheme palette automatically updates and displays that specific color's analogous and complementary colors. The analogous colors are the ones that show up next to each other on the color wheel inside of the small circles. The complementary colors are the ones that show up opposite these colors on the other side of the color wheel.

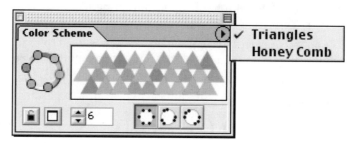

The color wheel inside of the Color Scheme palette can also be adjusted to display various types of color combinations based on the color that you currently have selected as the foreground color. In addition, the toolbar will display all of the colors in this specific group in order to allow you to quickly access them as you work on your projects.

The palette offers several different types of controls to allow you to access the different types of color combinations. Starting at the upper-right corner, the Views button allows you to select from two types of views: Honey Comb and Triangles. Each of these views will update the way the colors display in the right-side window of the palette. Moving down to the bottom-left corner, the Scheme Lock button allows you to temporarily lock the current color combination in both the Color Scheme palette and in the toolbar. To unlock, simply click the button once more. The next button over allows you to include the color of your background amongst your current color combination. As with the Scheme Lock button, this button can be toggled on and off. The next button over allows you to control the numerical value of the number of colors that will appear on your color wheel. Each numerical value has its own set of views, which can be set at the bottom-right portion of the palette.

Remember that the Color Scheme palette is there to assist you in using colors that match. If you'd rather follow an untraditional way of using colors and use your own color combinations, feel free to do so.

1-Minute Drill

- What is the significance of the colors that appear right above the foreground and the background color boxes in the toolbar?

- Which file and with what type of program would you need to change and work with if you were to change the location of any exported images from LiveMotion, within the exported HTML document that displays them?

Upload Files to Your Site

When it comes to uploading your exported files to your site, consistency in your directory structure is critical. However, this time directory structure needs to stay consistent throughout. Therefore, if you've exported your project as a set of GIF files, LiveMotion automatically created an images folder to which it saved all of your exported image files unless you choose to rename that folder in the Properties palette, in which case, the name of it would be different. In order to for the accompanied exported HTML page to display properly, all of those images need to stay as they are in the image folder, and the HTML file needs to be located at a higher directory. If you were to drag an image out of the images folder and place it in either a different folder or alongside the HTML file, that particular image will not display when your page is either previewed or viewed in an Internet browser. However, if you do have access to an HTML editor, you can both open and edit your exported HTML file, as well as set the location of your image(s) to whatever you like.

The same basic rules apply for any type of file that gets exported from LiveMotion. SWF files, unlike image files, are exported alongside your HTML file. Therefore, when you upload them to your site, they need to be located in the same directory. However, once again, if you'd like to have these files appear on different directories, you can do so by appropriately editing the HTML code in an HTML editor by referencing the file to the absolute path of the directory.

- The six colors that appear in the toolbar are part of a group of colors that were set in the Color Scheme palette.
- In order to change the location of your images that were exported alongside your HTML file, you'll need to edit that HTML file in an HTML editor.

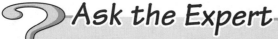

Ask the Expert

Question: Why is staying consistent in the location of your navigation menu and the contents of your pages so important? What if I don't want to have my site resemble Yahoo.com?

Answer: As mentioned before, these are only suggestions. However, most good sites will either be consistent in the location of all of their content as well as navigational area, or offer some sort of pattern as to where these features appear.

Question: I've already exported all of my files to a specific folder on my hard drive, now how do I create a web page?

Answer: You'll need to first browse the Web for a web hosting provider. Some are free and some charge by the month. The difference between the services varies. Free sites tend to use small pop-up windows that automatically launch when your site is viewed.

Question: How do I upload my exported LiveMotion files onto a web site?

Answer: You'll probably need to get your hands on a decent FTP application. There are many of them out there, and some are even free. Try searching on download.com. After getting the FTP application, follow the instructions sent to you by your web site hosting provider or search their site for more information.

Resources and Inspirations

When the first version of LiveMotion came out roughly two years ago, only two sites contained an abundant amount of information on the program, as well as user forums that allowed LiveMotion users to communicate with each other,

15

share ideas, and answer each others' questions—one of them is FlashKiller.com. The site, along with its name, was designed to advertise the power of LiveMotion; however, at that time LiveMotion 1 wasn't really a Macromedia Flash Killer as it still lacked several elements that Flash contained—mainly the ability to script files. A second site is the Adobe LiveMotion Forum, located at AdobeForums.com. Not only can you get answers from your peers, but also from the engineers that build the program. To this day, many of them continue to answer questions. I recently opened a new forum dedicated to a LiveMotion 1 and LiveMotion 2 discussion. Stop by if you have any questions relating to LiveMotion and any of the moderators at the forum will be happy to assist you.

As LiveMotion began to gain ground, dozens of LiveMotion sites came out. The following section will list several of my favorites (including my own). In addition, the section will also provide you with sites that offer free ActionScripts. Unfortunately, the sites that offer these ActionScripts will be written for Macromedia Flash users in mind.

In addition, this section lists several sites that offer free music loops for download. The music loops are edited in such way that when they are looped, the sound continues, thereby saving you both the headache and the money to go out and buy professional software that does the job.

LiveMotion Sites

- **Adobe LiveMotion Official Site**   www.adobe.com/products/livemotion
- **LiveMotionStudio.com**   www.livemotionstudio.com
- **StyleMotion**   www.stylemotion.com
- **Mad Doctor Phil**   www.livemotion.uk.com
- **LiveMotion Central**   www.livemotioncentral.com
- **Web Artimus**   www.webartimus.com
- **Cpros.net**   www.c-pros.net/intro.html

- Scooter King   www.idexworks.com/scoot

- TyFu.com   www.tyfu.com

- Kirk White   http://kirk-white.com

- TGIF Design   www.tgif17.com

- JAB Portfolio   http://homepage.mac.com/blitted/

ActionScript Resource Sites

- ActionScripts.org   www.actionscripts.org

- Flash5ActionScripts.com   www.flash5actionscripts.com

- Flash Move   www.flashmove.com

- Flash Kit   www.flashkit.com

- Cool Resources   www.coolresources.com

- Flash Zone   www.flashzone.com

- Flash Heaven   www.flashheaven.de/englisch.htm

Royalty-Free Sound Loops and Effects

- Daisy Chain Loops   www.daisychainproductions.com

- Were-Here Loops   www.were-here.com/forum/sound/index.shtml

- FlashSound Loops   www.flashsound.com

LiveMotion Forums

- Adobe Forums   www.adobeforums.com

- WWUG Forums   www.wwug.com/livemotion

- Flash Killer   www.flashkiller.com

- LivemotionStudio.com Forums   http://forums.livemotionstudio.com

- LiveMotion German Forum   www.livemotion.de

Project 15-1: Create and Export a Simple Web Site

Previously, we've created three pages that utilized a simple navigational menu that allowed us to jump from one page to another. The main aspect of the menu design was consistency. The same applies for the following project in which you'll create three separate files; however, you'll link them together by using the Load Movie script.

The first file of this project will display both the navigational menu and the content for that page. The other two files, however, will only contain their individual content. By using the Load Movie Script, you'll load these two pages on top of the content of the first page, and so on. In doing so, the file size of the other two files will be significantly smaller than that of the first since they won't contain the navigational menu within them; rather, the menu is transparent and available to you from the first file.

Step-by-Step

1. Create a new composition measuring 300×200.

2. Create three small buttons at the top of the page that will trigger your home page, the About Me page, and the Contact Me page.

3. Select the Home, Contact, and About button and create an over and down state for them in the States palette.

4. Create some type of content on the page that'll be relevant to just the home page.

5. Select the down state of the Home button and click on the Edit State Script button. Enter the following script:

```
unloadMovieNum("2");
```

6. Select the About Me button and enter the following script for its down state:

```
loadMovieNum("aboutme.swf," "2");
```

7. Select the Contact Us button and enter the following script for its down state:

```
loadMovieNum("contactus.swf", "2");
```

8. Save your file as **Project 15-1.liv** in your LiveMotion Projects folder.

9. Create a new folder in your LiveMotion Projects folder and call it **Project 15-1**.

10. Export your file as an SWF file to that folder and save the HTM file as **Home.html**.

11. Create the content for the remaining two pages. Delete the current content on your composition and create some type of content that is specific to only the About Me page (for example, a short bio or a small picture).

12. Delete the navigational menu from the page, as we were only using it as a placeholder for the About Me page, and save your file as **Project15-1b.liv** in your LiveMotion Projects folder.

13. Export your file as **aboutme.html** into your Project 15-1 folder located in your LiveMotion projects folder. (We won't really need the HTML file that'll get exported with the About Me page nor the HTML file that'll get exported with the Contact Me page. However, we do need the filenames of our SWF files to be exact in order for the scripts in the menu bar of the first file to work properly.)

14. Go back to your composition and enter some sort of content that is only specific to the Contact Me page (for example, enter a link to your e-mail address).

15. Once again, save your file in your LiveMotion Projects folder as **Project15-1c**.

16. Export your Contact Me page as **contactme.html** and save it to your Project 15-1 folder, located in your LiveMotion Projects folder.

17. Within your Internet browser, launch the home.html file. Experiment with your new scripted navigational menu.

Project Summary

As you might have noticed, the script entered for the Home Page button is different from the remaining two. The reason for that is that unlike the other two files, the Home.swf file will always be playing. When you click on the remaining two buttons, you're simply covering up a specific area of the Home.swf file with the new content. The script in the Home Page button simply instructs the player to unload any type of attached SWF file. When that happens, all of the content on the home page is apparent.

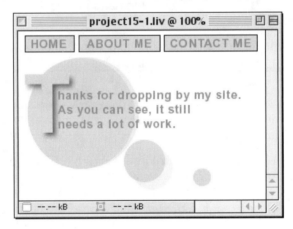

Many sites, including mine, use preloaders to load their attached content. Not only do they offer a cool effect, but they also let the visitor know that the content is being loaded.

Summary

This concludes our Beginner's Guide to LiveMotion 2. We've covered all of the features of LiveMotion, which you'll need to know in order to be able to create your own LiveMotion content for the Web. We've even covered some advanced features such as scripting the player, the timeline, and even creating our own LiveTabs.

The resource section of this module is rather short. However, by the time LiveMotion 2 hits the shelves (which should be about the time you're reading this book), tons of resources for LiveMotion 2 will be available to you. You're best bet is stay tuned to LiveMotion's official site, located at Adobe.com/products/livemotion.

Forums are a good way to get quick and easy answers to your questions. As stated earlier, Adobe's LiveMotion Forum comes highly recommended from both myself and many other LiveMotion users. You'll get quick responses, a warm reception, and, most of all, you won't be treated like a newbie. I've also recently opened my own third-party forums at http:// forums.livemotionstudio.com. I, or any of the moderators at the forum, will be happy to answer any of your questions as well as offer several LM2 examples.

☑ Mastery Check

1. Which palette allows you to enter URLs that correspond to their buttons?

   A. Transform palette

   B. Library palette

   C. Properties palette

   D. Web palette

2. What is the purpose of the Color Scheme palette?

   A. To assist you in finding colors that load quicker than those found in the Color palette.

   B. To assist you in finding colors that are not available in the Color palette.

   C. To assist you in finding various color combinations.

   D. To allow you to use neon type colors.

3. Colors that are next to each other on the color wheel of the Color Scheme palette are_____. Colors that are on the opposite side of the color wheel are_____.

   A. Analogous / complimentary

   B. Complimentary / analogous

   C. Dark / light

   D. Transparent / solid

☑ *Mastery Check*

4. Which is true about the following script:

```
unloadMovieNum("2");
```

   A. It will unload an SWF file named 2.swf.

   B. It will unload all SWF files loaded on level 2.

   C. It will unload the last two files that were attached.

   D. It will unload an SWF file that is numbered 2.

5. Which set of key commands followed by the dragging of your mouse, allow you to move an anchor point of an object?

   A. COMMAND-CTRL

   B. Option-Ctrl

   C. Command-Option

   D. Shift-Option

Appendix

Answers to Mastery Checks

Module 1: LiveMotion 2 Interface

1. What are pixels?

    C. A form of measurement

2. If you're planning to design your project for web use, a good idea is to keep your frame rate _____. On the other hand, if you're designing your project for a CD-ROM presentation, you should keep your frame rate _____, for smooth quality.

    Low, High

3. What's a quick way to access the tools in the toolbar?

    E. All of the above

4. How would you move palettes from one window to another?

    B. Clicking and dragging them

5. What's the significance of adding a file extension name during the Save process?

    A. It helps your LiveMotion application on a PC recognize the file.

Module 2: Work with Simple Shapes

1. Which of the following Palettes will allow you to adjust contrast of your objects?

    D. Adjust palette

2. A good example of layers is to compare them to the numerous _____ of an onion.

    skins

3. How would you go about creating a new style in the Styles palette?

    B. Select an altered object and click New Style in the Styles palette

4. In order to permanently remove a texture from your Textures palette, you need to:

    A. Drag it out of your Textures folder and move it to the trash.

Module 3: Work with Custom Shapes

1. Which one of these four choices displays the correct tools and palettes for creating and importing shapes?

   C. Pen tool, Library palette, Rectangle tool

2. Which function would you perform if you want your selected object to be brought in front of another object on your composition?

   B. Use the Arrange menu to bring the object forward

3. The _____ tool is used for drawing lines and curves on your composition. The _____ tool is used for editing lines and curves created by the _____.

Pen, Pen Selection, Pen

4. All the Combine functions enable you to combine either all or some parts of the selected objects. Unfortunately, not all of them let you use all the palettes available to you prior to combining your shapes. Which one of these doesn't let you use some palettes?

   B. Unite with Color

5. Which of the following file formats containing shapes does LiveMotion let you import using the Place command?

   D. EPS and AI

6. _____ shapes enable you to organize your objects on your composition. You can always _____ them to return them to their previous state.

Grouping, Ungroup

7. The _____ retains shapes inside until you decide to add them to your composition, while the _____ command automatically places the shapes directly on your composition.

Library Palette, Place

8. What's the quickest and easiest way to create a semicircle?

   B. Use the Ellipse tool and the Crop tool

9. If you plan to combine two overlapping objects using the Intersect function, which parts of the objects will remain?

   A. The overlapping parts of the two objects

Module 4: Work with Text

1. What's the purpose of adding text in your LiveMotion projects?

   D. All of the above

2. Unlike Word Processing programs, such as Microsoft Word, LiveMotion lets you add _____ to your text.

   D. Style

3. What's the purpose of the Break Apart Text command?

   A. To enable you to work on individual letters of your text

4. If you want to align all your objects along the Y-axis of the centermost object, which type of alignment would you use?

   A. Horizontal Center

5. Which of the following palettes remain the same and, in addition, enable you to alter the same preferences, no matter what kind of object you're working on?

   B. Transform palette

6. By applying color to your text object, ____ becomes colored.

   C. All of it

7. While using the Gradient palette, how would you adjust the amount of color used on one side of the object, as well as the other?

   C. By moving the sliders

8. Which preference is unusable in the Adjust palette while working on text and shape objects?

   C. Tint

9. _____ enable you to build on your text objects, while _____ let you give text objects a sense of depth and volume.

   Layers, 3-D effects

10. The Paste Special command enables you to paste _____ to your objects.

   Specific attributes

Module 5: Import Images

1. _____ type files are more practical to use for saving real-life images, such as those of people, animals, and the environment. On the other hand, _____ file types are more practical to use for images that contain artwork.

   JPEG, GIF

2. How would you import an image on to your composition?

   A. Use the Place command

3. What is the function of the Make Alias command in the Object menu?

   B. To create an exact alias of a selected object

4. Which palette enables you to build Alpha Channels and create mattes for images?

   A. The Properties palette

5. The Adjust palette enables you to _____ your images.

   C. Touch up

6. Which of the following palettes will have no effect on an image?

   B. The Gradient palette

7. To change an image object to a shape object, you need to select Color from the Fill With preference in the _____.

   D. Layer palette

8. Which menu command would you use to import a PSD file type into LiveMotion?

    D. The Place command

9. PSD is the native file format for which Adobe application?

    C. Adobe Photoshop

Module 6: Buttons and Rollovers

1. What are buttons in LiveMotion?

    D. All of the above

2. What's the difference between regular buttons and advanced buttons?

    A. Advanced buttons contain more detail

3. How many different States does the States palette enable you to create for objects?

    B. Four

4. The Normal State is the Default State for an object. On the other hand, the _____ State is the State the rollover object returns to once the mouse cursor leaves the object.

    C. Out

5. The Preview mode enables you to view your rollover objects in action, whereas the _____ mode enables you to continue working on your rollover objects.

    C. Edit

6. How do you create a State for an object in the States palette?

    C. Both choice A and B

7. What's the main difference between Rollover and Remote Rollover objects in LiveMotion?

    A. Rollover objects, unlike Remote Rollover objects, can change color.

8. What are Custom States?

A.   Custom States are States that can only be triggered by other Rollover buttons.

9. Which tool in the toolbar enables you to properly align the various states of either a Rollover or a Remote Rollover button?

C.   Layer Offset tool

10. The _____ buttons in the States palette enable you to trigger the States of other rollovers.

C.   Target

Module 7: Export Your Work

1. Which of the following file formats is LiveMotion capable of exporting to?

C.   HTML

2. What's the function of the Preview In command?

B.   It enables you to preview your projects in a Web browser

3. What's the purpose of the HTML file that gets exported with the Export command along with either a SWF file or an image folder?

D.   All of the above.

4. How many different settings are available to you in the Export palette?

B.   Eight

5. Which of the following statements is true for compression?

C.   I and III

6. _____ objects are made up of complex algorithms, which ultimately reduce the file size. _____ objects, on the other hand, are made of pixels. Unlike _____, _____ images are noticeably larger in file size. When resized and stretched, they appear pixilated.

A.   Vector/Bitmap/vector/bitmap

7. What will happen to a shape drawn on the composition once an additional layer has been applied to it from the Object palette?

B. The object becomes a bitmap object.

8. Which command enables you to export a specific object on your composition?

D. The Export Selection command

9. Which of the following commands lets you preview the file size of both individual objects on your composition, as well as the composition itself?

B. The Export Compression command

10. The Auto Slice Area command enables you to view which of the following?

A. The way LiveMotion will slice up your composition when exporting

Module 8: Introduction to the Timeline

1. What's the purpose of the timeline?

D. All of the above

2. What's the difference between the Shy and View buttons in the Timeline window?

A. The View button hides the object on the composition, while the Shy button hides the object on the timeline.

3. What's the purpose of the current time marker (CTM) in the Timeline window?

D. It marks the current Time Interval marker in the Timeline window.

4. What will happen to an animated object with a duration bar longer than that of the composition?

C. Object duration bars can't be longer than that of the composition unless their duration bars are independent of the composition.

5. How many Transform Components does the timeline allow us to edit for each object?

B. Seven

6. Which of the following statements is true when defining keyframes?

B. I

7. Which of the following elements in the Timeline window is used to properly select the location prior to placing a keyframe?

A. The CTM

8. For which of the following Transform Components of an object are Motion Paths used for?

C. Position

9. What is the main difference between MovieClip objects and ordinary objects?

A. A MovieClip object's animation is independent of the composition. Regular objects are dependent on the composition.

10. What is the difference between linear and auto Bezier Motion Paths?

B. Auto Bezier Motion Paths follow curved lines. Linear Motion Paths move in straight lines.

Module 9: Create Simple Animations

1. Which of the following statements are true?

D. II only

2. Which two major palettes are the attributes under the object attributes section associated with?

C. Properties and Transform palettes

3. How many different components and attributes does LiveMotion allow us to animate for any specific object?

D. More than 20

4. _____ animated objects within a _____ group will follow the animation of the overall object as well.

A. Individual/MovieClip

5. Which type of object in LiveMotion allows us to animate more of its attributes under its object attributes section than others?

   B. Text

6. Which of the following statements are false?

   A. I

7. How do layer components differ from both object attributes and Transform Components?

   A. Layer components are created by their corresponding palettes.

8. How many layers does the timeline allow us to animate?

   D. As many layers as the object contains

9. Which tool in the toolbar helps us move the position of an object's layer so that we may ultimately animate it using specific layer components?

   B. The Layer Offset tool

10. With which palette are the X offset, Y offset, width, and softness associated?

    B. The Layer palette

Module 10: Advanced Animations and Techniques

1. Which of the following commands allow us to simultaneously break down and animate the individual layers of either a PSD or AI file?

   D. III and IV

2. After breaking down the layers within a PSD file, how would we go about breaking down a subgroup of layers?

   B. Choose Convert into | Objects once more.

3. From which Adobe application is LiveMotion's timeline based on?

   C. Adobe After Effects

4. When using the _____ command to apply a copied animation from an animated object, the animation is created at the _____ of the selected object's duration bar.

   C.   Paste Animation / beginning

5. Which of the following will result from applying an animated style from the Styles palette to an already animated object?

   A.   The previous animation will be replaced with the animation from the style.

6. By checking the Ignore Color of First Layer option, what will result when applying this style to a newly created text or shape object?

   C.   The object's color will remain unchanged.

7. Which of the following benefits are true of using alias objects?

   C.   I and III

8. Which of the following interfaces of LiveMotion do LiveTabs resemble?

   C.   Styles and palettes

9. In order to create a LiveTab, you need to check on the _____ check box when creating a new composition. In order for the LiveTab menu to display your newly created LiveTab, you'll need to first place it in the _____ and _____ LiveMotion.

   D.   LiveTab / LiveTab / restart

10. Which new feature that we haven't yet covered is needed to create a function LiveTab that allows us to apply effects onto the objects in the composition?

   B.   Scripting

Module 11: Introduction to JavaScript

1. Which of the following codes represents the appropriate tags for introducing JavaScript to HTML?

   B.   `<script language="JavaScript">`
       `</script>`

2. Which of the following statements is/are true?

   B. III

3. What is the significance of variables in JavaScript?

   D. All of the above

4. _____ variables are the variables created outside a function and _____ variables are created within a function.

   B. Global/local

5. The ___ JavaScript operator adds the value to the right of the operator to the one on the left. The _____ JavaScript operator subtracts the value to the right of the operator from the one on the left and sets the variable to that amount.

   B. +/-

6. Which of the following is the appropriate method of writing a function?

   A. `function test()`
   ```
   function test()
           {
           //code here;
           }
   ```

7. Which of the following statements is true about If Else statements?

   B. I and II

8. Which of the following keywords is used to create a loop?

   B. for

9. In the following example of a condition in a loop (count=1;count<5;count+=2), what is the purpose of the last variable: count+=1?

   B. It represents the rate at which the loop will run

10. Which term is used to describe the initial part of an object in which you introduce various parameters and assign them values?

   C. Constructor function

Module 12: Scripting in LiveMotion

1. Player Scripts are composed from which of the following scripts?

   C.   Object Scripts, Rollover Scripts, and Handler Scripts

2. In which window of the Script Editor are scripts entered?

   B.   The right-side window

3. The _____ icon lets you know if a specific State or an Event Handler contains a script.

   A.   Star

4. Some Event Handlers and all States are _____-based events.

   A.   User

5. How are Keyframe Scripts executed during an animation?

   D.   All of the above.

6. Which of the following combinations of an Event Handler and an Object State are executed by the same type of a user action?

   A.   OnMouseDown/Down State

7. Which of the following is/are a system-based Handler Event/s?

   A.   I and II

8. When you enter scripts into the scripting window of the Script Editor, when are the <script language="JavaScript"> and </script> tags learned in the previous module needed?

   D.   Never

9. When a label is created, where does it appear?

   A.   On the timeline

10. Which of the following scripts is the appropriate way to call up a label named "1" that's located on the timeline of the composition?

   C.   `_root.gotoAndPlay("2");`

Module 13: Advanced Features of Scripting

1. Where can you find LiveMotion 1 Behaviors in LiveMotion 2?

    B.   In the Scripting Syntax Helper library

2. Which type of Behavior is the following script associated with?

    A.   Change State

3. What is the purpose of the very first label placed on the timeline when creating a Wait for Download script?

    D.   It allows the script to go back to it and replay the animation.

4. What's the purpose of a preloader?

    B.   It loops a continuous animation that plays until the file finishes loading in a web browser.

5. What's the purpose of the Debugger?

    D.   All of the above.

6. From which menu are you able to run and open scripts?

    B.   Automation menu

7. Player scripting controls the _____, while Automation scripting controls other _____.

    B.   Player/compositions

8. Which of the following sections of LiveMotion allow you to trigger scripts on the object on your compositions?

    B.   I, III, and IV

9. How does the Script window differentiate from the Script Editor?

    B.   It allows us to save its scripts into a JavaScript format.

10. Which of the following is true about LiveTabs?

    D.   All of the above

Module 14: Music and Sound

1. Which of the following palettes does the Sound palette resemble?

    B. Library palette

2. Which palette lets you alter the two types of Object attributes for an imported sound in the Timeline window?

    C. Properties palette

3. Which of the following isn't an Object attribute of an imported sound file?

    B. Pitch

4. Which of the following options lets your sound files play alongside an animation?

    A. Streaming Sound

5. What's the effect performed by the Pan Object attribute?

    A. It enables you to set from which speaker the sound is coming from.

6. What's the significance of the 65 in the following script?

    D. It tells the player to unload the movie on level number 65.

7. What will happen to a file that contains a Stop Script located on the 00s time interval on the timeline that contains the music file, along with other animated files?

    B. Neither the music file nor other files will begin playing.

8. Which of the following methods are the correct steps to take to create a Stop Script for a music file when you don't want it to start playing when the file loads in a browser?

    C. II

9. Which of the following is the appropriate way to create a script that will trigger a sound file named music1 to begin playing?

    A. `music1.play();`

10. On which level is the initial-playing SWF file located, in reference to other SWF files loaded on top of it?

    C. 0

Module 15: Smooth Design

1. Which palette allows you to enter URLs that correspond to their buttons?

    D. Web palette

2. What is the purpose of the Color Scheme palette?

    C. To assist you in finding various color combinations.

3. Colors that are next to each other on the color wheel of the Color Scheme palette are_____. Colors that are on the opposite side of the color wheel are_____.

    A. Analogous / complimentary

4. Which is true about the following script:

    B. It will unload all SWF files loaded on level 2.

5. Which set of key commands followed by the dragging of your mouse, allow you to move an anchor point of an object?

    A. Command-Ctrl

Index

T

INTERNATIONAL CONTACT INFORMATION

AUSTRALIA
McGraw-Hill Book Company Australia Pty. Ltd.
TEL +61-2-9417-9899
FAX +61-2-9417-5687
http://www.mcgraw-hill.com.au
books-it_sydney@mcgraw-hill.com

CANADA
McGraw-Hill Ryerson Ltd.
TEL +905-430-5000
FAX +905-430-5020
http://www.mcgrawhill.ca

GREECE, MIDDLE EAST,
NORTHERN AFRICA
McGraw-Hill Hellas
TEL +30-1-656-0990-3-4
FAX +30-1-654-5525

MEXICO (Also serving Latin America)
McGraw-Hill Interamericana Editores S.A. de C.V.
TEL +525-117-1583
FAX +525-117-1589
http://www.mcgraw-hill.com.mx
fernando_castellanos@mcgraw-hill.com

SINGAPORE (Serving Asia)
McGraw-Hill Book Company
TEL +65-863-1580
FAX +65-862-3354
http://www.mcgraw-hill.com.sg
mghasia@mcgraw-hill.com

SOUTH AFRICA
McGraw-Hill South Africa
TEL +27-11-622-7512
FAX +27-11-622-9045
robyn_swanepoel@mcgraw-hill.com

UNITED KINGDOM & EUROPE
(Excluding Southern Europe)
McGraw-Hill Education Europe
TEL +44-1-628-502500
FAX +44-1-628-770224
http://www.mcgraw-hill.co.uk
computing_neurope@mcgraw-hill.com

ALL OTHER INQUIRIES Contact:
Osborne/McGraw-Hill
TEL +1-510-549-6600
FAX +1-510-883-7600
http://www.osborne.com
omg_international@mcgraw-hill.com